Books by Natalie Gittelson

The Erotic Life of the American Wife

Dominus

DOMINUS

DOMINUS

A WOMAN LOOKS AT MEN'S LIVES

Natalie Gittelson

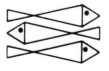

FARRAR, STRAUS AND GIROUX | NEW YORK

A portion of this book appeared,
in somewhat different form, in *Harper's Bazaar*.

Library of Congress Cataloging in Publication Data
Gittelson, Natalie.
Dominus : a woman looks at men's lives.
1. Men.   2.   Masculinity (Psychology)
3.   Sex role.   I.   Title.
HQ1090.G57 1978   301.41'1   78–1331

In memory of

Celia Siegel Leavy and Abraham Harris Leavy,

my beloved mother and father

ACKNOWLEDGMENTS

During the years in which I worked on *Dominus*, I have become indebted to hundreds of men, here and abroad, for the consideration they extended in talking to me about their lives and for the candor with which they shared their experiences. Most of them agreed that I might use their names. But as the writing progressed, I saw that if I did so, I could not wholly honor their candor with my own. To all of them who helped make this book, I owe inestimable thanks.

I also want to express my gratitude to some of the men and women in the United States and Europe who extended special kindnesses—and often hospitality beyond the bounds of mere courtesy—in providing interview sources: Betty Asbury, Eberhard Blum, Robert Brannon, Klaus Budzinski, Jacqui Ceballos, Gerard de Courten, Warren Farrell, Sally Gaines, Serge Goldberg, Estella Wallace Greene, Robert Greene, Dorothy Jones, David Kent, Nancy Klein, Jane Hutchinson Ogle, Joseph Pleck, Francesco Regaiolo, Susan Roberts, Felice Schwartz, Colin Shelley, Jane Stockwood, and the Reverend Robert Thomason.

I feel especially privileged that Robert Stein and Don McKinney read early drafts of *Dominus* and offered the discerning criticisms of content and style that enabled me to complete the book. I have learned much from both of them.

Roger W. Straus, Jr., gave richly of his support, patience, and unfailing good humor over the personally difficult years that this project was in work. He also suggested and encouraged my research in East and West Europe. These travels added immeasurably to my understanding of the implicit themes and meaning of *Dominus*.

I would like to thank my editor, Aaron Asher, for his discretion, his light hand, and his sensitivity in refusing to impose his own values on this work.

Janice Martin, my redoubtable ally, typed the manuscript with her customary high intelligence and dedication to detail, as she did *The Erotic Life of the American Wife.*

I am also beholden to Stanley L. Siegel, Esq., who contributed the amazing typewriter on which I finished the final manuscript; and with it, gifts of wit and geniality at moments when they were immensely appreciated.

But *Dominus* owes its greatest debt to my children, Tony, Eve, and Celia. I have been sustained in this work by their radiance in the face of adversity, their generosity of spirit . . . and not least, by their astute and discerning editorial insights.

CONTENTS

DOMINUS

INTRODUCTION

On a recent Sunday, two stories appeared in the Arts and Leisure section of *The New York Times* that, taken together, reflect some of the concerns of this book and something about its genesis. In one, Lina Wertmüller, the Italian film director, said, "Men and women—it's the same for me—they're only human beings. And in my pictures, they're usually symbols. Anyway, I'm against the smug, racist concept of male and female. The real problem of our future society is to establish who's going to wash the underwear."

In the other *Times* story, the American theater critic Walter Kerr discussed a new British play that had opened in New York. A husband and wife try desperately to conceive a child. The man wonders: Is it a child he really wants or merely proof of his virility? The play, Kerr wrote, expands "into what may be a metaphor for whole nations, for the species. Will life itself, at any level, continue to give birth?

"In a brilliantly written passage, the author sets the failed husband to bitterly remembering precisely what happened to the dinosaur," the critic continued. "With millions of termites devouring its giant legs, a dinosaur remained unaware that death and decay were already upon him; his cerebral equipment was too undeveloped, his capacity for sensation too limited, to warn him. 'What danger signal is the human brain not getting?' the husband asks."

The possible extinction of our species due to danger signals that we fail to apprehend, the need to confirm virility on the one hand and to decide "who's going to wash the underwear" on the other, may seem considerations on vastly different planes of consciousness—portentous, poignant, picayune. But just as they did in the *Times*, they also converge in the modern mind, across art and life, across genders and across oceans. Implicit in both is the issue of manhood and, even more strikingly, the fact that manhood has become an *issue*—knotty with confusion, riddled with doubt, the focus of controversy and debate, not just in New York, Rome, and London. A little while ago, it seemed as simple and incontrovertible as sunlight.

But in any equation, mathematic or moral or social, as one variable changes, it alters the other. And for more than a decade now, women all over the world have been probing the meaning and plumbing the matrix of womanhood. It was inevitable that, in the course of time, men would follow suit. When femininity becomes a matter for conjecture, so too must masculinity.

This was no new thought for me. As the seventies began, and with them the epoch of militant feminism, I was collecting material for a book about the then already more independent lives of women. *The Erotic Life of the American Wife* was a report from women themselves about how the revolution in female consciousness was affecting their own sexuality as well as that of their husbands. As the seventies draw to an end, and perhaps also the epoch of militant feminism, I am completing this book about men's lives. *Dominus* is a report from men themselves about how the present status and the new psychology of women has affected not only their erotic lives but also their entire experience—in office and factory, campus and kitchen, as much as in the bedroom.

Like those two stories in the *Times*, these two books inform each other. Reviewing my discoveries during the years they span, I feel obliged to make an observation that will startle only those astonished by irony: the so-called feminist revolution has transformed the consciousness of American men more dramatically, more decisively—and perhaps more dangerously—than the consciousness of women.

Gathering the interviews on which this book is based, I

traveled across the country from New York to California, and across Europe from Great Britain to Greece and Yugoslavia. I recorded the thoughts and voices of hundreds of men contemplating their lives with liberated women—wives and daughters, colleagues and classmates, mothers and mistresses. There was a steadily expanding literature about the new heroine of the seventies. She was on everybody's mind and tongue and television channel almost everywhere in the world. We knew her well. But what about the men with whom she worked, played, studied, and slept? How were they faring? How did they perceive her—really? Those who responded were always free to pursue their own ideas, wherever they might lead. I set out with no preconceptions and no rigidly formulated list of questions.

Later, pondering thousands of pages of notes and hundreds of hours of tapes, I tried to isolate the common themes that united—or divided—young men and older, white and non-white, rich and poor, middle-class and working-class, American and European. Although in the writing I have tried to remain in the wings, leaving the stage to my informants, this book is as much about my own experience of the people I met as it is about the people themselves. These are men, not as they appear in some neutral, objective, unevaluating eye, but as I, a woman, saw them; in fact, as they presented themselves to me. Needless to say, if I were a man, or indeed another woman, different transactions would surely have occurred. I have changed names and sometimes places in order to protect the privacy of all those who contributed to *Dominus* by honestly speaking their minds.

While no person is typical, many are representative, insofar as they exhibit similar signs of the same condition. And the more closely I listened to what men said (and left unsaid), the more clearly I heard similar ideas, attitudes, anxieties, and apprehensions resound. Although I have attempted to preserve each person's uniqueness and individuality, the blood and guts that make him who he is, the men here represent, collectively, a state of male affairs more prevalent than some readers may be willing to concede. I would have liked to write a more temperate, comfortable book, reflecting more currently popular views. But it is inevitable that you do not choose the book you write, the book chooses you. In the course of time certain rather vivid recognitions became inescapable. I present them not as gospel but as tokens—or foretokens. No epidemic hits every house on every street in town. It may spread, however, in direct proportion as it is ignored.

The time has come, I think, for women who write to stop echoing each other's ideas. "Don't rock the boat," one feminist counseled me as I began work. Men and women were still unsure of their new roles (or rolelessness), she said, and it would be premature as well as risky to examine the real-life consequences of the new ideology.

But that was three years ago. If, once and for all, we puncture the myth of unanimity, by now the boat must be sturdy enough not to sink. It does us no service, if it ever did, to continue to protect the women's liberation movement from closer empiric scrutiny than it has yet received. Real sisterhood—and more important, real humanity—lie in exploring together the furthest-reaching implications of our present assumptions. For even if it did exist, a consensus that encompasses only half the people is no consensus at all.

Dominus, in Latin, means master—

once a title of honor, accorded to men

1 | Who's That Sitting in My Chair?

He gave his name, Tom Enrico, and introduced himself as a "househusband." It was the summer of '72, long before the word—and the character—turned up on situation comedies and magazine covers. Over the squawky TV telephones of the day-time talk show in Boston, it still took a while to assimilate the masculine gender for housewife. "Men like me are flying in the face of our male heritage and of the culture, trying to do the right thing," this househusband explained with touching gravity. Laugh all you want, it was no joke—not then—to the man who wore the apron. "Mrs. Enrico felt that I had to take an equal hand in bringing up the children. I agreed that our kids' development and material gain were not compatible. It's important to revise the definitions of success in favor of the family."

He and his wife, he said, took turns staying home. "We switch around about every six months. I used to do community organizing, but now I take whatever work I can get at the given moment." He was not complaining—Enrico made that abundantly clear—he was just describing. "So far I've been employed in a hardware store, a men's shop, and as a caretaker around Boston University. Mrs. Enrico's in nursing. This is my period at home."

But he did not deny that playing househusband, although "fair and square," made him gloomy. "When I was going into homes as an organizer, 99 percent of the women I saw were just sitting in front of the tube. I didn't pay much attention. Today, I understand the real isolation of the housewife. I know why she has that great big urge to get out. When she's home, she spends her days glued to the box. Her lover is the television set."

He made a bold confession over the TV telephone. "Daytime shows upset my stomach," Enrico said. "The programs are geared to female fantasies. And the neighbors think I've freaked out. We live in an Italian-American neighborhood where fathers don't even put the dishes in the sink." He did not stifle a long sigh. It came hissing over the airwaves. "This role switch has made me much more sympathetic to what my wife endures. And it's a healthy situation in that the children really get to know both of us . . ." Then he reached the crux of the matter. "But it's no long-run solution to our lives. Because I hate my six months even more than she hates her six months."

Several books were subsequently written by and about role-reversed husbands as happy as mice in the house; and at last even television finally got around to recognizing, sometimes with a certain risibility, the domestication of the male. But long before it became a stylish topic, early househusbands like Enrico were already learning that doing "the right thing"— albeit with the best will in the world—often felt wrong.

It was during the heyday of those early-morning and late-night listener-participation shows that provided a kind of street-corner soapbox for the country, offering conversation, consolation, perhaps even catharsis, to those who could not sleep. I was embarked on the ritual guest-author tour, on behalf of *The Erotic Life of the American Wife*. It startled me at first that most of my callers were husbands and that they shared, with some fervor, a common concern: the second storm of female emancipation within this century was rising all around them. But was not liberation, after all, a "women's issue"? Why did men care so much? Listening attentively to those male voices, I realized that, even then, they had begun to see themselves as victims of a natural (or unnatural) force. The eye of the hurricane was speeding straight toward them. Reaching gale velocity, it was destined soon to shake the sexual status quo to its foundations and transfigure the landscape of American life.

Meanwhile, with this new dawn of women's rights, men's rights had entered a curious twilight zone. "I don't want to be an overbearing bastard and get Jill pregnant against her will," said Sam Nolen, a jazz musician in Washington. He wanted to become a father, he explained, more than his wife wanted to become a mother. "She might have the baby to please me, if I put on enough pressure," he mused. "And I've started to hate it when friends call up and ask, 'How are the dogs?'" But their two dachshunds did not disrupt his wife's daily schedule. "Jill's a concert pianist who practices seven hours seven days a week. What right have I to urge a woman with her potential to have a child she isn't sure she wants?"

Especially for those under forty, the balance of marital power was shifting fast. Most young wives now held the privilege of veto in matters that ranged from when and if to take a lover— or a holiday—to when and if to have a child. From patiently accommodating young husbands like Nolen and Enrico, whose wives were "entering consciousness" with the ferocity of a second birth trauma, came the recurrent story of female conversion. Details varied, meaning did not. During the short night of the liberation (the feminist movement was then still young), the missus had become a stranger.

Sometimes she did not even want to be called missus any more. Her husband had gone to sleep, so it seemed, "next to the nice, easygoing girl I married," as one gentleman caller in Baltimore said, only to awaken beside a woman smarting with the pain of centuries, seething with male-inflicted wrongs incurred not just during their few years together but throughout the whole history of her sex. Instead of private man and private woman, they were on the verge of becoming glassy abstractions to one another: oppressor and oppressed, master and slave. At some moments, he could have sworn that she seemed much more eager to depose him than embrace him. It was, said the Baltimore man, "unreal."

Almost all the honest, open-minded men who spoke to me on that summer tour were wrestling with aspects of the same general question: how male was too male? Later, a political-science professor in his middle thirties recollected, "It wasn't just the women's movement, it was everything that happened in the sixties that made us start to wonder what masculinity was really all about." The self-consciousness of his generation—not merely about the meaning of *dominus*—was so ingrained that the men themselves seemed unaware of it. "First of all, we had a crummy war. That tore our hearts out. But we also had the Weathermen and student riots, the assassinations, and Lyndon Johnson's macho. That curdled our blood. There were no more heroes, except maybe in the boxing ring. We were already beginning to question ourselves. The women's movement only encouraged us to admit it."

Of course, not all the men with whom I talked were lambs. Yet male chauvinist pigs, then a recently identified breed, were conspicuously absent that summer. Maybe they were too, well, pigheaded to yet acknowledge that this "women's issue" of emancipation would eventually overflow its boundaries and implicate them. However, judging from all I heard and saw, the proper label for most of the men of the early seventies would have been, not MCP, but MGG—for Mister Good Guy.

More than merely fair, they wanted to be just, in this baffling new confrontation between the sexes. Long before the nationwide struggle peaked over the ERA, most men were accepting without debate the essential validity of women's rights. As an indignant husband in a Harold Pinter screenplay observed, it was "an idea no reasonable man would dispute." If some female militants persisted in treating the principle of sexual egalitarianism "as though it were a breakthrough in human thought," they accepted that too—with a shrug or a smile.

The real trouble lay not in the principle itself but in what flowed from it. One night a caller in Philadelphia yearned openly over the TV telephone for the return of the "unreconstructed female. It's cool when a woman just likes to be what she is," he said. The talk-show host reproached him. "That's a repressive attitude," he warned. "But when women are losing their will to be women," said the caller with a tremor of anxiety that was to grow familiar, "how can men be men? What the hell have we got to be male about any more?"

It was part of a larger puzzlement. With the economic recession of the later seventies still some years away, many men were unable to understand the new lure of many women for "the job." For blue-collar men and white-collar men alike, more often than not, the job was a trap. While the paycheck might have made some rich (although it made most barely solvent), it had never made any man free. As far as they could see, there was little autonomy available in either office or factory. "Business," as some song or other went, "ain't nothin' but the blues." Why then did entering the labor market signify liberty to their wives?

"Separate bank accounts," one caller in Chicago suggested. "That's what they're after. It's not freedom, it's panic, that prompts women to work. There's no more security anywhere. Every wife's afraid her marriage will be the next one to go. And she doesn't want to be left without resources."

The enlightened new female attitudes toward their sex lives also confounded many men. Equality as perceived by women and eroticism as desired by them seemed antithetical. The quest for orgasm, even multiple orgasm, had been aggressively inaugurated. And some of the very same women who were radically revising the terms of femininity, turning "submission" into the dirtiest word in the language, were demanding ecstasy in the arms of strong and forceful lovers, as if ecstasy were one more civil right. "This so-called liberation of the libido has got more men mixed up than freed up," a caller in Cincinnati declared. "The dominant-submissive pattern still works best in a sexual sense. But maybe we men will soon get liberated enough to accept the submissive position." Nothing, it seemed, was too much for some of these good guys to hope.

Late one night in Cleveland, the thirty-two-year-old talk-show host himself, Harry Hopper, stayed up until early morning in the cocktail lounge of the Hollenden House, telling the story of his own home life. Delivering his commercials for automobiles and exercise salons, accepting telephone calls from insomniac listeners, he had appeared rather glib and calm as still water. Off the air, he was feverish with some of the same night terrors that were keeping many men in his audience awake.

"Practically every guy I know is in this thing. One way or another, their wives are flipping out," he said, cloaking himself at first—just as his listeners frequently did—in the easier anonymity of the third person. It was one of the ironies of the epoch: many an American wife, believing that she was coming into her own in a sane, healthy, responsible way for the first time in her life, discovered that, in her husband's eyes, she seemed to be coming undone.

Now he adopted the first person singular. "I have two lovely little girls, seven and nine. All of a sudden one day, Paula, my wife, says she's going back to work. She dumps the kids . . . on me. It's just lucky that I work at night. I take the girls to school. I pick them up. I fix their peanut-butter sandwiches at three o'clock." This Mister Good Guy settled back in his lounge chair and lit the first of many cigarettes. "When I met her, Paula couldn't wait to get out of the secretaries' pool. Ten years later, she couldn't wait to jump back." When he reminded her of her old distaste for the nine-to-five life, she responded, "Chauvinist!" in the then familiar mode.

"But that's not the worst of it," Hopper went on. The worst of it was that Paula had let him know that he was not, had never been, a good lover. After ten years of marriage, she confessed that he did not satisfy her sexually. She was only being honest, she explained—one of the cardinal prerogatives of the liberation. Soon afterward, she told him she was taking advantage of her right to know other men. "What the hell does that mean, 'know other men'?" he had asked. In a little while, he found out. She was sleeping with his best friend. All over the country, in big cities and small towns, a lot of best friends were turning out to be enemies. But the young cuckold of the seventies made concessions that would have been unthinkable in the days of his father—or his older brother. "Well, it's her body," Harry Hopper said. "She has the right to do what she pleases with it." Like many of his peers, he consented to the rhetoric of women's liberation with alacrity and without analysis.

"But anyway . . . I got goddamn angry," Hopper added uncertainly. Was he *supposed* to be angry, for God's sake? It was one thing to support, intellectually, the new code of sexual freedom; another to stand by and watch it burn your house down. "I told my wife if that clown ever darkened my doorway again, I'd kill him," Hopper declared. It was the first time he sounded really sure of anything. One could almost see the dazed, submerged male in him stir and, for a moment, come to life. "Well, Paula dropped him like a hot potato. But lately I have reason to believe that it's starting up all over again. First I lost my best friend. Now I'm worried that I'm going to lose my wife."

Maybe she was better off lost? Only crazies and religious people or the infirm and the elderly were still maintaining the sanctity of the old-time marriage contract against all odds. Hopper shook his head. He drained his glass and took a long, reflective drag on a fresh cigarette. "I can't face a divorce," he murmured. "I'm trying hard to stay loose and conciliatory. I've got to see Paula through this thing. My family means everything to me. And I don't want to lose the kids."

Although I did not know it then, *Dominus* was conceived on that cross-country tour. By the time the book quickened, showing active signs of life, the storm provoked by the new feminism had not abated. In fact, it had spread—from middle-class elite to working-class mass, from college graduates and their mothers and their grandmothers to young girls in school. Almost no woman was immune any more to its sharpening convulsions, so almost no man was left untouched.

But a sea change had occurred among them. Many of the

MGGs of those early days—their good will dissipated, their best intentions frayed by witting and unwitting rebuff—had given up trying to accommodate with grace to the exigencies (some now said the vagaries) of the liberation. They were turning into MCPs in what often seemed rather like instinctive acts of self-protection. "Anything is better than to live with the feeling that you've been deballed," one of the converts declared. He wore tongue-in-cheek insignia: cuff links with four tiny hooves and a curly tail. But his tone was deadly serious.

These pigs—as their creators christened them—were made, not born. Just as those who need to believe in saints invent them, so do those who need to believe in swine. "Whatever they are presumed to be, they will live up to—they will even live up to unconscious presumptions," a psychiatrist once remarked of women. It is no less true of men.

So it was hardly by sheer chance that the very first man I interviewed for the book that was to become *Dominus* turned out to be as "chauvinist" as they then came. Frederic Beekman, age about forty, started out with an elegy for days gone by—when even small men, by the fact of being men, loomed large in their own estimation. "My father ran a little grocery store, but he was a huge personality," Beekman said, relishing that size and scope perhaps more in retrospect than in reality. "The whole family revolved around him—uncles, aunts, cousins. It was a strong, terrific patriarchy. My father was the magnetic center. Without him the structure crumbled."

Beekman, a Northwestern University graduate and a Hyde Park bartender "only temporarily," recalled the Passovers of his youth. By profession he was an actor-director, but his paying jobs in the theater were rare. "Our house was the gathering place for the whole family," he remembered. "When my father lit into the Haggadah, it was performance, pure craft! He was Moses and the Pharaoh, Rabbi Akiba and Rabbi Hillel. Every year, it was more than a Seder, it was a celebration of . . . survival." If some Jews seemed particularly susceptible to that scourge, "male chauvinism"—always a symptom of more than ordinary anxiety—it might have been because they saw the continuing survival of a people linked to their personal survival as men.

"Like most guys my age," he continued, "I'm caught between the magnetic pull of the past and the technologized, androgynized, homogenized present. But the governing ethic of my life is my father's." His father might not have been quite the undisputed lord of his domain that the son remembered. No matter; it was the value both men ascribed to *dominus* that counted. Thwarted, it became debased into those cheap counterfeits, chauvinism and machismo.

At first, Fred Beekman hid behind the impersonality of abstractions. He shied away from intimate details. "Woman's energy has gotten misdirected," he said. "Essentially, it's service energy. Until now, it has always had its source in love. This is profound. It touches the core of her being. Denying that need—for protection, trust, reassurance—I've seen too many women go crazy." He repeated for emphasis, "Crazy. Maria among them." He was married to Maria.

And so the cloak of objectivity dropped. A kind of Old Testament intensity caused sparks of hurt and anger to flash in Fred Beekman's dark eyes. But he spoke of his wife as if she were a willful child, not mad. "Maria has the same delusions about what the world has to offer as her sixteen-year-old daughter. Both of them are romantic adolescents. They may have different romances, but their grasp of reality is zero."

Yet by her own standards, Maria was the prototype of the "take-charge, liberated woman," her husband said. Associate film editor for a national television network, "she's always held lucrative jobs that her friends who stay home find glamorous. But they've never been important enough to suit her. Maria feels that life has given her a raw deal. Born a man, she thinks, she would have been Robert Altman by now. That's Maria's romance."

Beekman went for more coffee. He started to sip it before he sat down again. "Maria's reality"—he sought a discreet way to describe it—"Maria's reality is delusions of grandeur. There are some gifted women in the arts with extraordinary resources; she's not one of them. She's pretty damn lucky to have the job she's got, supervised by a strong producer. Maria doesn't think so. She complains that she just follows orders. But as Robert Altman, she would be a washout. Making the smallest practical decision upsets her. Creative decisions would destroy her. I think sexual democracy is a lot of nonsense," he added. It was a crochety remark, aimed to outrage, not really a war cry. But it would have won him those letters, MCP, wherever they were awarded.

Then, unwilling to be accused of a faulty social conscience, he said, "Sure, women *have* gotten a raw deal through the ages. But have the ages been so all-fired kind to men? At least Maria's doing work that interests her." The proprietor of the tavern where he worked beckoned him back to the bar. He winced. "I hate this place," he blurted out.

Then he took another slug of coffee. Beekman did not enjoy hard liquor and people who did distressed him. "Namely, my wife," he said. "From 6 P.M. to 2 A.M., Maria's never without a glass in her hand. Why? Because's she's under too much pressure. Women like her were not made to take that kind of daily deadline pressure. It drives them to drink."

The proprietor was becoming impatient. Beekman nodded. His brief afternoon break was coming to an end. Abruptly, he disclosed that he had just walked out on his wife. "It still doesn't seem real to me," he said, apologizing for the tardy revelation. "The booze sealed the fate of the marriage, but that's just a shield. Maria's masking other problems behind it. She's fiercely competitive. She's full of self-pity. She thinks only of herself. I told her we had to get into therapy together or otherwise I would leave. She refused." Now he spoke slowly, weighing every word. "She refused on the grounds that she was afraid of developing to the point where her strength and superiority would threaten me. The only way to save our marriage, Maria said, was for her to remain weak and inferior."

Beekman put down his empty coffee cup in a way that made the tiny table jump. "Do I seem like the kind of man who needs a weak, inferior woman to make me look better?" He was short and stocky, but his chest was broad and he had a fighter's arms. He probably resembled his father.

"Maria thinks we're going to get it together again," Fred Beekman said. "But she isn't Jewish." He rose from the table, preparing to return to his station at the bar. "She doesn't know that all through history Jews have had to learn to pick themselves up and walk on." It was the way many men, Jews or not, were affirming *dominus* now.

The Reverend Richard Braden, faculty head of the United Student Ministry at a large Southwestern university, was just about as unlike Beekman as another man could be. He wanted to shed "the reactionary past" as much as the bartender would have liked to preserve it. He had purged himself of dreaded chauvinism, not without emotional travail, he said. He spoke with almost mystic zeal, laying out the imperatives of the liberation as he saw them. "We've all got to think in new, non-linear ways . . . to view the future as its own thing, not simply as an extension of what's gone before. We've got to divest ourselves of the old, traditional images of heterosexuality, of yesterday's dead heritage."

He was his own best example. "Since my wife's gone back to school on a full-time basis," Rev. Braden said with almost too much cheer, "I've had to learn all kinds of new roles. I spend a lot of time every day doing the things that Laurel once did." He named them with the buoyant yet slightly martyred air that was not uncommon among men. "I fix breakfast for the boys. I straighten up the house before I leave. I give Laurel her breakfast before she leaves. I take the kids to piano lessons at four-thirty. I drive the maid home on cleaning day. I wash the dishes every night. And once a week, when Laurel has an evening class, I cook dinner. My chicken cacciatore is very well received." He pronounced it with a flourish, smiling.

But that litany of chores exhausted him. Rev. Braden's tone became less hearty. "When your wife finds the courage to stand up and do something for herself, you've got to salute her—knowing all the while that it's bound to be at your expense. Most men want full-time wives. Professional men, like doctors and ministers, need them. I'm still not adjusted to my new life."

Looking sheepish, the pastor revealed the nature of his "worst dilemma" in recent weeks. "It's about who sits in the evening chair, if you can believe it. You see, it's always been my chair. Traditionally, the man comes home and he takes it easy and he sits down in the daddy chair, right? Well, these days, by the time I finish washing the dishes, there's Laurel, the mommy, sitting in my chair." He had to laugh at himself. "Now of course I don't think it's a deliberately aggressive act . . . and of course I'm not going to ask my wife to move. That would be petty. It's such a trivial matter. She's not usurping anything . . . important. But lately I've found myself wondering: What have I got left to call my own?"

In almost all men—Gentile and Jew, rich and poor, working-class and middle-class—the decline of *dominus* on the domestic front was unleashing powerful emotions. There were angry and anxious men; men who, dreading women, masked their dread in exaggerated displays of deference or, according to one psychologist, hid behind smoke screens of "studied neutrality, highly motivated and highly charged." Hostile men ventilated their hostility by the refusal to mask it at all or, in the oldest way, by compulsive sexual seductions. But perhaps the most grievously wounded were those who responded to man's fall from eminence by disowning *dominus* entirely. If women no longer honored the orthodox mode of manhood, they would not honor it either. The "daddy chair," they let it be known, represented nothing that they wanted.

With astounding frequency, American men used the vocabulary of exhaustion, inadequacy, and defeat to describe the way they felt about themselves. Many said "insufficient," some said "superfluous," others "unnecessary" or "superseded," "overwhelmed," "overshadowed," or "out of control." Demoralized, they resigned from once-esteemed male roles. Some of the steadiest husbands were turning slippery as mercury. Some of the fondest fathers were turning into strangers. Family men were turning into playboys. Straights were turning into gays. Old marriages and newer ones were breaking up like eggs in a Hollywood wind machine. Some patersfamilias, still trying valiantly to stick to the old routines, complained that they seemed to be playing in a deserted auditorium, while the audience and the rest of the cast had moved on to another theater.

Divorce and separation, as well as their social acceptability, were increasing everywhere in the United States. With less acceptability, so were the number of delinquent fathers, deserting their families; so were the number of frenzied husbands, battering their wives; and so were all the forms of violent crime. When *dominus* was obstructed from its normal channels, it had to erupt into rage.

Their new downgraded status deeply displeased most men. Yet few protested—except by indirection. Silence gave consent. Indeed, it made a noise like thunder. A nation of little Wilburs, it sometimes seemed, cringed under Big Mama's broomstick, accepting the reprimand to their entire sex. "It's the pussy-whipping of America," said the associate publisher of a distinguished men's magazine with uncustomary boldness. If his language was flippant, his tone was not.

This ad insults women, a catch phrase of early feminism, rapped male knuckles for purveying in their advertising a "denigrating image" of women. But even as reflected in the popular arts, the new age was shaping up as a massive insult to men. Few plays or novels, unless they were recapitulations of the American past, evoked the spirit of *dominus* and the memory of whole men. They were condemned as often in literature as in life as "inhuman monsters and sexual pirates." They were portrayed in television shows and movies as brutes, boobs, and incompetents. "The continuing inability of the American father on sitcoms to lace up the shoes of his own mind without falling off his rocker must be of some cultural significance. But what?" critic John Leonard asked.

Terminal self-doubt, maybe, engendered by Big Mama's ardent disapproval? It was remarkable that so many men seemed to think they had it coming. They were more often contrite than indignant before this avalanche of criticism, overt and implied. In the face of the rebuke to masculinity, there was, by and large, a modesty among men that amounted to self-effacement; diffidence that sometimes seemed like anguish . . . or fear, and ended in withdrawal. Occasionally a lone voice was heard. In *Boston Magazine*, Norman Alstar wrote about the male capitulation in the battle of the sexes. "Above all else, you had learned one thing," he said of his own generation, "not to be offensive to women." Thus, he explained, "men stood by helplessly as they watched women undergo radical transformations. So many felt a longing for male companionship, for a retreat from confusion . . ." Like some others similarly confused, he had joined a men's consciousness-raising group, where he found himself "telling my brothers how women had seized a powerful advantage in relations between the sexes, how men had been taken by surprise and made to feel guilty, how it was important that men come to terms with the new social realities and learn to reassert themselves."

Some women—although not often those who could engage the ear of media—longed for the return to an earlier social reality, as David Frost, the British commentator, pointed out.

"There's a curious double standard operating in America," he said. "In certain areas women have established an absolute power stronghold . . . and men think that surrender is the only road to acclaim. But the letters I receive from women all around America—forget about the letters from men—are pleading for more male leadership. They feel that they've gotten too much dominance over their men, and that their men are mice, and they wish they'd get out and lead them a bit more. 'I don't *want* my man to keep surrendering,' these women say." But by now, male surrender had become a conditioned reflex in the U.S.A.

"Impotence is the sea around us," said a natural scientist in Oregon. "We've living in an impotent time. Men have lost control of their environment, their government, their children, their women, their destiny, and, finally, of themselves. When you have no more control, you have no more caring. You don't even care much about sex, whether it happens or not."

He clung for a moment longer to the security blanket of "they." *They* felt not only "squeezed by the economy" but "overshadowed by women," he said. "Women's ambition has gotten beyond all bounds." Then, throwing off the blanket, he turned to his wife, also a research scientist. "It distorts you," he said. "You're like one of the macrocephalic creatures with the big heads. That head is your abnormal ambition." He turned away from her and told the ceiling, "She has a dream that consumes her." His wife did not look consumed, but composed. It was he who looked consumed.

Women, he said, had the big dreams now. Now it was they who wanted to prove their manhood. His eyes were fixed on his wife's face again in a mixture of anxiety, admiration, and envy. "I have always accepted you as a superior person," he declared, as if the superiority of women were an axiom of nature. "But there's this problem that's come up. When women begin to act on their superiority, men feel they're no longer necessary. It's difficult to accept the secondary position. I suffer under this thing."

The scientist lived in Oregon, but three thousand miles away, in New York, men were speaking in the same vein. "Every day you feel like a smaller and smaller molecule," said a public-relations executive. He ticked off some "revolutionary phenomena" that he described as "demolishing." "Perpetual orgasms in women . . ." (He had translated "multiple" to "perpetual" in his own mind.) "Battery-powered vibrators for sexual excitement, instead of the real thing . . . The input from femme lesbians . . ." (Women who, under other circumstances, would have chosen men as partners.) "The acceptance of autoeroticism . . . Artificial insemination, the pin-prick or electric-shock technique. Genesis without the male!" He shook his heavy, graying head, aghast.

"What's a man supposed to do? Is it any wonder he feels useless and uprooted? Any wonder he says, 'Let's sit this one out?' You learn to withdraw because you never know what the next contact will bring. The tumescence goes down before the evening starts. You let yourself be overwhelmed by women."

In Little Rock, Arkansas, a young minister mentioned his recent Sunday sermon. "I called my talk 'The Most Oppressed Minority.' Blacks have moved up like greased lightning. Women, the numerical majority, have become aggressive and effective beyond the dreams and fears of anyone. But the white, middle-class male? He's left out in the cold."

Sometimes he had become nearly unrecognizable. In San Francisco, a bemused novelist described some white middle-class males he knew, all softened into strangely blurred contours, exhibiting a shade too much refinement or a shade too much flesh. "They get plump like capons. The physiological changes make you wonder if it's really hormonal. Their voices change too. They get higher and shriller." If married, symbiotic alterations often overtook their wives, he said. The women grew manly in subtle ways. Their speech was blunter, their gait heavier, their eyes harder, their feelings toward children apathetic, toward men objective. They could make love off-hand. The novelist mentioned one friend, a married man, who waddled toward him on Market Street, grown not only plump but prissy. "Ah, there goes a woman who looks just like Mitch," he thought. Then he discovered it was Mitch himself!

The gender dimout had this predictable effect: the American flirtation with bisexuality expanded into a coast-to-coast affair. On a popular national television show, during which a whole series of documentary programs was devoted to *The Question of Bisexuality*, the middle-aged commentator apologized for feeling like a "square" because—compulsively heterosexual—he could report no liaisons with men.

If one could believe in the literature and rely on the information of many sex therapists, self-gratification was the salient "erotic" act of the times for both women and men. Narcissus, not Eros, now stood for our sexual aspirations. A sociologist pointed out that masturbation took the lead as "the principal mode of sexuality for American men throughout their lives, including those who have wives handy." "Handy" was his own word.

When *dominus* declined—weakening our heterosexual foundations, defaming the family and fatherhood (or substituting private definitions: the communal "family," the homosexual "father")—it perverted the meaning and substance of manhood, as manhood had always been understood. Not only the young and avant-garde were affected. Middle-aged banking executives in blue serge suits were almost as likely prey to the new male virus as boys in body shirts and beads. Some grew uncertain that they wanted to be men. They confessed gynecic longings: the wish to shed worldly obligations, the need to nurture, the itch to "experiment" with homosexuality, the urge to abandon regular work, the desire to cry.

But in this age of transformations, we transform vices into virtues by giving them new names. So in many places, this male retreat was touted as "the new sensibility." Male indifference to the primal act became a wholesome symptom of "omnisexuality," male irresponsibility and inconstancy became aspects of personal freedom, male caprice "flexibility," and male reliability the province of stuffed shirts and saps.

Although many women had clamored for an end to *dominus*, now some felt betrayed by its demise. "I've played the field," said an advertising copywriter of twenty-three with navy-blue eyeshadow, raspberry lipstick, and an already despairing sensuality. "Forty-six-year-old father figures, eighteen-year-old freshmen, bachelors who are desiccated at thirty-five. None of them like dirt, smells, blood, agony, eccentricity, or bad haircuts on women. Some of them don't even seem to like sex. Their main goal is to stay out of the rain." She told of her young colleague at the advertising agency, "driving that dumb white Peugeot his doting mother bought him, all sealed up in the front seat, wearing seven safety belts, to get across town." Then she spoke with some affection but without much hope of the person she would see that evening. "He's a nice friend. He's the sweetest friend. And at least he'll walk through a blizzard. But he isn't a *man*, you know." By then I knew. She knew. We all knew. "It's the decline of the best," she said.

2 | Manhood Redefined

Not infrequently the dying fall of *dominus* was heralded as an improvement of the species. Some thoughtful men, as well as women, now defined what it "meant to be a man" in exclusively negative terms. "It was a giving up [of] the idea that manhood has anything to do with sexual identity . . ." writer Dotson Rader said. "Manhood is the courage to maintain one's integrity . . . so you admit what you are—bisexual, gay, straight, left, right—and . . . you act on it."

In a collection of essays called *Men and Masculinity*, Dr. Sidney Gourard, a clinical psychologist, commented on "the lethal aspects of the male role." Sexual potency, he said, was "a tenuous base on which to ground one's existence . . . Trying to seem manly is a kind of work, and work imposes stress and consumes energy" which, he implied, was better spent elsewhere.

Like proclaiming revolutions where only skirmishes took place, revising the meaning of manhood to eliminate sexual identity and even sexual potency could not guarantee the conversion of a generation. Yet by the mid-seventies organized efforts were underway to institutionalize the new non-manhood and, as it was said, "stop sexism" at the source. An informal network of more than a thousand "men's groups" stretched across the U.S.A. Some skeptics claimed that the phenomenon was a "hype," a "media event," or a "sociological fad," on its way out almost before it came in. Meanwhile, the men's movement—intended to shatter the "masculine mystique," just as the women's movement attempted to shatter the feminine mystique—expanded. In fact, it was better organized at an

| 27

earlier stage in its development than its progenitor. And it was growing more quickly with less public attention.

Within its collectives the reluctantly male male could confront his disinclination in a sympathetic atmosphere, meanwhile building up the "motivation" and "integrity" to substitute another mode of sexuality that suited him better. Diligently reconstructing the male role, the men's movement was again reminiscent of the early stages of the women's movement, aimed at reconstructing the female role. But the women of the sixties wanted *in*—into the professions, into the political processes, into the world of affairs—while the new men of the seventies wanted *out*. Many voiced suspicions that the strain of being male was more arduous than the pain of being female— and femininity, after all, the best of the bad human bargain.

"How can we dispel all the negative images of women, so that we are free to become more like them?" one men's-grouper asked. "When will we be really free to care for kids, to wash dishes, to laugh and cry and kiss each other on street corners the way women do, admitting that we were wrong in our original image of what it meant to be a man?" Among both sexes, displeasure with self often took the form of envy for the opposite.

Besides these groups, larger and more formal men's conferences, with names like Men Supporting Men and White / Straight / Male broke out like a related contagion. Workshops (sometimes called "playshops") ranged from Male Friendship and Exploring the Male Mystique to Male Sexuality and Sensuality and Men as Predators and Prey. At these celebrations, as they were often termed, old fences fell to the ground. There was "very relaxed and effective communication" between gays and straights, a gay man reported. "Maybe it's *me* that's changing," a straight man said. One Men's Spring Weekend included discussions about "Men and Work" and "Faggots in the Men's Movement" as well as "experiential activities" like massage, dance, and poetry. "Naked men frolicking in the stream were a common sight, disturbing only campground officials . . . It happened for forty-eight hours in a utopian setting; it can happen every day in the real world!" a euphoric participant predicted of the male-to-male communion that charged the atmosphere.

Not to be outdone by women, men's-studies courses, "exploring the male experience," often for academic credit, sprang up on large college campuses and small. From Connecticut to California, dozens of men's centers, clearinghouses for "male concerns," were in active operation. Newspapers, magazines, and newsletters were flourishing too. M.A.N., Men's Awareness Network, gave as its goal "consciously creating awareness between, among and about men and men's issues . . ." *Male Bag* came from Detroit, *Men Talk* from Minneapolis, *Fag Rag* from Boston, and *Gay Sparks* from San Francisco. The Templar Press in New York published *Double F*, a Magazine of Effeminism. In Cambridge, the Massachusetts Institute of Technology installed a Men's Studies Collection in the Charles Hayden Humanities Library.

All these groups, conferences, playshops, college courses, men's centers, and newsletters converged around a single, radical intention: unbecoming men. Not incidentally, that was the title of one of the movement's first and most influential publications. Put out by the Times Change Press, this little underground classic of the "new humanism" explained "how we learned to be male, to oppress women and dehumanize ourselves—how we became 'men.'" When the word was not now mocked or trivialized or worried to death, it was enclosed in quotation marks, either visible or invisible, and barbed with connotations of tyranny and the sinister abuse of power. *Unbecoming Men* was subtitled "A Man's Consciousness Raising Group Writes on Oppression and Themselves" and, on its back cover, asked these questions: "Do you really *know* your 'real close' male friends? . . . Who was the last man you kissed? . . . Touched? . . . Made Love to? . . . Loved?" It seemed at times as if the first sex was just discovering—or rediscovering itself—and that the last quarter of the twentieth century might shape up as the prelude to a whole new epoch of man.

At the start of one men's group meeting in suburban Connecticut, a scowling young lawyer set the tone for the evening. "I did not come here to better my male role; I came to totally change it," he announced. He wore a short, coiffed beard, Gucci loafers, and a pink cashmere sweater, advertising himself unselfconsciously as a spoiled child of privilege. "The men here have to be supportive of each other, without reference to their relationships with women," he said. Others in the comfortable living room agreed. "Getting liberated," said a man with a Florida suntan, "means getting liberated from the whole man-woman thing." A few years earlier, I thought, he was the sort of man who would have been talking with the same zest about "getting laid." All these groupers, of course, had enough time on their hands, space in their heads, and money in their wallets to afford the exotic new luxury of worrying about "role."

There were some women present, but they had already been quelled into silence—perhaps shocked mute by the recognition that these men were openly acknowledging the need to sweep them out of their lives. In the feminist movement, especially at the beginning, the heterosexual life in one guise or another had accounted for practically the whole consciousness-raising agenda. Here, it hardly counted at all.

This early, transitional "mixed" meeting was an exact analogue for the first meetings of the women's movement—before feminists agreed to bar men from their gatherings, so that they might pursue what they deemed their own interests without distraction or inhibition. But rather than help heal the rift between the sexes, these "coed" convocations only seemed to emphasize it.

"Contempt," said a college instructor in his thirties, as if that emotion accounted for the whole complexity of cross-sexual hostility that had settled like a chill in the room. "You discover that your father has these condescending thoughts about women and you say, 'Hah! That's the way to be a man.' " Thus do we play "faggot games" with one another, he reminded his peers. Since it was viewed as manly to deride women, to support them was to take the risk of seeming "faggoty, feminine," he said. Patriarchal society—not men but *dominus* itself—perpetuated attitudes of male contempt. It was a nice, neat theory. The men in the room seemed convinced. Ideology exonerated individuals.

At last one of the silent women spoke. She was too upset to conceal her feelings. "I just don't understand what's going on!" she said, in the tone of one caught in a trap not of her own making. "We came here to learn to like each other better, not to confirm that men despise us. Why should it be this way? Who is the enemy?"

It was a question that echoed in a dozen such meetings as far apart as Milwaukee and Los Angeles. The arch villain went by many slippery names. "It's the *system* that has made men and women perpetuate each other's enmity," a man at Marquette University said during a mixed meeting on men's issues. "Women have been taught to demand strong masculine figures. They're programmed to want dominance and control from men. And then they bellyache because we're dominating and controlling them." "We all reflect our *culture*, so all women are in the game of picking winners," another man said. "They're always measuring a man, evaluating him, adding up his assets and liabilities." "It's a vicious cycle, imposed by *society*," a woman agreed. "Men are socialized into behavior that demands we must agree with them, care for them, submit to them . . ." "Men must take responsibility, but only because they're now the *ruling class*," another woman added. "They perpetuate the system because they have the power. And by doing so, they perpetuate their own power."

At Marquette, as elsewhere, this ritual heterosexual "rap," as some still called it, was soon terminated by a customary announcement. "All this stuff about relationships between men and women doesn't interest me too much," the ubiquitous male insurgent declared. "I came here to get into men's issues, not to find out what women think is wrong with us . . . or to talk about what's wrong with women. We must have separate agendas."

As always, it was as if a spell had been broken. The room came alive. "That's why we're opening up men's lib! We're trying to find some fulfillment of our own!" others called out. "I'm in a gentleman's group already. In my group, we're not worrying about how to relate to a female in bed. We've passed beyond that." Another complained: "I thought the purpose of this meeting was to help us relate to *each other*—emotionally, physically, and tactilely. But most of the evening has been taken up with heterosexual questions. I care about connecting with other men!"

The evening was moving toward its ritual climax. Male voices rose in steadily elaborating counterpoint. "Men must reach out to other men and touch those parts that have been repressed!" "Let's get together as men and know each other as men!" "My sexuality has been so controlled, so overcontrolled, by things that have been laid on me by the establishment . . ." a sandy-haired young man said. "But men have real feelings toward each other that we must now admit and express." He paused only briefly. "I am much more concerned with homosexuality than I am with heterosexuality. I relate better to men than to women. I have good feelings about men that are totally separate from the role trip that goes on in this society." Another pause, even briefer. "Right now, I am deeply involved with a man. It's even improving my relationship with my wife. I can give to my wife, give to my children more, in the light of this new love."

Dammed-up female anxiety burst forth all over the auditorium. One young blond woman cried, "I'm not anybody's enemy! And I'm not a lesbian. All I am is human, and I don't want to be shut out of men's lives. I'm entitled to my own self-image: homemaker, mother, sex object, *chick*. Women have put themselves down as women and now men are putting themselves down as men, and the result is just . . . miserable." She was very pretty and very made up. Her voice grew breathless and threatened tears.

"You're an enemy of the movement!" a middle-aged feminist cried. "I have six children and I have been put outside my function and made a thing. You're cooperating in my oppression, and your own, and you're perpetuating the system." It was surely the crime of the year—or the decade.

But the men were indifferent to the dialogue between the feminist and the pussycat—if that is what the young blond woman was. "We've got to learn to talk about our penises!" one of them declared, cutting through these "women's issues" impatiently. It was a common complaint at such meetings that most men, with their fear of "vulnerability" amounting to phobia, found self-revelation too painful to risk. They would talk about politics and the stock market, trade baseball scores and pale-blue jokes. They would objectify experience. But personal candor was usually out of the question.

It was also probably out of the question that they would learn to talk about their penises with ladies present. So as soon as these men and others like them grew more secure in the righteousness of their cause and the safety of their numbers, they finally flushed the other sex out of their assemblies. The all-male sanctum became the new movement's permanent cell.

Men and women needed to grow apart, they now explained, so that we could take stock of ourselves separately before coming together again on "a higher, more humane level of integration." Reconciliation, they promised, was only a matter of time. But the more vigorously the schism between the sexes was rationalized as temporal and trivial, the larger the seriousness of it loomed.

It was instructive to compare these men's-movement meetings, and their ill-concealed ambivalence toward heterosexuality, with what was happening on and off the highways of America. I was traveling by bus, trying to discover the country. From one coast to the other, the landscape was a jumble of gas stations and green frame houses, billboards and used-car dealers, Big Boy hamburger stands, motels and massage parlors, pockmarked at irregular intervals with drive-in movies, often darkened now because of dwindling attendance. One was constantly aware of the imminence of the obscene. On almost every Main Street in America there was a Coffee Pot, a Village Pub, a Smoke Shop, a Palace Theater—and a Denmark Book Shop, or some facsimile thereof, selling all the sex stuff unfit to print and featuring peep-show 25¢ Adult Movies. For an additional twenty-five cents, many offered glimpses of Live Girl Models. Massage parlors were mostly second-story jobs near the outskirts of town, set up in lofts over Laundromats and dim, dingy offset printing shops. Even in the once-chaste Bible Belt, men seeking the ministrations of "masseuses" never had to venture very far from home.

The dependence on the daily fix was clear enough: the coffee, the cigarettes, the fantasy trip at the flicks, the beer before breakfast, the lunchtime gin—and getting off for a quarter on kaleidoscopic scenes of kinky acts that the viewer would probably never work up nerve enough to copy in his own copulatory life. But two Americas seemed to clash head-on, sending out contradictory signals: Main Street conveyed exactly the kind of macho mystique that the brothers of the liberation were determined to banish from the land. Yet the men's-movement man, deep into his flirtation with femininity, often seemed no less flaky, no more sound of soul and mind, than the Main Street man, with his booze and his broads, his pornographic paraphernalia, and his grandiose self-delusions.

The Main Street brute and the latent homosexual described two sides of a coin. They were both parodies of manhood, rationalizing male incapacity and the failure of nerve. The macho cop-out was to dominate by bragging and bluster and, when *dominus* went *dérangé*, by rape. But the cop-out compounded perhaps was to repress the wish to dominate at all.

As many men grew doubtful of their proper roles, many women grew more confident. They tightened up their lives with masculine resolve, narrowed down their focus to concrete and lucrative goals, and moved out toward horizons of tangible achievement. Women were talking to each other now about enhancing their managerial competence, about carving pathways to corporate success through the world of privilege and money, about wielding the instruments of political control. They often took their professional lives more seriously than their sex lives—which were viewed as diversionary and peripheral to the real thing(s): influence and affluence.

"Who's who and what's what has gotten mixed up in the minds of adults," said a marriage counselor in Akron, Ohio, once a Middle-American stronghold of the straitlaced and conventional. "Fathers and mothers aren't sure any more quite how to be a man or a woman. So how can kids be sure of anything? They've inherited enormous sexual-identity problems from their parents. But if the older folks can't help themselves, how can they help their kids? That's why middle-class teenagers are running away from home and turning to drugs and getting into trouble in such large numbers. They're scared stiff."

This alarm and confusion could harden into desperation. William Shannon, writing in *The New York Times*, declared, "Many families no longer adequately perform the nurturing and supporting function that children need, emotionally and intellectually . . . The rate of suicide among children aged ten to fourteen is twice as high as it was twenty years ago. For children aged fifteen to nineteen, the rate has tripled . . . Since 1963, crimes by children have been rising at a faster rate than the juvenile population . . . The rate of armed robbery, rape and murder by juveniles has doubled in a decade."

Shannon boldly charged the working mother with neglect

(somewhat obscuring the fact that very often she remains in the job market out of financial necessity). "What is astonishing and depressing is that in families where the husband is present, 30 percent of mothers with infants work and more than one third of those with children under six do so . . . A young child needs a one-to-one relationship with a loving adult if the child is to grow into a stable, confident person. A full-time mother best provides that relationship." Not unusually, he settled for the female parent as the primary psychologic one, ignoring the impact and importance of the strong (not motherly) father.

Where *dominus* failed and fathers became irrelevant, since they were at the heart of family life, families suffered heart failure too. In some influential circles, the institution itself was declared moribund. "The arts have told us what parenthood was like in a romanticized, unrealistic way. The arts never concentrate on things like screaming infants, dirty diapers, or the discomfort a woman with a swollen body feels," said non-mother Ellen Peck, president of NON, the National Organization of Non-Parents. "By confining women in the role of child bearer" (in Madonna paintings, as well as others, that glorified motherhood), "men controlled the bodies and minds of women," added art critic Barbara Rose. Another feminist excoriated "the man in the gray flannel suit who fills our minds with pronatalist fantasies." The male advertising copywriter, she said, was "the impregnator of impressionable and vulnerable women everywhere . . . and so it is up to us to charge Madison Avenue with child support." Many wives seemed on the verge of telling husbands to go have their own babies, if they wanted them so badly. A film, *Rabbit Test*, about the world's first pregnant man, appeared.

Unbecoming men? Unbecoming women? Was it really what anyone had in mind? Maybe so, Richard Todd said, writing in *The Atlantic*:

A decade ago, a general theory of American society, subscribed to at several levels of sophistication, held that one thing wrong with our country was its gutless men and oppressive women . . . Our boys were growing up deprived of a traditional sense of male dominance, outlets for masculine aggressiveness were disappearing, women, particularly devious, embittered, bitchy women, were having all too much to say about the tone and substance of our life . . .

It could be that we were reaping the whirlwind. The "deprived" boys of the sixties had matured into the "gutless" men of the seventies, and oppressive women, asserting that it was they themselves who were oppressed, were having more to say than ever about the tone and substance of American life.

3 | Across the Gender Chasm

Vir, in Latin, means man. Virility and virtue (from virtus: manliness, strength, valor) have a common core, linking masculinity with moral excellence. In ancient Greece, where the concept of supremacy did not menace men or women, tyrannos was an honorable term. And "bully" has come down from the German Buhle, meaning lover. It may be as old as the human race, the need of men to master. But with our American love of betterment and our literal definition of democracy, we prefer to reinvent the world. We demean mastery as a variety of oppression, leaving many men only crippled and defensive alternatives from which to choose: machismo, the false face of strength, or effeminacy, machismo's other profile.

In any culture, there are always those who court internal strife—in their own interests or in what they conceive as the long-range interests of society. "Destroy the present to improve the future" is an ancient slogan. And within any movement presuming to be revolutionary, not excluding the movement for "human liberation," programmed intimidation can stifle into silence other, softer voices that might raise hard questions.

Yet our real foe may be our own innocence. The innocent desire to free the "second sex" from subservience and imposed passivity created phallic woman. Active, hard, and thrustful, wishing to enter rather than to be entered, she sometimes comes to "venerate all that is male, while at the same time disdaining all that is man," I wrote in The Erotic Life of the American Wife. Now, striving to be free of the need for toughness and dominion, the men's movement created vaginal man.

Soft, moist, and open, he venerates all that is feminine, it might be said, while at the same time disdaining women.

It seems not too hard to understand. Incorporating masculinity within herself, a woman can fear man—and need him—less. Expressing his femininity, and thus delivered from the rigors of *dominus*, a man can conquer his dread of women as well as some of his disgust.

What Ovid had once termed "the horrific condition" of effeminacy, some men now proposed as aspiration. In California, an innovative social psychologist conducted men's-group workshops in which participants, through the use of "guided fantasy," exchanged their own bodies for those of women.

The psychologist-leader of the fantasy tour was a huge, ruddy man with a full beard and eyes as bright as blue marbles. "We work through all of women's life experiences from menstruation to menopause," he explained in a voice whose depth and resonance would have startled me even if he had been talking about chopping down trees. "We fantasy ourselves into sexual intercourse, playing the woman's role. I encourage the men to go down on themselves," he said.

In another consciousness-raising exercise, workshop members went even further, divesting themselves altogether of their most vital parts. The imaginative task was simple and straightforward. " 'You have a disease of the genitals,' I tell them. 'Your testicles have become refracted, your sexual capacity is gone. Say goodbye to all that.' "

These tasks and others like them were designed to enhance empathy for the tribulations of the other sex and affirm the new belief that sensuality could be more—or less—than "cock-centered." "I learned about my whole body as a sensual apparatus, about its all-over eroticism," one man declared.

He also learned about the inessentiality of the penis, at least in regard to the heterosexual life. Unencumbered by that organ, an obsession with intercourse was per se impossible. The focus and the source of sensuality could switch to less trouble-some appendages whose function was more dependable, such as the fingers and toes. From one point of view, it was an ex-tremely refined form of female oppression. A man might pro-pose finger sucking and toe touching to women as an alternate erotic style (and some women might even accept it), but who would dare propose such meager tokens to, say, male gays? Among them, the phallus still reigned.

From another point of view, "saying goodbye to all that," however symbolic, was a gesture of self-castration. "It's power-ful what comes pouring out," the workshop director said. "Masculine sexuality is still so locked in with genitality that these exercises evoke all sorts of powerful reactions. Some men cry, 'God, what a relief! I've been bound up with my cock all my life. Now I'm free at last of chasing women.' Others say, 'That damn thing had such a will of its own, it took control of me.'" One way or another, the response of the group invariably signified that a heavy load had been lifted. Liberated at last from the panic of maleness, at least in his workshop fantasy, the gelded but no longer harried man could now anticipate taking command of himself and his life. Sexual need did not stand in the way of self-mastery.

It is hard for women, whose sexuality is all internal, to grasp the strange, uneasy truce that sometimes exists between men and their genital parts. But a great many of them, straight and gay, seemed to be experiencing some version of the same phobic response. Julius Lester, a father himself, wrote in his essay "On Being a Boy":

That thing was always there. Every time we went to the john, there *it* was, twitching around like a fat little worm on a fishing hook. When we took baths, it floated in the water like a lazy fish and God forbid we should touch it! It sprang to life like lightning leaping from a cloud. I wished I could cut it off. But I was helpless. It was there, with a life and a mind of its own, having no other function but to embarrass me.

Some persons, like Solomon Julty, who referred to himself as a "sexually dysfunctioning man," put their intellect to work to salvage the pride that their sexuality no longer could. "Potency and impotency," he wrote, meant respectively, "powerful and without power." Thus, Julty's acknowledged dysfunction—impotence—became for him a factor of heightened humanity.

If it is my role to be potent, then I must become a potentate, a ruler. My license to rule then resides in my scepter. Thus, pleasure and satisfaction arrive by my command, not the woman's. Playing the power game is risky. I don't want to get into bed wearing a tottering crown.

Not all men flaunted their flaccidity with defensive pride. Some sought therapy with fluctuating success. Many, rightly or wrongly, blamed their impotence on the women in their lives, variously described as "overbearing," or "undermining," "domineering," or "powerhouses" who paralyzed male response. "No salmon could swim upstream against the waves *she* made," one man grumbled of his former partner.

Two British social scientists and sex-role theoreticians, Rhona and Robert Rapaport, tried to respond reasonably to the new American threat of the powerful woman. Balancing the rights and duties of the sexes should not imply that women "must do what men are doing," or vice versa, they said. "Equity in sex roles is different from equality. The far more radical concept is fairness in the allocation of constraints," the Rapaports argued. But beyond the sociologists' locution lay a sound idea. "At different moments, each role—male and female—may carry different constraints; and the inequities of one moment may be set right at another." These ethics of moderation—suggesting that, in any union, the sacrifices by each partner of the prerogatives of equality might balance out over time—were a radical innovation in the sex-role debate. "We do not want to move from one prison to another—from a traditional to an egalitarian prison," the Rapaports warned. "Self-realization must be the goal, not equality. We need a multiplicity of norms in family life . . . Every family must plot emotional topography of its own." Indeed, within some families, the need might not even exist to "set right the inequities," Rhona Rapaport said. One woman's bitter sacrifice was another's act of love.

Most feminists were not impressed. One cautioned that the English knew too little about American life to propose useful remedies for our ills. "In the United States, there is danger in seizing on the milder concept of equity," she said. "It could make ominous inroads in the concept of equality. There is grave danger in tinkering with the concept of equality here."

Yet that concept or misconception (depending on where one stood in the Great Debate) was fostering much sexual disorientation. Men were talking about "macho women," those to whom the "power trip" was everything. Early in the life of the new machisma, a young graphic artist combined sex and power into what she called her "macherina number." She inserted a series of photographic self-portraits, as advertisements for herself, in *Artforum*. One, which might have been called "Female Artist with Giant Dildo," was calculated to mock the penis as a kind of gross, vestigial organ. In another photograph, announcing her California art show, she presented herself in a clipped, mannish haircut, wrinkled trousers, and motorcycle goggles, leaning against her Porsche. "I meant it to look tough, mocking . . ." she explained of the picture. "Toughness, machismo, has existed so long in our culture, and women used to feel very threatened by images that were tough. But now they are learning to say, 'However tough you can be, I can be tougher.'"

These "macho women," or macherinas, were male impersonators, emulating men at their stereotypical worst. But this age of transformation had also bred their opposite numbers: vaginal men who desired penetration in the manner of women. And homosexuals were talking impatiently about "macho gays," those who refused to submit to penetration.

"What do straight men fear most in homosexuality?" one gay male asked. "Being penetrated," he revealed. "Men do not like to be penetrated. They don't like anyone to get inside them, psychically or physically. A 'man' doesn't let anyone into his body, any more than he lets anyone into himself."

"But we seek homosexual experiences precisely to *let* somebody in," an older gay said. "It's not just penetration of body space. During my fifty years of straight life, I never gave conscious thought to penetration. That's not the paramount issue. Competition, physical prowess, winning out, needs like that . . . Those are the things that bug men and make them homosexual. What worries straight men is not penetration. It's that they're afraid of losing their Marlboro image by becoming gay."

Another homosexual spoke up for vaginal man. "Besides, most gays are counseled on how to accommodate for penetration with some technology. Articles in gay periodicals advise us about how to *enjoy* being penetrated," he said.

The gay plot thickened. "There's homosexual machismo, just as heterosexual. There's the guy who always has to be the inserter, the butch guy who won't reciprocate, who won't allow himself to be penetrated. *He's* the big problem and he isn't available to the technology." These macho gays, suffering a kind of anal "vaginismus" on threat of penetration, were imitating the female dysfunction of women threatened by sexual surrender. Unable to connect with females, their natural subjects, they were unable, even so, to give up their male need for domination.

The vision of genderlessness (or more accurately, gender crossing) fevered the imaginations of some very good men. In California I talked to a burly, sun-baked Angeleno who looked more like a muscle-bound heavyweight boxer than a sex-role revisionist. Yet he wished for nothing more, Bruce Delaney said, than to escape from the vulgar stratagems of what he called "the old balls game."

With none of the customary prologues about the Southern California climate or the crazy traffic on the freeways, he launched into an eloquent description of his male maladies. "These are the times that try men's balls," he said, as if some flippancy could soothe the pain. "The macho charade" was to blame for his unhappiness, he believed—as well as the obligation that accrued from that charade, to "live up to this heavy masculine image of mine." By his own testimony, he had the soul of a butterfly trapped in a gorilla's body. Many such men blamed their hulking physiques for the same dilemma. Delaney spoke passionately not of his passion for women but of his distaste for the "onerousness of gender," complaining that it had almost drained him of strength, vitality, and love of life.

"I want a world that offers all of us all the help we need to move across the gender chasm," he said in the dreamy tones of a visionary. "I want a world where men and women have freedom from the inhibitions of their sex; and internal or external sexuality with the same or different sexes is of little or no significance."

But gender (which springs from the same semantic root as genital) is inextricably bound up with sexual distinction. In most languages, that which is not masculine or feminine is neuter. "Well, maybe bisexuality has to come first," Delaney reflected, responding to that idea. "But this is certain: men have to move on from where they are now." He launched into what was already, to me, an old refrain. "We have been denied long enough the expression of human qualities available only to women. Masculinity is a very bad trip." And then, with sudden urgency, he asked: "What bends me so out of shape that I want so badly to change?"

Yet homosexuality did not appeal to him, nor did sexual

impotence afflict him, Bruce Delaney declared. "My whole experience has been straight. Oh, I have had brushes here and there with gayness, but there was never any sexuality in them. It was a matter of opening myself up, admitting to myself that . . ." His thought dissolved in mid-air. He grasped for words he could not find, then settled for an anecdote about a men's group he had joined, discovering only afterward that "all the other men but me were gay." The sensitivity exercises that produced this revelation also reeked with familiarity by now. Group grope was beginning to seem the most direct route to personal awareness that some men could find.

"First we felt our own bodies fully dressed. Then the leader suggested that we take off as many clothes as we were comfortable not wearing. Everyone stripped. Naked, milling around in the middle of the room, suddenly I realized that I was aroused. I held another guy's penis in my hand. This is kind of neat, I thought. Yet I had no desire for sex with any of those men." That was the main point he wanted to make—lack of any real sexual desire. "It was just very freeing," Delaney explained of this, to him, intriguing new experience—arousal without action and without object. Women too, whether friends or strangers, could satisfy his stirrings with a chaste embrace, he said.

Bruce Delaney was not the only man to view this lack of desire for consummation as a positive theory. Nevertheless, he grew rather wistful as he recalled how one by one—with varying degrees of tact but unvarying determination—the three main women in his life had dumped him: two wives, one mistress.

This last alliance was just now breaking up. "For five years, there was tremendous valuing, respect, and love between us. It was very important to me to take care of Vicky. It was important for me to be there, with that gift—caring—in my hand. I had little chance to exercise it in caring for men. The value of a gift is in wanting to give it," he said softly, "not in whether the gift is accepted or not. So Vicky can't put me down by her rejection, because it's the giving that I value." He sighed over his latest domestic debacle and the need to pick up the pieces of his life again. "But now . . . it's nasty for me. I don't look forward to four lonely walls and a bed. Women can face living alone more easily than men. So sure, I'm going to do some crying over it. But I'm going to survive."

Delaney's voice grew stronger. "Thank God I have some men friends for the first time in my life," he said. "I can cry on their shoulders. They can say, 'Hey, I understand!' " Until recently, "men could share nothing of human depth with each other. If they had emotional problems, they went to women," he declared. "But that's changing too. There's a lack of sympathy among women for men. They've stepped out of the frame. They're concerned with their own lives now. They're not playing the feminine role any longer." He paused to reflect on the recent past. "We grew up with the idea that women are supposed to smile when they're angry. Now they're plenty angry, and they're not smiling any more. So it's men who have to hear each other out when we're in pain." Delaney did not seem entirely displeased with this new state of affairs.

As the old order faded, speculation rose about what growing up in the new world would bring to a generation already traumatized by change. DO CHILDREN NEED SEX ROLES? *Newsweek* asked, as if, like snowsuits in winter, parents could drape them on offspring or not as they saw fit. On the East Coast, one psychiatrist replied in the affirmative oblique, a handy form adopted by those who wish to take sides without really seeming to. "Mothers who don't want to be mothers and 'liberated' women . . . are robbing their daughters of their sexual identities . . . These kids are being taught at a crucial stage in their development to hate their wombs, their bodies, the whole idea of having and caring for children. And the fathers are teaching these boys to retreat from their male responsibilities," he said.

On the West Coast, another psychiatrist replied with the

same studious indirection. Answering the sex-role question with neither a yes nor a no, he alluded to "an enormous increase in passivity" among young men, combined with the refusal to work and, in many minds, the equation of masculinity with compulsive violence.

So it was that the society grew slowly more transsexual. Some men (and fewer women) became so overwhelmed by the desire to turn into their opposites that they elected to cross the gender chasm by means of radical surgery. Dr. Richard Green, the author of *Sexual Identity Conflict in Children and Adults*, cautioned that "cutting off your penis" does not, in itself, turn a man into a woman. "It may make you a man without a penis," he warned. But the cherished right of self-determination, combined with an overload of penile anxiety, was leading more and more men to take the risk of undergoing irreversible sex reassignment. It was the American fantasy of infinite possibility come true: the grand illusion of a post-civilized yet primitive-again society in which nature was viewed as the raw material of man's manipulation.

Psychiatrists had already coined a descriptive phrase for the agony of self-distrust that, in its most extreme form, led to the removal of the penis and the testicles—or less often, to the grafting of male organs on women. They called it "gender dysphoria," a disorder characterized by anxiety, restlessness, depression, and dissatisfaction.

Sometimes this dysphoria became so acute that the victims did not wait for professional intervention. There were already a number of do-it-yourself jobs on the medical records, probably owing as much to unsupportable gender panic as to the five-figure surgical rates. "Cases are turning up in the emergency rooms of hospitals," one physician said. "This man comes in and he has amputated his own penis, because he hates it so much."

Was that because nobody ever loved it enough? The doctor answered more gravely than the question demanded. "There are

studies that show mothers and fathers cause serious gender confusion when the child is only two or three years old. If you ask
the parents of the adult transsexual about his early childhood,
they say, 'Oh, no! We never dressed the little girl in pants . . .
or treated the little boy like a girl.' But the victim of early
confusion responds quite differently. He says of his mother,
'Oh, yes! She always thought I should have been a girl and she
was never shy about letting me know it.' "

It was a sticky question—what could cause gender dysphoria
in the young? Some Connecticut families thought they knew.
At the height of the hullabaloo against sex-role stereotypes, several sets of parents threatened a lawsuit, charging that the
policy of the local elementary school which required sixth-grade
boys to take Home Economics could lead to "effeminate ten-
dencies." Did well-intentioned teachers or parents who gave
girls tool kits and boys baby dolls stir dangerous dissatisfaction
within the maturing sexual self?

No one could offer a certain answer. Few cared to try. Dr.
Green said, "It is the disquieting reward of the 'expert' that the
more data he collects, the more research knowledge he collates,
the less he is *sure* he knows." The "why" of male femininity
(and female masculinity) was too complex and too mysterious
for even the best authorities to untangle. Nevertheless, out of
his long empirical research, Green compiled a list of factors that
seemed to contribute to femininity in men. The most important were: (1) parental indifference and (2) parental encouragement of feminine behavior in boys during their earliest
years. He also noted "maternal overprotection . . . excessive
maternal attention and physical contact . . . inhibition of
rough-and-tumble play . . . and maternal dominance in a
family in which the father is relatively powerless."

However, many behavioral scientists, including a specialist on
human sexuality, Dr. William Simon, were not frightened off
by the gender dysphoria bogey, whatever might be its ultimate
source. "Our old friend, gender training," Simon said, was

simply the plague of an "uptight" society which—despite trans-sexual surgery and other less dramatic signs of getting looser—had not yet really thrown off the iron grip of sex roles. It was gender training, he insisted, that still prevented men and women "from experiencing the full range of potential human exchange. The real revolution of our time will be the sex-role revolution, not the sexual revolution," Dr. Simon promised, "because it will free us at last from the restraining stereotypes of masculinity and femininity."

This prophecy was still recited like a mantra in many quarters, but even mantras cannot make dreams come true. Simon, who, as senior sociologist at the University of Indiana's Institute for Sex Research, worked with Professor Alfred Kinsey on his famous *Report on the Sexual Behavior of the Human Male*, added a new coda: "The important distinction is not whether a man is heterosexual or homosexual or bisexual, but whether he is monosexual or polysexual," he said. "*Mono* means trapped in a single script. And no matter what the gender nature of the object you're 'doing your thing' with, if you're monosexual, you're limited to a particular kind of role in a particular kind of sport." He pitied most the poor limited male "who's trapped into heterosexual monogamy." For that monosexual marital system, more widespread than any other, deprived him of "the chance to sustain and elaborate his erotic commitments and increase the possibility of testing them in a way that would enrich his capacity, so that he can become not only a more sexual person but a much more complex emotional person."

In this view, polysexuality is the fount of human richness; and monosexuality the fate of those with impoverished imaginations and stunted sensuality. "There are supermasculine, heterosexual men who like making it with women, but who also like fucking fairies," Simon explained with a bland air that could render almost any idea reasonable. Now he revealed the "trap" in the masculine role. "When a male engages in sexual activity with other males, he enters into the unhappy realm of cocksuckers. That's a fall from grace that involves, as it were, a permanent stigma," the behavioral scientist said. "All other sexual commitments are seen as rationalizations for this fundamental perversion that now characterizes his nature. Men fear it like the plague. You can see that in so-called liberated, swinging circles, where women have a very easy time handling each other but men get very nervous and very uptight with other men. It's our rigid notions of gender that make homosexuality in any guise an inevitable and irreparable indication of faulty masculinity."

The truth of the matter, Simon said, is quite the other way around. He saw faulty masculinity as the lot of monosexual (i.e., heterosexual), not homosexual man. "Men who are exclusively homosexual are far more polysexual in the sense that they can engage in sexual activity from many more angles, playing many more roles," he explained. "This may be the critical distinction: how many ways can you engage in and experience the sexual? That's much more important than whether you are free to stroke one kind of genitalia as against another."

Across the gender chasm, freed of our masculine and feminine selves, we would discover the profound and vibrant sexual lives that now elude us. That was the siren song of the reformation. But a chord was missing. For this world without *dominus* was also a world without love. "Experiencing the sexual" was usually separated from experiencing ardor or sometimes even affection. And no one—not even the most eloquent hawker of the superliberal new mores—had explained how Eros could survive in the absence of the very force that gave it life.

4 | "Dominus" and the Single Life

"The way I live is very selfishly," said Ned Miller, a West Coast newspaperman of modest renown and immodest good looks. He said it without arrogance but also without alibis. Eros, for him, was rather beside the point. The point, for him, was Ned Miller.

By a rough standard, Miller was today's bachelor to the teeth—which he displayed often and to excellent effect. Whereas yesterday's bachelor often remained one because of some deep-seated conviction, true or false, that he couldn't please a woman (or at least *the* woman) on a permanent basis, Miller's generation of single men didn't want to. What's more they were proud of it (or at least unashamed). Their self-esteem lay in having the courage to refuse traditional male responsibility rather than accept it.

Like almost all those engrossed in themselves, sometimes to the exclusion of all else, Miller defined "selfish" in his own sweet way, positively not pejoratively, as a respectable, neutral, descriptive word. "It just means placing my own needs and desires first. I date a lot, but I don't get involved," he explained, after politely disclaiming the description "bachelor." It implied, Miller felt, a lack of ties with women. "Involvement means demands . . . on my time, my feelings, my life."

Although, he said, he appreciated the opposite sex, he did not appreciate demands. Inevitably, they would annul his freedom. And almost any woman, getting close, would be disposed to make them. In his perfectly fitted burgundy sweater and matching pants, he looked like the catch of the year: svelte yet muscular, self-contained yet amiably conversational, with nice gray eyes, a warm smile, and none of the prissiness or male insecurity with which yesterday's bachelors often turned off women. Miller ran the lively-arts department of an important daily newspaper. Socially, he ran with the liveliest crowd in the city. In short, he was a man whom almost any discerning mother of the old school would have welcomed as her son-in-law. At first glance.

On closer acquaintance, one felt a subtle chill in the spaces around him, not uncommon among those who have learned to love themselves most of all. And the spaces around him were vast.

"I have lots of friends, but no relationships," Miller said, expressing surprise that anyone should be surprised by that. "It was a *de facto* decision. I never really thought about it as a moral issue." Steering clear of close connections came naturally to him, he explained. Relationships themselves, not the lack of them, would have been disturbing.

"By my own choice, I have always lived alone." It was a preference that grew more commonplace every day. "You take much more shit with a roommate . . . of either sex. And when I see what some of my friends go through—the energy drain, the suffering, the hassles that come out of shacking up, then breaking up—I can't help wondering, What do they need it for? Marriage, the legal paper, is beside the point. Some people who live together are more married than married people. It's essentially the same thing." He wanted, above all, to feel no pain. Remoteness was safer than relatedness. He could conceive of no kinder destiny than the hassle-free life. Miller's goal was not happiness (who knew what that was?) but, less presumptuously, a life without . . . shit. Everyone knew what *that* was: the inevitable detritus of close human contact, always a consequence of "getting involved."

Ned Miller lived clean as a whistle. No female moods or menstrual emissions sullied his psyche or his sheets, no baby vomit stained his lapel, no cat hairs laid a furry mist on his wine-colored trousers. And he calculated precisely at what cost he bought such fastidiousness. "I have opted for a level emotional life without peaks of joy but without valleys of despair. I have opted to sacrifice the peaks and the valleys . . ." he said, seeming reconciled to his sacrifice and quite at home on his plateau.

Of course he had normal sexual appetites; probably he could satisfy them almost as matter-of-factly as he ate breakfast. One could imagine him acting out the whole erotic drama to its culmination without once uttering a sound, without even sweating. He might have been emotionally impotent in his very bones or frightened out of feeling at an early age.

"I'm a perfect child of the fifties," Miller said, with a glint of melancholy. "My parents were divorced after thirty years of marriage. My father walked out on us. I don't think he was designed to be married in the first place. Like me, he never liked having people around. But in his generation, you were married or you were nothing. Even when I was a little kid, he was never a father to me in the conventional, cliché sense. Bouncing on the knee, off to the ball game, going fishing with Dad . . . I didn't know from such things." It would have been unfair to blame this man for the trace of self-pity in his tone. The fifties, that was the decade of the Family.

However, Miller refused to regard himself as a special case. And of course, he wasn't. "It's not just my family. It's families in general," he said. "I see what happens everywhere. No matter how well you start out, you can't guarantee that your son isn't going to wind up a junkie and that your daughter won't get knocked up by age twelve."

His own childhood caused him to view fatherhood as something less than alluring. "I can only see kids as an ego trip. And I have no cosmic desire to reproduce myself," Miller said. He told of his best friend, Richard, a victim of that once-widespread desire. "Dick and his two sisters grew up under a repressive father, worse than mine, who also deserted them when Dick was quite young. His mother was a saint, but that didn't help her kids very much. One daughter married a lunatic alcoholic. The other, who's thirty and divorced, is having an affair with an eighteen-year-old boy. Dick married an English girl . . . strong and dominating, like his mother, but without the saintliness or the sanity. His wife is crazy. His kids are crazy. And he's going to pieces. His goal was to create superboy and supergirl. 'I want to teach them everything I know, everything I ever learned,' he said. But Dick's son turned out a shiftless bum. He left home early and wound up as a doper and a drunk. His daughter was picked up in Little Rock in a drug-and-sex ring. With the dreams that he had for his kids, how could he have failed so badly?"

Every bachelor has such a story in his repertoire, proving that married life is inevitably a misadventure. "So I just go put-put-putting around," Ned Miller said, "grateful that it's not my agony." He made the serene sound of a child playing with a toy boat in the bathtub. It could not capsize under heavy breakers, the way a real boat could in the open sea. On the other hand, it could not take much of a journey in the bathtub. But Ned Miller hardly had the soul of a daring adventurer. Sooner or later, the adventurers marry, if for no other reason than to find out what it's like.

With no great enthusiasm, he allowed himself to be drawn into a hypothetical discussion of "getting involved" with a woman. "If I hooked up with some lady, once I made the choice, I wouldn't run around. My ego couldn't stand it if she ran around, so how could I?" (The double standard was not so much becoming extinct as reversing itself. Many men insisted on sexual fidelity, now that many women did not.) "She would be between twenty-seven and thirty-five, professional at something interesting, with an income of more than two hundred dollars a week. She would have to pull her own weight. And we would have to have a place big enough for both of us to live separate lives . . ."

But why bother hooking up, only to remain apart? Miller

quickly lost patience with that pallid fantasy and turned to topics that fascinated him more. "If I have one ambition, I'd like to stop working." He sighed, with the unrequited love for sheer inertia that he shared with many young unmarried men. "I'd just like to be able to live comfortably at a modest level, say twenty-five thousand a year." He conceded that he had a very good job. "On the newspaper, I do only what I care to do. I answer to nobody. Nobody's breathing down my neck. I have 99.9 percent control. Actually, I could get away with murder if I wanted." But the job tied him down, without lifting him up. "I have too strong a sense of responsibility," he declared. "I should see more, read more, listen more. But it's all beginning to sound the same. And I don't want to feel I have to go on working forever, saving up my shekels until the very day I go to Sun City to retire . . ."

His uncle, an independent filmmaker, had "made a mil" on one of his recent pictures, Ned Miller said, and was just about to go into theater production with an original musical comedy. "I thought of investing a few pence in his project, say five grand. But my uncle doesn't want the money. 'Take your five thousand, apply for a leave of absence, and invest in yourself. Write a novel and sell it to the movies!' he told me."

Ned Miller looked both intrigued and apprehensive. "I'm not a bad writer," he said. Then his voice dropped. "But my problem is . . . I have nothing to say." It might have been the price of disengagement.

Many unmarried men announced with apparent sincerity that they hoped to give up their single status "someday." But very few, whether sooner or later, dreamed of marrying a girl like Dad's. She was not only outmoded, what was worse, she was costly. Owing in part to the high-priced economy and in part to the new sociosexual environment, the most attractive of wives was she who required no upkeep; whose middle name, was, so to speak, Self-reliance. Today's bachelor had little patience with yesterday's non-salaried "homebody type" who wanted to stay near the stove, take care of babies, and, in turn, be cared for by him. There was no shortage of such women, but their kind had become so *déclassé* that many had fled into that famous American closet where the embarrassed and ashamed took cover.

Darren Danieli, an investment banker in North Carolina, voiced stylish doubts about the genre. "A man and woman ought to have a lot in common intellectually before they take a chance on marriage," he explained, with a bachelor's customary caution. "Then, unless she's working too, *he* grows . . . and *she* takes care of children." These men almost invariably equated work outside the home with constant female evolution. It was intrinsically mind-warping, they seemed to believe, to dust a window blind or flush a diaper. As soon as a woman became a homemaker, so many bachelors thought, she stopped growing and started shrinking.

"It's too easy for a girl to get stagnant when her life is circumscribed by pediatricians, diapers, and cleaning the house. If she's a real *person*" (that was the word with all the cachet), "if she's intent on building a career, just like her husband, she's more apt to have an active brain." He did not add, "and an active bank account," but he might have.

One glance at Danieli revealed that his own personal upkeep was already exorbitant. Unlined and beaming like a baby at almost thirty, he could have posed for a fashion poster of Young Executive Most Likely to Succeed. One of his colleagues called him "a typical man on the move." Spiffily dressed and shinily shod, the better to move fast, he was resplendent in a French silk tie, cuff links made of semiprecious stones, and an expensive watch that performed several auxiliary services just short of offering an hourly weather report. His winter and summer holidays required, respectively, extensive sports equipment as well as extravagant wardrobes. Early on, he had acquired habits that could only be called sybaritic. Any woman who wanted to participate with him in his lush and busy life had to be able to foot her part of the bill.

As a Southerner, Danieli supposed that the girl he married, if and when she came along, would probably be a Southerner too. "But I'm in no hurry to find her. Meanwhile, I'm having great fun looking. I date a number of young ladies, ranging from a nurse of twenty who's not very stimulating, because she's so young, to an older woman of thirty-two. Women become more interesting as they grow older," he said. "If marriage happens in five years . . . or ten, that's fine. Right now, the social pressure is all in the opposite direction. Everyone I know who's married warns me: 'Distrust it. Go slow.' I could just as easily bollix up my life with the wrong marriage as improve it with the right one. I don't want to make any mistakes."

He was almost as wary of women mesmerized by their careers as those mesmerized by their kitchens. "Pushy, inconsiderate, self-involved, and come-uppy," he called them. "They try to impress men with their independence by outshouting them and outmaneuvering them. If they didn't really force the issue, they might not make so much progress," he admitted. "But I don't have to marry one."

Well, a man couldn't be too careful. Or could he? Exercising extreme caution about getting married sometimes seemed more than merely prudent. It also provided the perfect excuse for disengagement, for steering clear of unwanted entanglements. Most bachelors, even those who insisted that their single status was only temporary, were members in good standing of the "me decade," as the writer Tom Wolfe called this narcissistic era. Their minds were concentrated on the upward climb.

"I wanted good things to happen to everybody, but me first," said a smiling young stockbroker, selected by *Playboy* to represent his getting-richer-quicker generation. He and his peers were "selfish about their success," the magazine noted with up-to-date approval. They didn't worry about what they could afford, only about getting what they wanted. And what they wanted was to get the goods—those racquets and records, sleek automobiles and opulent apartments (formerly called "Playboy pads")—that signified success to them. "Experience collectors," the magazine labeled these anxiously acquisitive young men. But the experiences that they collected, when amatory, tended to be swift and shallow; when otherwise, faddish and ephemeral.

By and large, they deified objects. Getting more and more was an almost religious aspiration, and spending money for it something like an act of sanctification. But if bachelors elected to bestow this grace upon themselves, it was not always just because they spent more than they made, even when living alone. Some men so rich that they could have kept harems in several countries shrank from matrimony too.

Many charged, expectably, that the new autonomy of women was alienating *them*. "Girls don't want to get married any more, unless they've really got nothing better to do—or they're queer for owning oil wells," an oil-refinery tycoon in Texas said. Others issued the opposite complaint, less cynical but almost as widespread: women had yet to achieve *enough* autonomy to suit them. In New York, one of the country's wealthiest young bachelors, who did not wish to be known as "the playboy millionaire," reported that "the old patterns of dependency" still clung damply to some of the newest women. "But I just don't feel comfortable with someone who likes puttering around the house; someone who expects me to be her entire emotional life," James Campbell said. Only in the past eight months, this heir to one of America's great fortunes had endured sixty "dates," by his own careful reckoning. ("I hate that word," he admitted, after using it.) But he had all but dozed through most of them. None of the chosen was sufficiently emancipated, or sufficiently intelligent, to interest him for more than a few hours—or for a few evenings.

In his many long years of unmarried life (Campbell was forty), he could count only three "serious commitments. And the last girl I lived with relied on me so totally for everything that it was frankly distressing," he said. "It was I who decided who we saw, where we went, and when. She was living off what I was giving her, economically and every other way. She wasn't introducing me to any new ideas or to any new people, and she wasn't earning any money either. Living as my dependent, she was eroding her own self-respect." More or less as a favor to the girl—to save her from her own worst self—he abolished their provisional household.

Sharp female intellect was really what pleased him, the millionaire confided. "There are lots of attractive women all over the place, but most of them have let their minds go to sleep," he regretted. " 'Damn it, you're not using your wits,' I want to say to them. 'If you don't feel challenged and excited by what's going on, how can you hope to come across as very smart?' "

Like many of his poorer cousins, Campbell believed that intelligence and dependence on men were antithetical in the female personality. The former was as high up on the scale of human values as the latter was low down. He outlined the contemporary conformations of Ms. Right in a brisk and businesslike tone, as if describing a new automobile design, still in its experimental stages. Predictably, she was no old-fashioned girl. She was a self-motivating, self-propelling "woman of accomplishment, above-average beautiful, with a high metabolism; that is, eagerness, mental acuity, open-mindedness."

Growing nostalgic, he recalled the only woman he had ever known who nearly approximated this vision of femininity. "She was so very bright; an IQ of 160," he sighed. "She worked for ecology and energy, but she was interested in those things very narrowly," Campbell declared. "Ecology and energy, that's all."

Even when her range of concerns approached the global, however, such a woman eliminated herself as a prospective wife. "She's hard to groove with," the millionaire explained. "When you're both creating your own busy schedules every day from the top down, it's almost impossible to interlock." He proposed a hypothetical case. "She's a high-powered correspondent on a weekly news magazine, meeting a story deadline. How can she promise to show up for cocktails at six sharp and be free for dinner at a certain hour?" All the better women were occupied elsewhere, prisoners of schedules with which his own could only clash.

Sex occupied a back seat in Campbell's limousine—and not very often at that. It was boringly available. He could take it or leave it. "There have been many periods in my own life when work was so important that I became sexually uninterested," he said. Campbell's work was mostly of a philanthropic nature. He did not actively participate in the family enterprises, but he enjoyed poking around in public affairs with his long check-book. "When I get absorbed in a project, it's not difficult to spend months and months without sleeping with anybody. I don't feel deprived."

This ability to forgo the life of the flesh for loftier, or at least more cerebral, pursuits was viewed as a sign of strength. Few of the bachelors I met seemed to yearn for erotic engagements with highly charged, sexual women. They preferred plainer fellowship from girls. They doted on the straight-from-the-shoulder sort of pal whom Humphrey Bogart once described as "a real Joe." They valued her because she was good at playing cribbage, or the piano, or jokes, or the stock market. If she was good in the kitchen and good in bed, that was—sometimes—a bonus. But not always. For many a bachelor liked his own cooking best; and as for the lesser art of copulation, well . . . even the lowest animals were good at *that*.

It was widely assumed that the younger the man, the more he appreciated this bland, rather boyish girl named Joe. Freshly scrubbed and as forthright as he, she was still turning up in her blue jeans and sneakers on nearly every campus in America. But, in fact, the younger the man, the more exasperated and the less infatuated he tended to be with Joe. After all, he had grown up with her. She had reached her apogee in his own generation. He knew her better than anyone else. She had been reared on the omnipresent women's-studies courses, glorifying worldly accomplishment, in the high schools and colleges they attended together. On television, the mythic figure of Mary Richards (a.k.a. Mary Tyler Moore) had ratified the new ideal of femininity for all the children of the seventies, male and female alike. In the ever-hungry media—dazzled by dollar signs and signs of more dollars—the self-serving, self-supporting bachelor queen was ritually anointed.

"A young woman's first priority today is herself. Openly so. A job is more than a way of earning a few extra dollars. She expects to get somewhere," said *Glamour*—like *Playboy*, a magazine influential enough in its readers' lives to create behavior as well as reflect it.

But even among these youngest unmarried American adults, the sexes were already out of synch. In this society as in the older one, as the women grew more outward, opening to the world, the men grew more conservative. Somewhere on the way to maturity, probably from old movies like *Intermezzo* and *Gone With the Wind*, they had caught a heady whiff of the past. And they liked it. Those natural feelings of *dominus* that had been squelched or exhausted or denied in the preceding generation were once more rising within them.

"I've got to find out about love," said one undergraduate athlete who had experimented briefly with what his social-science professor called "scorecard sex." Superficial connections and casual attachments were making this young man uneasy. But how to find out about love, whose first priority was always the Other, with a young woman whose first priority was herself? "My sex life has no meaning at all. It's as if I'm plugging into some machine—no face, no feelings, no sharing," the worried athlete said.

This faceless, unfeeling, unsharing "machine" was the girl named Joe in one of her many guises. Elsewhere, Erica Jong had christened her a connoisseur of the "zipless fuck," unencumbered by emotion or sometimes even by acquaintance. Her older sisters might still have been somewhat apologetic about self-assertion, somewhat wary of sex for sex's sake, some-what timid about displaying their militance "up front." Joe was not. She took all that for granted. Hers was the first generation to feminism born.

"The prime thing coming out right now is selfishness," said George Davidson, a college senior in Maryland, about the Joes of his acquaintance. "The girl I'm living with is awfully goal-oriented, much more than me. She's already got her master's degree in drama and speech. But now she wants a doctorate in psychology more than anything else in this world." His red beard spread out like a bright, bushy napkin over his blue denim jacket. Although he thought of himself as "atypical" (almost everyone did), it was not only his looks that marked him a child of his times.

College men all over the country seemed to be living with the same woman now. "My girl was counting on getting her master's at the end of the year," one said on another campus in another state. "Now that she realizes she's not going to do it, she's super fucked up. She may agree to get married," he explained, "but she doesn't want to be a wife."

George Davidson expanded on the wedlock question. He too, he said, "would like to get married after graduation—and I'd like to have kids. But Berry doesn't see it that way. It'll be a long time before she'll be able to think of a man as any more than a sometime thing." Davidson did not like to think of himself as a sometime thing and it showed in his troubled green eyes. "Having a baby in the foreseeable future would mess up her life, my girl says. If she were to get pregnant, she'd get an abortion right away. But I wouldn't pay for it. I've told her that," he added sternly. Refusing to become her accomplice in an act which he did not approve affirmed *dominus* for him—at least a little. "I don't believe in abortion. I think that's a form of selfishness too. Sexual actions should have consequences and people should accept them. A life without consequences, it can make everything sort of meaningless."

He was responding to the mores of the generation just before him, the generation that had misplaced its moral compass. "About childbirth—I just don't believe a woman has the sole right to choose. That's pure propaganda, aimed against men," Davidson said. He spoke with more forthrightness than many bachelors ten years older. "I've never seen a woman get pregnant all by herself. It's half her partner's doing and half his responsibility too. It won't ruin anyone's life to carry a child for nine months. But with lots of girls, I think they just would rather maintain their slim figures."

Davidson owned up to some male resentment. "Sure, I wanted to get a real life going. But I got no cooperation from Berry." After she had turned down his offer of marriage "more than a couple of times," he decided that, upon graduation, he would take a trip with a male friend, "a kind of American grand tour that could last two or three months . . . or two or three years. What the hell, maybe floating's an okay existence," he said. But his voice vibrated with indecisiveness. "In any case, we're going to Texas, Mexico, South Carolina, Utah, and Washington. We're putting together a little traveling minstrel show. I play the recorder; he plays the kazoo and harmonica. We'll have pantomime and music and try to make some bread that way . . . at coffee clubs, supper clubs, at the beaches."

But he did not pretend that the prospect enchanted him. Davidson had misgivings even before he hit the road. "People my age think they want to be free. That idea—of freedom—has been handed down to us. But it's no solution to anything. Free to be what? Free to be unemployed, unattached, unhappy?" He scratched his long sideburns, not the only man lately to ponder the real meaning of liberty.

"Well, one of these days, we're all going to have to grow up, including my girl. Berry thinks she's sophisticated. But being scared of commitment, of getting married and having kids, that's pretty infantile, isn't it? I believe her emotions haven't yet caught up with her intellect, although she's two years older than me."

The popular movements toward liberation, Davidson felt,

were essentially movements "toward selfishness" too. "Group things, and group think, turn me off," he said, reviewing some current group fashions. "Hare Krishna, the Moonies—I'm not one of them. As for the 'people' movements . . . well, who's not for people? But my mother was always a career woman, and I didn't grow up thinking of females as second-class citizens. Lesbians, gays, and others like them, they're really the second-class citizens. But I don't feel part of their crusade."

As it was so often true, beneath Davidson's beard and denims lurked an extremely traditional male. He returned to the subject that was most on his mind. "When I met my present girl, I only knew that her name was Berry Bergmann. That could have been Swedish or German. But no, it was Jewish!" This had extra-religious significance for him. "For some reason, I can't get away from Jewish women. Of course, I've got nothing against Gentile girls. But the last three or four women I've liked, all of them were Jews. Maybe it's the standard myth of 'Eat, eat, eat' I fall for every time. Not that they give me chicken soup." He smiled. "But, well, I guess I thought Berry would be more of a, you know, a nurturing woman." Behind his frazzled beard, his face broke into a broad grin, vivid with self-awareness. "After all, she's not only Jewish, she's two years older than me."

The young men of the seventies may have been "reacting negatively" to their parents' marriages, as some educators asserted, yet for many of them, it seemed to result in the wish not to overthrow the institution but to improve it.

Raleigh Jones, a community college sophomore in Massachusetts, was even younger than Davidson. His cheeks were still almost as smooth as a child's and he might not quite have reached his full height, but he too already had marriage on his mind. "Less regimented than my mom's and dad's" was the way Jones described the kind of union he would like. He had known his current girlfriend, he said, since they were both freshmen in high school. "We were childhood sweethearts, you might say. I get attached to someone very easily, and if I like the relationship, I want it to last. But my girl's not so sure about marrying."

He ran down the familiar symptoms of the antiwedlock epidemic among college women. "Jenny says she wants to go into retailing, not into the maternity ward. She thinks that someday she might even get to be vice president of a fancy store like Neiman-Marcus in Texas. Well, that's fine when you look at it from an objective standpoint. And I wouldn't want to hold anyone back from anything, least of all her. But when it's happening in your own life, you feel differently about it." Nevertheless, just as older men did, young Jones prided himself on his tolerance. "No matter how I feel, I try not to get into a rut and insist, 'It's all wrong.' That would be close-minded."

He produced a photograph of Jenny—tall, slender, blue-jeaned, and steely. With tons of blond hair and layers of green eyeshadow, she looked like a cheerleader of the fifties rather than a Joe of the seventies. "She's very strong-willed," Jones said. "So what can I do? I just let it all ride along, seeing what happens, where it goes. Forcing it to come together unnaturally, that wouldn't be any good. I was brought up to appreciate a nice home, a family, and dinner on the table every night. But Jenny's parents are divorced. She's awfully unsure."

Those girls who were more marriage-minded than Jenny did not appeal to Raleigh Jones. "They're just out to find men . . . and they're after the richest man they can find. They come up here, look around, sort out the prospects, and attach themselves to the most likely guy. This state has more colleges than most countries do, so it's not hard for girls to get around." Young men, he said, were "caught in the squeeze between these husband-hunter types who want to marry for all the wrong reasons and girls like Jenny," for whom the fate of a "housewife" had become the worst fate of all: no excitement, no appreciation, an abrupt closing down of alternatives.

" 'My mom was a housewife,' Jenny says, 'and when my father left, he asked her, "What did you ever do for me? Cook hot dinners every night?" ' I'm not Jenny's father reincarnated. But she sort of thinks I am." His sigh was heavy for one not yet twenty. "God, I don't even know how this whole thing got started, do you?"

The sexual seesaw teeter-tottered nowhere more wildly than on these campuses of the nation. The constant push toward equality, perhaps stronger in college than anywhere else, often had the effect of shaking young male and female equilibrium. At the University of Georgia, a dozen or so undergraduate men were talking about women in the same engrossed way that young women used to talk about men. "I see it as a situation similar to what's happened to blacks in recent history," said a mathematics major, sitting behind a tall stack of textbooks. "Now it's women who want to form an exclusive society. The smartest girls have decided to make their own way in the world without male help. I see no need for separation—why can't men and women work together?—but *they* do. They just don't trust our intentions."

"Those are the extreme cases," his classmate demurred. "The much more common case is the woman who would like to relate to men on a completely equal basis. She doesn't want to take a separatist position, but circumstances force her into it. It's still pretty difficult for college women to compete equally. Lots of old male professors put down female students in subtle little ways. It's their defense against seeming intimidated."

But in almost no time the talk turned toward marriage. "I would say definitely, absolutely, that I would contribute *more* than 50 percent," vowed a small, freckle-faced fellow whose sparse goatee only emphasized that he had just turned the corner from puberty. "For a marriage to be successful, it can't be just a fifty-fifty deal. That way, someone's going to come up short and it'll turn out forty-sixty. So you have to take that extra mile, that extra leap. It has to be 60 percent or 70 percent that you contribute!"

The other men looked impressed. Then the boy sitting next to the goatee said, "But even if you're contributing *all* you've got, that's still only half, only 50 percent."

"No. That's my whole point," the goatee responded. "You *can't* just contribute all you've got. That's never enough. There's always more you can contribute. If it's a sincere relationship, equality is a stingy idea. In a sincere relationship, each always gives *more* than his share." This was not the way many of their less idealistic older brothers would have talked.

A senior, majoring in biology, brought up his—possibly—impending nuptials. "I'm engaged right now. My fiancée and myself are in the same field. We want to go on to graduate work. Of course we'd like to be together. But if she gets into one school and I get into another, we don't know what we'll do. Who makes the concession? So my fiancée says, 'Let's stay engaged . . . indefinitely.' To her, marriage just means limitation." He had the wan and worried look of so many men his age. "It's a very different situation than it was twenty years ago. Girls were less likely to want graduate education then. And even when they did, the choice was clear. The male would have chosen."

These young college students, while often less cynical, had no fewer problems with women than men twice as old. "I don't want to live up to any stereotypes set by anybody—whether it's superconsciousness of my maleness in the old way, or superconsciousness of my liberatedness in the new way," said a quiet, thoughtful boy with horn-rimmed glasses. "But where's the alternative? Practically whatever I do and whatever I say, I know that I'll still be called sexist. You're talking to a girl about, oh, anything and suddenly her eyes get hard and she brands you a sexist, even if you've only said, 'Gee, you've got a nice new haircut there.'"

They agreed that communication between men and women

had become ridden with pitfalls. "Some subjects, like rape, you can't discuss with girls at all," a pre-law student brought out. "They're just too sensitive. There was a specific problem at the law school. Women use the library late at night and some were accosted on the way to their cars. The initial response from the faculty was, 'Get a man to escort you to your automobile.' Well, the idea that maybe women did need male protection enraged them. We're stuck with this society, we have to live in it. But the minute you say that to a woman, she accuses you of being reactionary. We shouldn't accept the society, she says, we should change it. They see themselves as a revolutionary class."

"If a man slows down his car and whistles, some girls spit, only because—as yet—they're unarmed," a female student at an Eastern college had said earlier. "Reports of attempted rape are a dime a dozen. The next step will be to make flirting a federal offense with shooting permissible on sight. The way some people talk, you begin to think, Why not arm all the girls with rifles, electrify all the fences, set up a twenty-four-hour police system, and assign each of us a guard dog?" Then she relinquished her tart tone. "But arming yourself against men, even if it's just psychologically, is arming yourself against the whole rest of the world. I'd rather take my chances."

A young man at Emory pursued the same general theme. "If it's not hostility between men and women, it's apathy. That goes for sexual apathy too. I mean, of course, there's plenty of sexual *activity* . . ."

"Too much," a freshman cut in. He had curly hair and serious brown eyes. "There's an awful lot of loose-goose shacking up on this campus. A fellow comes into his dorm and finds that his roommate has decided to bring his concubine home for the night . . . or for the rest of the semester. That's upsetting. First, because it's an infringement on privacy. The rooms here are small. Two people's pushing it, three's intolerable." He described the situation in his own suite. "My roommate lives with his girlfriend. But it's more or less just a body-warmth arrangement. The only thing they're really concerned about is getting into law school or medical school. The competition is forever increasing. They're so involved with their studies that they never take time off to get really involved with each other, except sexually. That's apathy, in caps."

"You're damned if you do and you're damned if you don't," another sighed, talking about sex in the dormitory. "You're led to believe that platonic friendships are fine; that you can develop relationships without a lot of sexual politics. So you accept a girl as an asexual person. Then she lets you have it because you're not playing your 'male role.' And when you tell people that you're just friends, that there's no action, *they* say, 'Oh, you're not sleeping together? Why not, for God's sake?' "

Finally, one freshman made the case for chastity. And nobody laughed. "For me, it takes a long relationship to become intimate with anybody," he said. "I totally believe in sexual fidelity. I don't believe in sex without love. I don't believe in loose-goose shacking up. I'm totally against it—for myself. If Alf wants to shack up and Steve wants to shack up, that's fine with me. It does not affect me. But personally, I could not have sex with someone I could not love. And I do mean *love*."

He was encouraged by the raptness of the silence to continue. "I want to wait until I get married to have sex. My parents and my grandparents and my mother's ten brothers and sisters all got married and stayed married. They've given me the feeling that sex with a person is really a sacred thing. And so is marriage. The girl I go with thinks I'm crazy," he said. "But I'm not crazy." Then he added, gently apologetic, "Of course, I'm afraid I'm unique. Maybe odd's the word for it."

He was not as unique, or as odd, as he suspected. The old romance of gender beckoned many of the young men of his generation. They were beginning to express their respect for *dominus* in some old and unexpected ways.

5 | Blacks: Gender Euphoria

"Manhood in this country has many meanings, but a central theme is clear," Drs. William H. Grier and Price M. Cobbs, the psychiatrist-authors of *Black Rage* wrote in 1968, referring to white society. "Men are very early taught that they have certain prerogatives and privileges. They are encouraged to pursue, to engage life, to attack, rather than to shrink back . . ."

Within a decade that theme had grown muddier than the Mississippi River. The tides now ran the other way. Now white men were questioning their prerogatives and privileges. And blacks were engaging life, attacking adversity with courage, and relishing the rites of *dominus* as if they were still sacred.

After all, good, old-fashioned masculinity had always been the black man's dearest dream. Up until a little while ago, "we were still working across the tracks in menial, degraded jobs, when we were working at all. We were beggars, or worse, in white society. Emasculation was the net effect," said Randolph Green, a banking executive in the Carolinas. "Now we treasure the so-called male role and the chance to try to live up to it," Green declared. Almost every black man made the same point about emasculation and followed it up with the same vow.

Husband and father, lover and master, breadwinner and decision-maker—these roles were not traps to him but the belated triumph of centuries. After three hundred years, he was at last throwing off the long slavery of caste, at last learning what it meant to live as a man. The word was no joke to him. He had been a "boy" too long to fail to honor it. There might be some more setbacks to black ascendancy along the way, but his destination was not in doubt. Personally, his prevailing mood could best be described as gender euphoria.

That "growing sense of black potency," noted by Roger Wilkins, among others, had hardened in the crucible of the seventies. New York attorney and Wisconsin laborer, Southern politician and Northern administrator, California cabdriver and Georgia college professor, all were as eager to take on the trust of manhood as some white men were eager to shuck it.

Samuel Archer—rangy and strong, married nearly thirty years, the father of four children—was on the administrative staff of an Eastern university. "Gender euphoria" did not quite define the mood of this mellow but hard-nosed realist. "Gender-rooted" was more like it. "We do not need group instruction to help us 'rearticulate our masculinity,' " he said, chuckling. "We do not need help in 'getting it on' or 'getting off.' We don't worry about sex. Either we do it or we don't do it, but we are not hung up about it. We are not confused by the differences between masculine and feminine. We *know* who we are."

Blacks, he said, with no false modesty, were a minor miracle of human evolution. Not only had they learned to adapt in a hostile environment, but their powers of adaptation seemed to increase in proportion to the hostility directed toward them. "None of us is supposed to exist," he reminded me. "White society has been organized for the purpose of destroying us. When you run into survivors, you run into strong men, men who have made peace with themselves."

The peace had not come easy, Archer was not alone in pointing out. "A great deal of psychic damage was done to black men in their attempts to fill the male role. But that has only made it more precious to us. We were always at a quite huge disadvantage from the standpoint of earning a living. The jobs that carried more prestige and more income went to black women. Historically, they were better educated; and they were liberated from the first, simply because of the economic realities." This imbalance put a strain on black male self-esteem, and on the self-esteem of the black family, that was only just now relaxing, he said. As blacks moved up in society, slowly gaining status and respect, they were beginning to feel better about themselves as men. "And by that, I mean as husbands and fathers. There is no other way I know to be a man."

His own father had taught him that manhood was fixed not by a set of chores but by a state of mind. "You did what you had to do to keep the family afloat—and you thanked God for the opportunity." Distinctiveness was a trick of the survival trade, handed down from father to son. "As a boy I behaved like my dad did. He died recently. He was always a tower of strength. I changed diapers just like he did. I washed dishes too. I cooked the Thanksgiving turkey every year. And I enjoy getting up early, so I was always pleased to give the children breakfast. My wife never asked me. It wasn't a question of volunteering for jobs out of some misplaced sympathy for her. I did what I wanted to do. I participated naturally—as a father. So it was always a joy to me."

Dominus did not reside in the trivia of who-does-what, but in the unstressed authority of the head of the house. Everyone knew who was boss, Sam Archer said, because the boss knew. "But I still iron my own shirts, because I press better than my wife. On the other hand, there are lots of things she does that I can't do, like working the sewing machine. Although I can sew a mean button," he added, flashing his quick smile. "It has never bothered me a bit that some of the things I do are not peculiarly male activities. There has not been a moment in my married life when I felt my manhood was in jeopardy."

He was the fulcrum of the family, the generator from which its main energy flowed. He did not undervalue his influence and power, but it would have been outside his nature to abuse it. "You succeed in life when you find a woman who complements you as a man. That I did. Without ever having consciously worked it out, Agnes and I have always taken a team approach to the perils that we face. That's because both of us are human and both of us are black."

Nevertheless, he was not oblivious to the subtleties of the sexual hierarchy in any race. "My mother was one of the early liberationists," Archer said. "Her strength was not outweighed by my father's. Yet she never usurped his role. Now I've got a daughter at Yale who's as bright and tough intellectually as my mother was. And my wife, an artist, is as sharp and outspoken as either of them. But not one of these ladies was ever mixed up for a minute about who was the man of the family." No woman whose strength of character equaled the strength of her intelligence would be caught dead trying to take over traditional male positions, he said. "Men are more comfortable with women who are free enough to acknowledge male superiority. And women who acknowledge that superiority are more comfortable with men," he declared, at least half seriously.

When it came down to the etiquette of sex, Archer was an unconflicted traditionalist. He shook his head over "this new thing of women making advances to men, articulating their right to choose partners and then discard them. Most men are very sentimental. Contrary to legend, they have deep feelings about the women they take to bed. When they believe it's just a fling, because the women lead them to believe it, something fundamental goes out of the relationship. Men may be initially flattered by these advances, but it's our natural role to be the sexual aggressor. When that's taken over, we are cut down in our maleness."

He was also clear in his feelings about militant feminism. "What happens to a society when women turn on themselves, and turn against men, and abrogate their positions as mothers and wives? It's a total and complete violation of the values of biology," he said. "Women have a biological destiny they can't control, that's how it boils down. They secrete certain hormones, whether they like it or not. Of course, no one can oppose their rise to the level of their abilities commensurate with their expertise," he added, echoing just about every man in America, "even if they go so far as becoming chairmen of the board at General Motors or General Foods. But except for the most exceptional women, it will be at the exclusion of their inherent biological demands."

While he deplored that exclusion, he respected the dynamic

that gave rise to it. "One of the basic strategies of revolution is to polarize as much as you can. So it's no surprise that the major thrust of the feminist movement has always been to polarize against men. There's no other way to revolt, except against those whom one conceives as the enemy. But I have to wonder: When does the recognition by women of their rights begin to represent a threat to us?" Sam Archer answered his own question. "When it constitutes a basic attack against the family. Because the family is our only true protective environment." His voice grew warmer. Family was his favorite subject. "We live in a time when it's a mortal sin to be yourself. We're staggering under massive doses of camouflage. There's got to be that one place in the world where there's no need for camouflage, or for artifice, or for playing games. There's got to be that final sanctuary."

He did not share the familiar ambivalence of the white middle class about the value of parenthood. It carried heavy obligations, like all other rights and privileges, Archer said without resentment. "Life is a series of sacrifices for those you love. What's important is establishing priorities. Once you bite that bullet, you've got it made. All of us are seething with unfulfilled ambitions. But you give up your dreams gladly for something better than dreams. You give them up for those you love. If you fulfill your ambitions at the expense of the welfare of others, you're an animal, that's all." Sam Archer was the least equivocal of men. "Family," he breathed. "Hell, that's the only thing you live for. It's there that we survive. Otherwise all of us are homeless."

Even for blacks who had cast off marital ties, family often remained the proving ground of manhood. They were less likely than white men to appreciate the liberties and non-alliances of a bachelor's life.

"We got divorced because she thought I wasn't paying enough attention to the marriage," said Stanley Burns, a taxi driver in San Francisco. He wore a white knit fisherman's sweater, a purple visor cap, and a gold ring that commemorated his high-school graduation. "I was traveling back and forth to Dallas, where I grew up. I was spending too much money, trying to find a nicer berth for both of us than this old taxicab. But she said we was going off in opposite directions. Maybe we was. Sometimes you have to part with something to find out how much it means to you."

The clang of a passing cable car interrupted him. "But I was shocked, and that's no maybe, when they served me with the papers down at the garage. It really shook me up. I didn't think she'd go through with the divorce proceedings. Because we had a good thing going there. We really loved each other. But women today have a tendency to act in haste at the early signs of dissatisfaction. Still, it taught me a thing or two. The divorce gave me time to get into my own life, to figure out where I'm at and where I would like to go."

Where he would like to go, Stanley Burns said, was "back to where I came from, back to her. I miss the comfort and fulfillment of having a real home life. You feel less free, but more like a man. My wife's in Bath, England, with our six-year-old daughter. She's working for a law firm there. I wrote to her that I'm beginning to get myself together. I'm into vegetarianism in a big way, studying up on nutrition in books and courses. I've got definite plans to develop a new organic food."

Some friends from Los Angeles, whom he had met through one of the courses, had agreed to stake him to a journey to Switzerland to present his plans to chemists there. Of course, he would take a side trip to Bath. "I guess I won't rediscover Granola, and maybe the chemists will tell me I'm talking to the wind," he said. "But if I get back with my wife and daughter, I'll be satisfied. I used to think this damn taxi was my prison. The real prison is being nothing to nobody."

"Upside-down economics," Alfred Norton said, had thrust him back into the single life. "She didn't know how to live with a man, she lost interest in giving him his due respect," he declared, of his former wife. "They making more money than you, they just get a swelled head. Ain't anything can touch 'em."

He worked in a printing plant and "pulled down a pretty good salary. I mean it seemed good, until hers got better. With a few extra bucks from showroom modeling, she got stubborn, dominating, nasty, mean, and rude. Some women, they're alley cats when they are born, and some turn into alley cats when they get older and richer."

Norton laughed, then admitted his loneliness. "A man gotta have a woman or he don't know he's a man—someone sincere and honest, sincere and true. Men are jive-time friends. They're summertime friends. But for the everyday, all-day, all-season friends, I still have to bet on the woman."

He could recall a time when wives were less feisty and husbands less frustrated, he said. "There were five sisters and two brothers in my childhood home. We boys and my father, we didn't do anything housewise. My mother fixed my father's dinner and my father's bath. She washed his back for him every night of his life. Now she seemed to enjoy that, she would laugh and laugh, running him down with the soapy water."

He pushed back his visor cap and scratched his head, remembering. "We had a regular family life. You don't see that much any more. My sisters cooked for us, took care of us boys, because they wanted to. They even used to fight for me in school, since I was the youngest one. 'Don't you mess with my brother!' they used to say. That's what I mean by family feeling."

Alfred Norton confessed to a sense of loss that, by now, most white men took for granted. "There was a mother to me in every one of my sisters. So I guess I came to expect that of a woman. But there was no mother at all I could find in my wife. That girl was just turning into an accountant."

Other blacks were coping with other challenges to *dominus* besides the conventional ones of role. They were defending themselves, not only against white society and often against their own women, but also against some of the men of their own race.

In a country living room deep in Georgia, a group of black college professors and their spouses were discussing a recent unsettling incident of black-to-black harassment. Blaming it on sporadic small robberies, the black campus "Gestapo," an economics professor explained, had erected a fence that closed off the college grounds to faculty members after class on evenings and weekends. This act and the consternation it created, the professors believed, was probably a prelude to the rumored desegregation of the all-black campus. It would cause the firing of some black instructors and the hiring of whites.

"The letter of the law can break the will of the people, *if* the people let it," a music professor warned. " 'Only men of limited ideas take for law what the words expressly say.' And I quote— from a white man!" The gathering erupted into laughter. Racial integration might be turning into a Jekyll-and-Hyde phenomenon in front of their noses, but even that was not enough to bring them down.

"There is a black administrator among us, in the highest echelon, who is receiving reinforcements from the white culture. He put up this fence to limit our authority, to coop us up and keep us in our places," a professor of history explained. "He has this kind of Hitler feeling. He gives orders and expects us to abide by them, regardless of how we feel. Maybe he thinks we'll get angry enough or fearful enough to resign without a fight."

Antagonism from the white world was never unexpected. But how were they to endure the betrayal of brother by brother? Beer was passed, music played, and laughter rose as the group examined that solemn question. They would not grow glum in the face of circumstance. They were inured against it by time and trials.

"Last Sunday, I needed some books from my office. I was arrested for driving my car across the campus by a member of the Gestapo," the professor reported. "Why, that illiterate policeman couldn't even spell the word he wrote out on my ticket. Trespassing: t-r-e-s-p-i-s-i-n-g. Now, that's not what I was doing!"

"But what kind of men are we that we don't resist?" a professor of philosophy asked when the laughter died down. These men could tap a multitude of feelings within minutes. "The whole thing is really tragic, because we aren't doing anything about it. I gripe as much as anyone, but that's just stirring up noise. Why don't I act? What am I waiting for? Where is my manhood?" Young yet, in his early thirities, William Foote was one of the campus sages. He had recently published a thin, fevered volume of verse. "I'm not so sure I'm as free as I should be. When men create values, they falsify life. Something constricts under the pressure of those values. I built a house here, the worst thing I ever could have done, because I became fettered to this community. If I lose my job, my project perishes." He was at work on his doctorate, an existential interpretation of the life and times of that defender of the oppressed, Don Quixote.

"Maybe it doesn't matter to the cosmos if I starve to death or if I become a bum. But I married Patricia. I am responsible for her. There's another value. The mere fact that I have to take care of this woman here—and I do have to take care of her—means that I must choose to suffer, bear the brunt from my superiors, accept just a little more crap than I accepted before. We're constantly abandoning our freedom in the name of love . . ."

Patricia, his fragile wife of twelve weeks who had written the preface to his book of poems, maintained a respectful, worried silence. Her skin, the color of milk chocolate, was moist with emotion. She wore a brown knit pants suit, a white satin blouse, and as many gold chain necklaces as if she still lived in the large Eastern city where she had studied for her master's degree in English. While her husband held forth, she leaned forward in her chair, forehead puckered, mouth tight. Then, clearing her throat, she spoke at last: "*That* could be your manhood, William. Abandoning freedom in the name of love . . ."

The philosophy professor gave her a haughty glance, deadly as it was devoted. "If I had it to do all over again—if I could get women out of my blood, which I cannot—I'd drop out of school at tenth-grade level," he said to his audience, flourishing his can of beer. "I think any black man who goes beyond tenth grade is unfair to his black heritage. With a strong healthy body like mine, I could be making $350 a week as a construction worker. I cannot make $350 as a Ph.D. I'm poor because I'm intellectual, that's the case."

This was nothing new to his colleagues. For black men, as well as white, educationally up was sometimes economically down. They were sympathetic but silent.

Like any natural star, the poet regarded silence as a vacuum to be filled. "When I first heard that all behavior was an expression of the energy of the libido, it infatuated me," he said. "And when I decided to work on my doctorate, I knew that had more sexual overtones than academic. On the sexual market, my stock goes higher as 'doctor of' than some guy's who's working in a plant. Why, I have seduced a caboose full of white women just because I have a mind," he declared. "If I want to take some white women to bed on the basis of my intelligence, that's easy. It appeals to their sweet, foolish vanity that I come well equipped in more than one direction. Yet intellect in white men turns them off."

He was enjoying his impromptu dissertation at least as much as his audience. "Now with or without my Ph.D., the black woman's too tough to crack. She's so uptight about everything, especially sex, she never even gives me a smile. If she does, she thinks that means I think she's available. But white women, they smile just for nothing. See, the whole thing's predicated on a smile."

He blew his breath into the triangular aperture on top of the beer can, as if calling for closer attention. But only Patricia seemed restless. "When I was at the University of Mexico, white girls were a dime a dozen at the local bars. But black girls don't go to local bars in Mexico. Why, even in a Georgia supermarket, if you offer to help a black girl pull her buggy out into the parking lot, she believes you're trying to make her. Of course black women are far superior sexually to white women," he said, "but you got to marry them before you get them into bed. And even then, they're tough to crack."

The poet's wife poured some Scotch into a glass without ice. She sipped it very slowly.

"But what is worse than my mean and poor motivation for remaining meanly poor," William Foote continued, already high on too much beer and the right of free speech, "my black brothers feel abandoned by me, you see. They feel I am not authentically black any more, that I have severed myself from them. Because as a professor, I represent a symbol of authority . . ."

He sent up ideas like kites and watched them float in the sky all at once, charmed by their color and variety. The campus-fence kite dangled beside the white-woman kite and the black-authenticity kite, their tails miraculously untangled. Pausing to puncture another can of beer, he released some questions to fly around the room. How could a black man express his negritude most advantageously for himself and his race? Did true manhood lie in the refusal to assimilate? In the determination not to fade out into the white world but to stubbornly maintain his own distinction?

"Could I get a word in edgewise?" the professor of education shouted while William Foote was catching his breath. The crowd roared. Sitting stage-center on the frayed green velvet couch, the poet-philosopher bowed. His head touched his knees. Even Patricia smiled.

"In Jackson, Mississippi, when segregation was segregation, I went to a theater that was all black," this professor recalled. "It was one of the most beautiful black-owned theaters in the nation, a proud enterprise. But it's deteriorating now. The black educated upper middle class have deserted it. They have found other places to go."

"That fine black motel in Perry, the Ebony, it's run-down too," another added. "The Forrest Arms, the University Hotel, all finished. Everybody with a dollar in his pocket and a degree up on his wall goes to the Hyatt Regency and the Marriott and the Holiday Inn . . ."

"There are men on television, you can't tell they're black any more, if you're not looking straight at them," the professor of history said. "A few years ago, their speech would have given them away. It would have had some distinction."

Integration, that incorrigible Jekyll-and-Hyde, could attack *dominus* while seeming to advance it. The private ambition to become "more white," by negating blackness could negate identity too. Men, Foote said, could sacrifice self-pride, self-possession, finally self.

Women could too, Patricia declared. She sipped her Scotch as if a little bit suspicious of it. Her voice had a fine, high, bell-like ring. "You absorb the aspects of a culture," she remembered, of her academic experience up North. "I saw my blackness fading. There was no collard greens and no cornbread. My life style was changing. My values were changing. So I came back down home."

"Even at home, we're traitors," her husband said. "We're traitors, just as much as that treasonous black brother who put up the fence. We have got to decide pretty soon whether we want black solidarity and cohesiveness or whether each man's for himself."

His wife put down her glass. "Can a man be a traitor to his marriage too, as well as to his race?" Patricia asked. William Foote gave her another freighted look. Without sentiment, it throbbed with many meanings. No one appeared discomforted by the evident tension of this Saturday-night encounter. But perhaps they were all resigned to the fact that marriage, by its nature, was tension-making.

"Monogamy is in opposition to human consciousness. Marriage is a betrayal of man, man betraying himself," said the poet. "We should have a free fluidity of alternatives. I can know one woman only through many women. No other way of knowing one woman exists."

Patricia stared at him. Any one of those kites he raised seemed sturdier than she did. She looked as if a soft wind could blow her away. He was goaded on by her vulnerability. "The more adaptable the wife, the greater the intelligence, the more accepting she is of her husband's affairs," he asserted. "And she herself should be capable of having three or four men in her life at a time. The more limited the intelligence, the more threatened by 'the free exuberance of nature.'" He loved quotations, whether accurate or not, as much as he loved dramatic statements. "Nietzsche said, Live according to the true dictates of consciousness. Heidegger warned against inauthentic lives." For punctuation, he broke open another can of beer. The foam shot over his silky pale-blue shirt.

"I guess that does not answer my question," Patricia said. Her tiny voice was trembling. "I was not asking Nietzsche or Heidegger for anything. I was asking you for a simple yes or no."

Now a small, wiry man with big, knobby hands and a head like Gandhi's spoke in support of the poet-philosopher. "I am an African. My father had thirty-eight wives. Since I've lived here, I've had more women than my father had," he declared in an accent as rich and dense as mashed potatoes. "I think I could take care of 108 women sexually, if you just give me six weeks," he said. "William is right. Monogamy is wrong in terms of male consciousness. It will not foster the manhood of American blacks." This little man of such large aptitudes might have been anywhere from forty to sixty years old. He was sharing his household with a fifteen-year-old bride, sent to him from his native Nigeria.

Most of the others were not shocked by the sexual radicalism that he and the poet advocated. Perhaps they had long since come to terms with it. But Patricia was blinking back tears.

"American blacks have commendable ambition," the little Nigerian said, speaking in an exotic rhythm that made six short words sound like one long one. He did not take breaths between phrases. "But sooner or later, they've got to find a way of hooking themselves on with the Africans. Otherwise, they'll evaporate as black men. They'll get bleached out. It's happening already. Blacks are torn between and betwixt. Monogamy goes against the free expression of our nature. We feel pride in ourselves on one hand, humiliation on the other . . ."

"Acceptance by the white world, that's what we're all still after," the professor of music said. "Nothing's changed. It's sort of a classical thing. We used to give theatrical programs around here. If a white person showed up and enjoyed the program, you wouldn't hear anything else during the whole next day but, 'Even the whites enjoyed it.' William's right. We're not our own men . . ."

"We're goddamn snobs!" the poet-philosopher cried exuberantly. "Not only about color, but about class and education. Snobbery is an effete characteristic. I guard against it. I accept people wholly on the basis of character. Whether you're a sixth grader or a seventh grader, you come to my parties. You'll find Ph.D.'s, M.D.'s; you'll also find fifth-graders."

He clung to the spotlight. "About three months ago, I decided to burn up some land. And you know what? The fire got away. It almost took down the town. Old fella down the road, Mr. Halson, probably a third-grader at best, he came and he fought and he fought. I walked up to my own house and sat down on a pile of sand and said, 'I just can't fight no more, my Lord.' But this old man fought the fire until he got it under control. Where were my Ph.D. buddies when that fire was running rampant? I couldn't find them. I sent for one and he sent back that he was having a party! 'Tell Dr. Foote I'm in the midst of a party. I have guests.'" The poet-philosopher mimicked his doctoral friend in a high-pitched voice, crooking his little finger above the beer can.

"That wasn't me, was it?" the professor of history cried in falsetto, mimicking the poet's mimicry. Once more the gathering was regaled.

"No, we looked for *you*," the poet said, wiping the mirth from his eyes with one hand and his beer-stained blue shirt with the other. "We couldn't find you. You was probably buried up to your neck in six feet of books." One more kite was launched. "Education is just like religion. Worse than worthless."

"Some people need their religion. It's all the faith some people have left," Patricia murmured.

"Well, the first time I started teaching was the first time I borrowed money," the Nigerian said. This brought down the house again. "If I laid bricks for a living, I would not just be richer, I would feel better too. Now I carry some pills in my pocket from the doctor at all times. The upheaval of doing something with the educated mind makes me nervous. But laying bricks wouldn't be as big a challenge as my classroom. Education is an instrument for people who have abandoned life for intellect," he finished sadly.

A beautiful, high-strung psychiatrist, the wife of the music professor, defended education with flashing eyes and many gestures of her long, eloquent hands. "How else can you learn the skills and techniques and strategies necessary to deal with the system? How else except through education can you plug into a certain kind of job that gives you your status, authority, and power?"

She told of her days at a university medical center in the Deep South, "where I was the only black and the only female. I found it to be a very trying experience. White male professors worked hard to flunk me out. All they wanted to do was to be able to say, 'This nigger has messed up down here.'" Her elegance belied the words. She was dressed in flowery chiffon and her long pink fingernails were shaped like perfect moons. "But it wasn't only the professors. One psychiatric attendant took the batteries out of my pager in the hospital where I was working in Emergency. He was the kind of honky who would lynch me as soon as look at me. But I kept on fighting for my education. Because it strengthens you. It makes you adaptable. And that's what you got to be."

The poet-philosopher leaped again. "Where's my authority? Where's my power?" he asked the psychiatrist. "I'm a poor, starved-out poet nobody reads, writing a doctorate nobody will quote. Christianity's serving the white man, not the black," he said, as untroubled by his non sequitur as by the fact that his wife had closed her eyes and seemed to be sleeping. "The church encourages us in our passivity: God will take care. Well, history gives each phenomenon a chance to prove itself. Religion has had more time than any phenomenon I know. But what has it done for the black man? Now I will never ask a person, 'What do you do in your bedroom at night? Do you treat your wife as a human being or a stick of furniture?' It's the same with prayers. They're a private matter. But on Sunday, I play six sets of tennis as a therapeutic release . . . and I know that I feel better than anybody who goes to church."

"There's still such a thing as blasphemy," Patricia said. She did not open her eyes.

The poet regarded his wife as if she were an interesting artifact he could preserve or destroy, depending on his whim. "And there's still such a thing as having a baby," he said. Nobody seemed surprised. They all took the unexpected for granted.

"But at thirty-three, I'm too old psychologically," he went on. "A baby would mean too great a loss of freedom. When a man cries for freedom, you can only stand back."

"Since you have such a feeling for private matters, why are you discussing this baby of yours right here?" Patricia's eyes, open now, were wet.

"Because economics has turned sex into a travesty and that is a public concern," he said, never at a loss. "I can't afford to bring another William Foote into the world. You know how much it costs to get a William Foote into the world today? Eight hundred dollars!" he cried.

"Too old, too poor, or too little freedom? Which is it stopping you? When you got so many reasons, maybe you got none," his wife said. She blew her nose. For a moment it seemed that they were alone in the room, equally vulnerable to one another. Then he clambered back behind his torrent of words.

"When economics and technology move in, we have to redefine the behavior of the bedroom," Foote proclaimed. "Sex is not procreative any more. Whatever does not produce, that's perversion. Husbands and wives participate together in homosexual relationships. That's perversion. Oral sex is perversion. Anal sex is perversion. I pervert you. You pervert me. A rectum is a rectum is a rectum . . ."

Patricia sobbed.

"You're superior to me, therefore tears are beneath you," her husband told her. His voice was rough with feeling. "A black man is inferior to a black woman. From time immemorial, from this day forward. Inferior." It was a male preoccupation exclusive to no race or class. Foote picked up the beer cans and piled them into a tower. Then he rose from the couch and addressed the gathering unsteadily. "But the American white is a savage! And next to him the African is a civilized man."

"That thought is 122 percent correct," said the Nigerian, with his admiration of exact numbers.

The poet's glossy blue shirt stuck to his body, plastered with sweat. He looked worn out but victorious, like a wrestler after a match. "I detest America with what you might call a silent impotence," he said in tones of love and agony. "America is a callow country, a sensuous whore at too young an age. Europe is too old to be a whore and Europe knows it. It's safer there for black men."

Patricia's sobs grew audible. Nobody looked embarrassed.

Nobody offered consolation or even a handkerchief. They just let her cry, as if they knew it was good for her.

"The white man perishes as I perish, for I perish as he perishes," her husband raved. "My survival is my decadence." He demolished the tower of beer cans with a blow of his hand. They rattled all over the floor. "If I could run out naked with my testes dangling in the air, if I could cut the heads off two white women and four white males, I would vote for my own death. If I can take with me ten white men—twenty-five white men!—I'm willing to sacrifice every white friend I have, even those I love . . ."

"If there is no God, then how can you be God?" Patricia cried. There was still no attempt to calm her. Excesses of feeling did not alarm these men and women.

"Black people have a state of rage like the one Cobbs was talking about," the psychiatrist mused, referring to one of the authors of *Black Rage*. "We're in a state of rage after all this long time," she declared.

His wife's soft cry passed over the poet-philosopher's head. "You have every right to consider me a half breed, a degenerate," he said, not to her, to everyone. "But we are dealing with responsibility here. I am responsible for being black. Responsibility implies a debt. The mere fact that I was not present at my own conception to offer opposition to it does not absolve me from the responsibility of having been born, of being human, and of being black . . ." His perspiration dripped on the shaggy pale-green rug. He was perspiring so much that he seemed fueled from inside.

Patricia gathered up her handbag and scarf. It was not quite clear where she was going. "Why did you marry me, William?" she asked.

He responded as if to the jury of his peers. "I am an existentialist," he said. "I believe in absurdity. I married her to learn how to die. With her in my house, I negate my freedom. I accept the ultimate negation of freedom that is death."

Patricia started for the front door, but she stumbled. The hostess, a grade-school teacher, had not spoken all evening except to inquire politely, "Will you have another drink? Will you have some cheese?" Now she helped her guest into the bathroom. Patricia threw up with the door wide open. "William is really saying, 'I'm ready to die for you, Patricia,'" the hostess pointed out as she sat on the edge of the tub with a towel in her lap. "He cares about you very much. That's why he's so angry."

Mrs. Foote was leaning over the bathtub. She raised her head, took the towel from her hostess, and wiped her mouth. "I know," she said. "I just never want to lose him, that's all."

In one of his poems, William Foote had written (under his real name):

> Make mine Beauty hard
> And masculine
> And difficult.

In her introduction to his book, prepared before they were married, Patricia Foote had written (under her real name) that such a man, "searching for the why of existence . . ." was "carried along by time" and not time's victim. "His state," she wrote, "is one of euphoria."

6 | Blacks: Getting Whiter

"We may be getting on to the day when the only thing left about us that's natural is our hair," William Foote had said about those black men who infiltrated white society and adopted white ways. "And the truth of it is, most of us like it better that way."

Indeed, many blacks less complicated, pent-up, and passionate than the poet-philosopher emulated the style of the larger culture with, apparently, fewer pangs of conscience and consciousness. Sometimes in their understandable urge to "get whiter" in a society that still despised blackness, they could turn into carbon copies of middle-class men—in almost every way except one. The fervent aspiration toward *dominus* hardly ever deserted them.

Robert Dwyer, thirty-four years old, married, and the father of two children under two years old, worked as a top-ranking executive for an influential, all-black business organization in the Northeastern United States. Only the place of his employment and the shade of his complexion set him apart from his Caucasian peers. Deliberately or not, he had erased the other attributes of race. His Ivy League diction, his Brooks Brothers jacket, his gilt-engraved attaché case, and his upwardly mobile attitude were all almost whiter than white.

"Sure I have certain needs that are not unlike the white man's," he admitted, tracing the knot in his paisley tie with well-manicured fingers. "I'm very ambitious and I'm materialistically oriented. I like nice clothes and nice cars as much as the next guy. Through acculturation, I was hung up for a long time on fair skin and straight hair in my picture of the ideal woman. I didn't want a cantankerous black girl bitching about this and that," he said with a rueful smile. "So when I decided to settle down, I fell for a girl whose physical and mental attributes were all wrong, just the opposite of that picture in my mind. She was black all through, wore an Afro, and knew her own mind. For instance, she was very quick to tell me that she did not intend to work once we had a family. My original thought was that I would like to marry someone who would assist me financially. 'No soap,' this little lady said. 'You fought so hard to be a man, then be one.' "

Now he could grin at the memory of that challenge. "Before the first baby, she had worked for several years. We saved enough money to buy a house; then she got pregnant within a year after we bought it. In another year, she got pregnant again. At first, I was laid low by the responsibility of three people, all leaning hard on me. But it kept my motor running. I'm the sole provider for my family now and I'll never rely on my wife's income again."

"Black women have been the dominant persons in the home long enough," the female psychiatrist in Georgia had said. "White men, by keeping black men down, have made sure of that. Now it's incumbent on us to give support to our men, to promote them, not compete with them. In the white world, women have to work out strategies for freeing themselves from the stranglehold and decision-making powers of white men. For us, it's different. We have to work out strategies to help our men accept decision-making powers and the dominant role, if we are ever to know the luxury of relying on them."

Not everyone agreed with her. "The fact is that lots of black women are finally getting it together for themselves and lots of black men are floored," a professor of psychology—white, female—said. "Those women have been beaten down and beaten up at least as much as we have. Maybe they're really making some sort of mass decision now to spread themselves out like tablecloths in the name of supporting their men. But if that's so, it's just poor economics . . . or misplaced sentiment. And they'll be sorry."

Nevertheless, most black men took it for granted that most black women construed their present mission in life as "pushing their men up front, assuming a lesser role for themselves, so that we get proper recognition. This isn't taking a back seat," Robert Dwyer insisted, "it's a conscious effort on the part of black women to mold different, more domestic lives than white women seem to want, without doing anyone a favor at all."

Dominus, however, was a two-edged sword. Many blacks in their new ascendancy resented the female possessiveness that the recurrent phrase "our men" implied. They were so damn tired, they said, of black women telling them how to feel and what to do. They wanted to be their own men now. Some saw the insistent support of their "cause" by black women as "a desperate attempt to keep us in line." It was, they felt, a new incarnation of the old black matriarchy, "engineering our lives, the same as ever, and tossing us around." What the authors of *Black Rage* had written was still substantially true: "Black men develop considerable hostility toward black women as the inhibiting instruments of an oppressive system. The woman has more power, more accessibility into the system, and therefore she is more feared, while at the same time envied."

In one breath, John Lexington, a black television journalist who ran a Sunday talk show in New England, spoke of the small but expanding black feminist movement as "a positive impulse for all concerned. It's directed not against us but toward white society in the name of all black people." But in the next breath he said, "I would also suspect that, in part, it's designed to inform the black man of his obligation to 'the sisterhood.'" His tone mixed respect with indignation. "Most of the women still believe that most of the men are 'talking black and sleeping white.' But in a truly free world, if that's what we're doing—which all of us are *not*—it's none of their business." He himself had twice married black women. Nevertheless, he was annoyed at the idea that private relationships could deteriorate into political imperatives. Dating or marrying black to "oblige the sisterhood" smote the eyes of many black men with visions of entrapment.

Moreover, they were often quick to acknowledge an affinity of the oppressed that crossed racial and sexual lines. "There is a natural reservoir of sympathy between black men' and white women that's impossible to dam up forever," John Lexington observed. "We've always been the last hired and the first fired. Now that's coming true all over again." Like so many black men, his blind spot about black women prevented him from viewing them as equivalent victims of oppression. "We have generations of fear and resentment to get over," he said, harping on the black man's obsessive awareness of the "matriarchy." "What does a man want most of all? To be his own boss. Freedom entails the right to make your own mistakes. But black women are chronically manipulative, although they say it's in our best interests."

The black man, however enlightened, tended to idealize the "warm, soft, feminine" white woman, just as many white women idealized the black man. And to further complicate this doomed interracial romance (doomed because it was so deeply sunk in fantasy), the white man held fast to his own myth about black women as submissive and supersexy. There were unresolved emotional crosscurrents flowing in both directions. These dreamy, mutual illusions would almost surely fade with increased familiarity. But until blacks and whites knew each other better, they would continue to feed on their fancies—nourished no doubt by the attraction of opposites.

Nevertheless, black men were not wholly without grievances about white women, especially feminist women. "Those ladies intruded on the civil-rights movement at exactly the wrong moment. Their timing was bad and their judgment was poor," Lexington recalled. "White male society was already frightened by the new upward mobility of black men . . . and then along came the feminists with their own power push." The rise of blacks and the simultaneous rise of women menaced white men, he said. "What's really ironic is that the feminist movement grew out of the civil-rights movement and then helped blow it to smithereens."

Black feminism sometimes called forth a circular stream of consciousness—from initial emotional resistance to heightened consciousness back to resistance. "I used to think they were just a gang of crazy ladies going to lots of meetings. Then I began to ask myself, how could I be involved in black causes, preaching and fighting for the rights of my people, while ignoring the rights of women?" said Upton Church, the director of a settlement house near Boston. In his work with welfare and one-parent families, he explained, he had become aware of children's books in which "all the women of *any* color were housewives, secretaries, and maids. They had a very limited number of options. There was injustice in it. I got some jolting new insights; among them, that I was treating my secretary as my daytime office maid. It was very convenient. It was working so well. Then she let me know that it wasn't working so well for her. 'No more coffee, no more sandwiches,' she said one day. 'You've got a car. Why don't *you* drive over to the diner?' Well, I learned to live with it." He shrugged. "After all, where in her job description did it stipulate that she had to be available to go out and get my sandwiches?"

He told of his friend Mary, "a poor, slaving secretary who suddenly realized she would still be doing her boss's job after he was dead, but even then, she'd never get his title or his salary. 'It's important to organize,' I said to her. 'There's not a man alive who's going to do you or any other woman a favor. Organize a mass rebellion. No company is going to wipe out hundreds of female employees if they all protest at once. In union there is strength.'" Upton Church screwed up his face. "Well, she tried, but she couldn't get that strike off the ground. When you're forced by society into inferiority the way women are, as well as blacks, you begin to believe that's all you deserve."

At that point, his intellect stopped talking and his emotions took over. "Yet I resist the whole thing," he confessed, of black feminism. "It's not an evil resistance. It's based on natural power. Men are jealous of their power. They're misers of power. They want to hoard it. They don't want to lose what they've got. Seventy-thirty is all wrong as a ratio, even if it's in my favor. Fifty-fifty, that's fair. But that's not how life works out, is it? And if I got to live in the outhouse for you to live in the main house: baby, forget it!"

Black women themselves sometimes regretted "going professional," as John Lexington had put it. "You may ask, do I believe black women can be overeducated? No, I don't believe so. But they do." It was not the educated woman per se, but her female insecurity, that made sexual problems for black men, he explained. "Take my first wife, a Ph.D. She had troubles with her femininity. *I* had no trouble with it, she did. But it was up to me to assuage all her self-doubts. Now, that took superhuman effort. Finally, there was just no way."

His old exasperation rekindled. "Women Ph.D.'s complain they can't find men who are easy with them. That's because they're uneasy with themselves," he said. "My wife felt she had sacrificed everything that went toward making her feel feminine, clawing her way up the ladder. In her own eyes, her doctorate in social psychology made her suspect as a woman. I had to make it clear to her every step of the way that, in my eyes, that wasn't true. But the strain was terrific. I was smothered, suffocated, by her effusive bursts of love—occasioned by genuine feeling, I think. But I couldn't reciprocate on the level of intensity that would satisfy her. My inability to do that increased her self-doubt. And her self-doubt made me feel like a failure." It was the same syndrome some white men described whose striving wives, they said, suffered from the same general anxiety.

The second time around, John Lexington married a girl of more modest achievements. But he only traded one set of stresses for another. "My present wife has much less formal education. She's cheery and she sings all the time," Lexington said, as if her cheeriness might be the result of her rudimentary schooling. "However, she's really no less ambitious. She's gone back to school for classes in home economics, hoping to organize homemaker programs in low-income communities. On weekends, she's a political volunteer. In my first marriage, there was no financial dependence, but a great deal of emotional dependence. Now that's reversed. This time, I'm the sole breadwinner and I'm subsidizing my wife's academic career." He seemed not entirely oblivious to the irony of having divorced one educated woman only to educate another.

Steven Hunt, a strapping six-foot-six Kentucky bank executive still living in the shadow of his past as a star football player, also wed "a shy, sweet, simple little girl" after a disastrous first marriage to a tougher, stronger woman. Like so many blacks poised on the brink of the white world and afflicted with the nervous uncertainties of assimilation, he felt alienated from both races and unsure of acceptance. Marrying a woman who was all acquiescence and admiration could sometimes stabilize a man—whatever his race—and solve a lifelong crisis of belonging.

"When you got yourself a wife who really needs you, that's when you begin to make it," Hunt said. His first wife had needed nothing from him, he explained, but to share, vicariously, the thrill of the celebrity that then surrounded him. "After it was too late, my mom realized I had been caught by one of those 'team girls.' They're like the groupies in rock music, attracted to the world of an athlete because of its glamour and glitter. Then a severed Achilles tendon knocked me off the field. I couldn't play pro ball any more. The excitement was over. I came home one day and the house was clean. My wife had split. It was the classic case of a black American princess, spoiled rotten by her family's money and her Bates College education. She never came back again."

Hunt then shed some of his youthful innocence. He also developed a taste for the *dominus* that had grown increasingly elusive in a society of autonomous women. But before he met "the young, naive girl, the fragile flower" who was to be his second wife, he bumped around from job to job, chasing some small, illusory chip of the American dream. "In Akron, where I grew up, I was lucky enough to meet some influential white people and learn what political clout could do." He landed "a nice little berth at Goodyear—and the whole world opened up. I had my own bachelor house, my own car, all the women I wanted. I was in heaven, so to speak. But I was miserable as hell."

It was the first of several worlds that Steven Hunt tried and found wanting. His odyssey resonated with that frustration and discontent familiar among the new black bourgeoisie, caught so often between two flags, one white, one black. "I knew fairly quick I didn't want *that* game," he said of the automotive industry and its adornments. "To me, it was meaningless. I didn't give a damn whether we sold one more tire, whether one more girl came by the place, whether I made one more thousand dollars . . ."

"A jazz man from way back," and already disenchanted with life within the "power structure," Hunt "took off to Columbus with my musician buddies. I picked up my horn, packed my suitcase, called my secretary, and said, 'I'm sick—permanently.'"

Playing the clarinet in Columbus gave him a truer sense of himself—for a while. "No one expected me to live up to an image—football star, business executive, happy husband, Don Juan. I was my own man." Then one more white friend, the son-in-law of a state official, ricocheted Hunt into banking, the dead center of the power structure he had disowned in Akron. "It was a young bank, not hung up on traditions and concepts, and it was obvious they wanted a black guy on the board." Now the brass plaque on his shiny mahogany desk read

VICE PRESIDENT. But Steven Hunt looked trapped and uncomfortable in his trim banker's clothes. A black Goliath swamping a white wage slave's cage, his powerful shoulders seemed about to burst the seams of his pale-beige plaid suit. His prim steel-rimmed glasses were like a Halloween disguise on his swarthy, open-air face.

He enumerated the compensations of his imprisoning life. He had bought a house "in the most fabulous white section of town." His young wife was pregnant, which, he said, "excites me no end." And most important: "I'm breaking through the plantation attitude in this part of the country singlehanded. Whites here are still patronizing their little black children, their black slaves. They haven't really started to see us as equals." His move to the suburbs seemed to assuage his desire to share in the tribulations of his race. "I wasn't trying to bust a neighborhood, I was looking for a safe and decent place for my family, and eventually other black families, to live. 'If I don't do it, if the house niggers don't do it, the field niggers never will,' I said to myself." "Field niggers," in his terminology, were working-class blacks. "House niggers" were middle-class. Nevertheless, he looked uncertain. "The vice president of a bank, moving into a neighborhood of low-income blacks, that would have caused even more resentment. Besides, who would I have helped that way?" He shrugged his huge shoulders, straining against the thin cloth. "But now nobody likes it that I've moved to a better place. I'm frowned on by blacks as a deserter of my own people. I'm ostracized by former white friends as a climber. If my new neighbors accept me, it's as an oddity, a curiosity. I get more smiles than angry glances when I walk down my street, but I might as well be some six-toed creature escaped from the zoo."

Sitting so high on the totem pole, Steven Hunt was still hounded by the queasy feeling that he belonged nowhere. It was a common plight of the black bourgeoisie. "What nobody seems to understand is that essentially I'm the same as any white guy," he said, in the voice of so many others. "I have exactly the same aspirations as the rest of America. I want a beautiful house in the suburbs, a beautiful car, beautiful kids, and a beautiful wife. But now, just as I'm getting next to some of that glory, it's losing its meaning. The block-long Buick isn't the status object that it once was. And before I even settle down, those charming people I was going to live next door to in the suburbs are running away, back to the center city. Because if I'm going to live out there in that big house and drive that big Buick, they've got to prove those things don't mean much any more."

When he took off his steel-rimmed glasses, it was as if he had removed a mask. "It's all turning inside out before our eyes. Blacks find themselves going after air, after pictures in the air. We're left with their mirage—and we're going to be left with their golden suburbs too." His voice had grown weary. "So much chasing . . . you reach for the moon . . . and you've grabbed a handful of air." Steven Hunt gazed at the gilt plaque on his desk that said VICE PRESIDENT. "How high is up?" he asked. "I'm thirty and I feel like fifty. Where have I got to go? I'm *there*."

In the South, the rise of the black bourgeoisie had other allied effects. It had virtually annihilated the overt taboos against sexual segregation. Black-and-white couples could dine and dance together publicly now from Tuscaloosa to Charleston. Obvious harassment was declining. Barriers of color and class had fallen, bringing that much closer to consummation the potent interracial romance.

"Sure I have sex fantasies about black boys," one coed in South Carolina admitted. "But I also have them about passion-crazed priests, Chico Marx, redneck window cleaners, and college professors with frayed tweed jackets and pot bellies." Almost anyone, she intimated, appealed to her erotic imagination more than most of her young white male peers.

"Oh, there's no doubt that white girls would like black boyfriends now," said the associate dean of students at the same college. "So many white men have sort of hit the skids. It's not only the kids either. Lots of older guys who once thought they were gay blades are finding out they just can't cut it." She was blond and pretty and her voice dripped Carolina honey. Not so long ago, it would have been unthinkable for a young woman of her age and station (over thirty, upper-middle-class) to be unmarried by choice, tooling around in her own Toyota and talking about "threatened white men" with her nose in the air.

"But the black guys aren't asking white girls out any more, the way they once did. They've learned that it's an insult to their own women. Black girls stick together. Some of them at the university had it out with the black men. They put their foot down: 'No more white dates.' It's had a big effect. The appeal to the black male conscience has prevented most of them from dating white girls ever since." She herself—this young, bright, blond Southern woman of aristocratic origin— maintained "a father-daughter relationship," she said, with an older black man whom she described as "a beautiful person. We have dinner at least once a month, and although we do not sleep together," she noted carefully, "I adore him."

But the appeal by black women to the black male conscience, while widespread, was by no means unconditionally successful. North and South, the black man and the white woman remained secret lovers. Interracial marriage, however, brought frowns and grimaces to most black male faces. Black men married to white women were among the most alienated, least accessible, and touchiest people in the country. Sometimes courteously and sometimes brusquely, they insisted on their "right to privacy." "I consider my personal feelings to be nobody's business but mine and my wife's," one black gentleman said. "Why should I allow our marriage to be exploited for the benefit of racists and voyeurs? When you fall in love, the color of the skin is irrelevant. And it is not a crime against two societies. But you spend the rest of your lives dodging rocks thrown from both sides." He observed that all their friends were interracial couples. Even this man's black business partner was married to a white woman. They lived within a subsociety of their own, not by preference, he said, but because neither race had yet learned to tolerate miscegenation. Almost no black man found this double jeopardy remarkable.

"A man has to consider the hell he's sure to go through in a mixed marriage," the Georgia poet William Foote had said. "And as soon as he considers it, he says, 'A thousand times no.' Love, yes. Intimacy, yes." He addressed a hypothetical white mistress. " 'You want to meet me in my one-room apartment? It starts snowing on Friday afternoon, snows until Sunday or early Monday morning, and we'll still be there together, snowbound together, for a day or two or three . . . The gods themselves insure the clemency of the heavens. They participate by providing some natural shelter for us, some privacy for our love . . .' " He gave up his reverie. "But marriage? Never. It demands too much. I could never deal with the hassle involved in interracial abuses, with those looks and stares on every street. You don't avoid them, I have heard, even in places like New York.

"It's not quite the same for the white woman," Foote went on. "She can sever herself from her family and her people if she so desires, more easily than we can. In any black-and-white love match, anywhere in the country, it's the black man who cops out when it comes to marriage.

"Consider my family structure," he continued. "I'm the oldest of twelve children. I come from south Georgia. I got to be able to go back there with a free spirit and a free mind to see my little sister Julie, who is eight years old. I can't have any white woman hanging on my arm to hold me back. I may love this woman dearly. Taking her to bed, that's private. But marriage, that's public. It's a social institution. It brings two families together, just like in the days of the Capulets and Montagues."

Intermarriage, most blacks believed, was not a survivor's game. Nevertheless, some brave souls played it. "Proximity accounts for interracial marriages," Robert Dwyer had explained, "as much as guts. A man who marries a white woman has entered the white world long before the wedding. Take my cousin at Bowdoin College. He had very little contact with other blacks during those four years because there were so few on the campus. But he had always been unhappy in a totally black environment. Until he was nineteen, every one of his friends was white. So, all things accounted for, it was natural for him to marry white. He said to his mother, 'Mom, I'm getting married. She just happens to be white.' Well, his mother was crushed, but she didn't let on. 'Your father and I always let you make up your own mind,' she said. 'I hope you know what you're doing. If you think you got the answers, okay.' "

Some blacks—especially younger ones—might be more tolerant than others of the interracial union, but few blacks besides the interracial partners themselves really understood or empathized with it, said a city planner in Louisiana. He told of a "black activist" who married a white woman, also radical. "Just because you married her, that goes to show all white people aren't bad?" his friends asked. In reply, the activist said that he too deserved "a piece of the pie." To him, his white wife represented worldly achievement. But her radical friends were equally perplexed. " 'Why she got to set with that nigger?' " they asked, the city planner reported.

"America is a nation of niggers, victims, downtrodden people," black congressman Ronald Dellums said. "We have among us women niggers, student niggers, hard-hat niggers, gay niggers, child niggers, over-sixty-five niggers, yellow niggers, and nigger niggers. But the ultimate family is the whole human race, niggers and honkies together."

The races were growing closer every day. But, as in any other family, that by no means settled everything.

7 | "Dominus" Abroad

Toward the middle of the journey, I went to Europe in search of some perspective. Was the spirit of *dominus* dying in white America alone or throughout the whole Western world?

With the seventies nearly over, the Continent was in the throes of its own women's revolution. No country in the West or East was without its own species of militant female—what the French called *les femmes mecs* (roughly translated as "he-girls" or "tough-guy women"). In Italy and France, Germany and Switzerland, Sweden and Finland, Holland and Austria, Yugoslavia and Rumania, as well as in England, determined enclaves of women—both enamored and resentful of the power and strength of men—were loosely organized into some version of a crusading feminist movement. In many places, they had either sidestepped the passive phase, consciousness-raising, or passed beyond it. Instead, they were invading, or preparing to invade, male turf, *"pour battre les hommes, les phallocrates, sur leur propre terrain,"* as the French magazine *Le Point* put it. Even the new feminist magazine called *F*, while priding itself on non-militance, carried an article in its first issue entitled *"Priez Dieu, Elle Vous Ecoutera"*: Pray to God, She Will Hear You.

Except in England and in West Germany, the men's movement was in its infancy. Not only those male supremacists, the "phallocrats," valued themselves as men. Most Europeans still took for granted the age-old rights and privileges that *dominus* implied. And European women, even those entering society's mainstream, valued themselves as women. By and large, they could honor *dominus* without dishonoring themselves. "It is a comfort to know there is someone in command. That in itself is freeing," one wage-earning French wife said, speaking for many. Neither European women nor European men seemed unduly impressed, as a rule, by the female autonomy implied in a weekly salary check.

They were as high on heterosexuality as if it had just been discovered. They could even indulge in a little light romantic comedy. Said Jeanne Moreau, the French actress, on the subject of *la femme libéré*: "To me, being free simply means having the freedom to choose the man to whom I will become a slave."

The times might be trying, yet most Europeans seemed more than ever to depend on each other for the zest and gaiety that made survival worth the struggle. In Paris, middle-aged couples promenaded arm in arm, stopping to feed each other fresh strawberries or scoops of ice cream, kissing with their mouths full, bursting into laughter that rang with all the old delight of being opposites. Bathtubs in the smallest hotels were still big enough for two and bidets shone like crystal. For a couple of francs, lovers could linger all evening over a carafe of wine or a café filtre. Waiters smiled.

"To deny the existence of distinctions is a form of fanaticism," said Henri Marais, a Frenchman high up in government circles. "Men are still men and women are women, regardless of whatever job they hold." If the French were fanatics, their fanaticism might lie in the other direction, he said. "Maybe we stress difference too much—if that is possible."

He himself had been married for eighteen years to an American. "My wife returns to Paris in a state of shock each time she visits her family in upper New York State," he revealed. "She believes that sexual ghettos have begun to build up in your country that in time will come to match your racial ghettos. Once she used to hope to live near her parents again—but no more. She says it is a sterile atmosphere, notwithstanding your hypersexuality. There is much talk of loving, but little love. I think we do what comes naturally more naturally."

This view of our sexual scene, which he attributed to his

American wife, was also held by Europeans poles apart in age, place, temperament, and political affiliation. Gilles du Vivier, a handsome, Sorbonne-educated native of Paris in his middle twenties, was more than a decade younger than the government official. A self-proclaimed *"intellectuel de gauche,"* he wore shoulder-length hair, a long, curled-down mustache, and a flowing Byronesque bow tie that exploded over a heavy white cardigan sweater unraveling at the seams. Like many of his young peers in the international counterculture, his attitudes toward European women surprisingly resembled those of older, more conservative men.

Even the most radical women he knew, du Vivier said (and he knew, he added, the most radical women in France), were friends of all the people, rather than each other's friends exclusively. As feminists, they pressed for change, not in the name of women's rights, but in the name of a socialism that cut across sex, race, and class. This view of radical women, dedicated to a philosophy of egalitarianism that was in no way sexually competitive, was expressed everywhere in Europe. Yet the same men who held it were unsympathetic to what they considered false liberalism and feigned beliefs.

In France, the world's first Minister of Women had already lost her job. Françoise Giroud—the controversial Parisian celebrity and, for a while, women's advocate—had not been received with blind faith. "Most French feminists saw her as a traitor, a figurehead of the regime. Her mission was to mollify women, not to help them," du Vivier said. "It was a trick that didn't work."

"Giscard d'Estaing made some loud liberal noises and Giroud was one of those noises," a French Jew added. "Oh, the administration hoped that if radical women saw one of their 'sisters' supposedly in charge of their problems, they would come round and give up their radicalism," he speculated. "But Giroud was no leftist, nor was she accepted by the left. And in France, that is where feminism has its whole meaning."

It was clear that most European women, whatever their politics and whatever their age, were sending out signals to men of interdependence rather than independence, cooperation rather than cooptation, alliance rather than self-actualization. "Maybe American women need it," Françoise Giroud had said, of enmity toward males. "When you want to fight, you design an enemy, so they designed man. But he's a false enemy. There is no enemy. That's why it's so difficult for us to fight." Whatever else Frenchmen might have thought of the former Madame le Ministre, they accepted that message as sent.

Even the occasional tempests of *les féministes agitées* that now and then blew up in the streets of Paris blew over quickly and agitated very few men. "Of course, we know they exist," said Alan Cartwright, an American art critic living in Paris with his French-speaking Swiss-Italian wife. "They have an organization, headquarters, a name: *MLF: Mouvement de libération des femmes*. And sometimes they do have their uprisings. Sophia's all for it," he added with none of the emotion, for or against, that many men across the ocean spent on feminism. "She thinks there's been enough beneficial fallout to make the fuss worthwhile. As for myself, I don't feel it as any kind of change. I'm not personally aware of it in my own life." Sophia Cartwright was an art historian, editor, and publisher. The Cartwrights had no children. Yet within their marriage, under the strong light of her personality, his male sense of himself had apparently not dimmed.

Alan Cartwright leaned back in an easy chair in his Art Nouveau flat. He picked up where Marais and du Vivier had left off. "There's no strong revolutionary movement here—although, philosophically, this is where it all began." Simone de Beauvoir, he recalled, had written her seminal work on the women's revolution, *The Second Sex*, not far from his own front door. "But even among feminists, there's nothing at all in France like the situation you have now in the United States. In Europe, the movement's not a women-for-women thing. Those who fight do so for social causes—not for themselves. Not against men or at men's expense or for the extra privileges they believe men have. They want higher pay for everyone, reforms in the educational system for everyone. They'll get out there and carry placards and block the highways, if it comes to that. But it's coed all the way. The sexual struggle really doesn't exist in France," he said.

In French-speaking Switzerland, it seemed all but unknown. Twenty-eight-year-old Gerard LeVesconte shared his apartment, and his life, with a young woman of twenty-six who owned and operated a beauty salon. A bachelor in name only, he worked at night as a hotel clerk to avoid the subjection of what he called "a nine-to-five, shirt-and-tie existence."

He and Lisette, his housemate, almost never went to American movies, "or even French," he said. They cared more for mountains and rivers, sunlight and starlight, eating and laughing and sleeping together. They greeted the women's uprising with polite lack of interest. "It's happening in France," LeVesconte shrugged, as if that country were forty thousand instead of forty miles from Geneva. "We don't really care about what the French do or think. We don't need their movements . . . and we don't need their movies. We live two times better than the French. They have two classes, rich and poor. In Geneva, everybody who wants to work can make good money. We have no poor, no underprivileged, no oppressed— either men or women."

As for power, both Gerard LeVesconte and his Lisette were equally immune to its seduction. They were either somewhat above it or somewhere beneath it. They did not aspire to upward mobility. They did not expect work to provide either emotional fulfillment or pathways to influence, but only a modest income, the means of existence. The Swiss prided themselves on their precise habits of industry, yet the job was a means, not an end in itself. "To be free," said LeVesconte, "is everything."

"I do what I want with my days," said the night worker grandly. "Today I went to France in my boat. My girl was with me. We had a barbecue and we made love. Then we came home." His smile proclaimed that it had been a perfect afternoon.

Lisette had quickly learned to love Gerard's tranquil, free-style life. She ran her beauty shop with a partner, another woman, so that each could relieve the other and take off for brief holidays on the spur of the moment. "Working half the time, they make twice as much money in Geneva as anywhere in France," he said. He himself had spent a year as a waiter in a restaurant on West Fifty-sixth Street in New York. He did not wish to return.

"American men are too often unfriendly—and also the women. Swiss girls don't ask for as much as Americans," LeVesconte said. "Here, girls are happier with little things—a sail, a trip to the stores, to the movies. They expect not so much of life. Those who are unmarried, if their men work at night, they get together with their friends, they laugh, they joke. It is enough." Lisette, although French and somewhat more sophisticated, was learning a lot about Swiss simplicity.

In their easy, uninsistent ways, he and she were more equal than many couples who made equality a grim point of honor. They could merge with each other, yet maintain separate identities. They agreed about what mattered—and it was not vying for supremacy. Just to live and be happy did not seem an impossible dream.

Even in West Germany, in some ways almost as American as the U.S.A., men and women seemed less personally ambitious and, so, less susceptible to the acquisitive-competitive appetites of materialism. They too cared more about being than becoming. (Yet compared to the East Germans, most West Germans considered themselves arch-materialists.)

Kurt and Marthe Schellhammer, both German by birth, had been married for eleven years and lived in West Berlin. Kurt played the flute for a living. Marthe worked as a freelance production assistant on American and other films on location in Germany. Fluent in German, English, French, and Spanish, she was much in demand among international film crews traveling in Europe. But when her husband was invited to spend an academic year—and then another—as a visiting artist at an American university's Center of Creative and Performing Arts, Marthe gave up her job to follow her husband. It was never a subject of discussion between them; it was simply the way it was.

"She has no work permit. So in the States she does nothing," Schellhammer said. "But you see, she is not so ambitious for her career. She takes it as vacation time and spends it in the thrift shops, buying old dresses." Collecting funky thirties' clothes was Marthe's "fun thing," he said. "When we first arrived, she got involved with the wives of some professors at the university," he recalled. "Afternoon teas, all kinds of shit. But finally Marthe said, 'It's impossible for me. They talk only about their husbands and how much money they make.' Yet at the same time they support the feminist movement and feel resentful of their situations. In America, many women are not so sure about the lives they want."

If Marthe had misgivings about her own wifely role, she kept them to herself, letting Kurt lead the way. He spoke with assurance for both of them. "*Küche, Kinder, Kirche*—it does not appeal to us. It is too old-fashioned. We do not hope to have this tied-down family life. I like to travel around. I make concerts here and here and here." Kurt Schellhammer wore a garnet velvet smoking jacket over blue jeans, and with an expansive wave of his arm, he encompassed the globe. "In my scheme, it would be impossible to have a wife who is always at home with the children. I could not be at home enough with them to please her. What would she do?" He waved his arm again, this time indicating emptiness. "Marthe must have her own life and her own personality and her own pursuits," he said.

Yet by mutual consent, her "pursuits" depended on her husband's. Hers were part-time, only semiserious, and subject to sudden stops and starts. His were full-time, serious, and primary. In eleven years of marriage, at least as Schellhammer told it, neither of them had wanted to modify their design for living. Husband-following was one of the unspoken agreements between this West German man and wife. The alternative—living apart almost as much as they lived together—was for them unsupportable.

Even among the intellectual elite, when it came to the terms of matrimony, most of Europe seemed a stronghold of conservatism. Antonio Molti was the mayor of a small town between Milan and Venice. A worldly and enlightened Catholic, educated as an economist, he spoke English with more grace than some for whom it was a household language. He earned his living as a banker in Milan. But in the elections to repeal Italy's divorce laws, Molti confessed that he had not brought himself to vote.

"I do not wish to prevent divorce," he said, "but personally I do not believe in it. It has very negative consequences—for the family and the society. Yet when there is no other course . . ."

During his long term as mayor, Molti said, only four marriages had dissolved in his town. He regretted each of these dissolutions in a very personal way. Europeans, whether of the left or the right, did not take divorce lightly. "Of course all of them were necessary. It was better that they parted. But for myself . . ." He shook his head. Marriage, once undertaken, was for life.

Molti's own wedding was imminent. In nine days he would be married in Düsseldorf to his German fiancée, a student of medicine. His mother, his sister, and many other relatives would travel to Düsseldorf with him to celebrate the marriage rites. It would be a solemn ceremony, respectful of the ancient sacrament. His wedding to him was a momentous occasion, anticipated with sobriety and joy.

Until recently the couple had spoken only English to each

other. Then Molti's bride-to-be had learned Italian from him. "It would be harder for me to learn German," he explained. "Much harder." He appeared to defer to his fiancée's superior talent for languages, but his eyes twinkled. Perhaps it was more seemly to communicate in his tongue than in hers. *Dominus* might demand it. How else could he retain a sure command of their conversation?

After the wedding, the mayor revealed, his wife would finish her studies in medical school in Germany. He would return to Italy to pursue his career in finance. Unlike the Schellhammers of West Berlin, they would travel between two countries.

It seemed a liberated style of life. "Liberated"? He examined the word thoughtfully. In the American sense, it meant nothing to him. "After my wife-to-be receives her degree, we will build a family," he explained. Her medical education would be useful, of course, in the rearing of children. "That is our intention. Until she becomes pregnant, she will practice medicine. Afterward, who knows? For her, medicine is secondary. First is the family that we want. That is liberated," he asked, "or not?"

Many young Europeans, however, were indifferent to traditional marriage. Yet they were still keeping their heterosexual contracts—if not always on the terms laid down by establishment society. These children of liberty often took the position that old-fashioned monogamy was "not enough," but the last thing they wanted was to lose each other, or the sense of family, in the swamps of sexual anonymity.

In Paris, Gilles du Vivier spoke for the young throughout Western Europe, "Freedom is the great word now. All of us want some decent position in society, some money, and the freedom for loving. Men want many women and women want many men. It is no longer enough to love only once. I am not acquainted with a person under forty years old, not a single person, who has not divorced or broken up his marriage." He gave his Gallic version of the "fast fuse" life, in which Americans were also caught. "Everything is going faster now. One has the impression of a big river that flows, taking us along, whether we desire it or not. There are so many sexual opportunities that even if we don't want to separate, after a time we are pushed into it. This was not so twenty years ago," he said, with some nostalgia for a more tranquil past he was really too young to remember. "Today it seems strange and funny if one stays married for more than ten years. It's not at all that we grow to hate each other. But everybody changes." He shrugged, not insensitively but with resignation. "It comes to be very natural to separate with great friendliness, to take other partners."

Even so, love between the sexes remained at the heart of life. "We are making new kinds of family now—but still family—in which it gives more pleasure to live," du Vivier explained. "All those who love want a child, and even some of those who do not love. But there is no sexual jealousy and no interest in the possession of the other. We do not speak the language of property or protection, only of loving. So we are more free than our parents.

"Yet when real problems come, we have traditional reactions," du Vivier added. Freedom notwithstanding, in time of trouble, even the radical young sought the consolation and support of parents and family. "Although I myself am never intending to get married!" he exclaimed. "I think it is bourgeois. It doesn't mean anything to me, the legality of it." Then he announced with unmistakable male pride and, once more, in the voice of his generation: "But already I am a father." Matrimony might be beside the point, but this primary assertion of manhood was not.

"In France, natural children have the same rights as legitimate children," he explained, as if that finally stamped marriage as superfluous. "If the mother requests it, the man is obliged to give his name to the child. Or the child may take her name. But even so, even when the mother rejects the father's name, she may still claim a pension and be granted money from him."

As marriage became less routine, he said, new styles in fatherhood were developing. "Some men—there are already many thousands in France—now keep their children. We used to say *filles-mères*, girl-mothers, of those who became pregnant by passing strangers. Now we say, *un père qui est une mère*, a man-mother. More and more often, it is he and not she who takes the responsibility for the child of a chance meeting. There was no love, no feeling, no living together. Yet the man wishes to prove himself as a father."

About his own son of twenty months, du Vivier said: "This was very much different, the fruit of a long relationship. I lived for three years with my friend, his mother. She now lives with another man, also my friend. When we left each other, the child was no longer an infant. And I am very much in love with my baby, but I am not obsessed." He paused, then delicately explained, "It is not altogether certain that he is mine." Blown but not buffeted by society's libertarian winds, du Vivier said, "Well, in a way, it is good not to be certain. I feel more free that way. If I am sure I am the father, I feel, 'I must have that baby!' Then I am no longer free."

On the subject of his former mistress and her new man, du Vivier's view was characteristically "liberated." "I see her as my friend first and then as his woman. It is not very important for me that she is with him. I do not intervene between them." Then suddenly intense: "But I have a certain strong influence in the life of my boy . . . of *our* boy." If the parental dyad had become a triad, well, he was an open-minded man.

As he outlined the extent of his possibly paternal influence, it was hard for me to tell where the new sensibility began and the old patriarchal one ended. But for du Vivier it was easy. Twelve years ago his older brother had married a girl after they conceived a child. "If my brother had not married her, my parents would have been scandalized. Yet the same thing has happened to me and my parents know nothing about it. If they did, they would no longer be scandalized and no longer insist on the wedding." The old sensibility was dead, he insisted. And "the big river that flows" carried both generations with it.

Another of Europe's multitude of unwed fathers, a young

Viennese of thirty-one, said, "I see my son about once every eight months. That is enough for both of us. It is good to know him, good to know that he is here. But I expect nothing from him, because I give him not much of myself. Children in close contact would bore me." He too professed a "long relationship" with his son's mother. They had lived together during most of her pregnancy and for six months after the birth of the child.

An American girl—his casual friend, but "not his sleeping companion"—said firmly, "Men like him, in close contact, bore *me*. They want the thrill of feeling like men without the day-to-day commitment that goes with it." But for many women, half a loaf of maleness was better than none.

In much of Europe, except among some members of the decadent aristocracy, only two modes of life were acknowledged: heterosexual and homosexual. Within the middle class, bisexuality was usually the occasion for either laughter, bewilderment, or scorn. A Londoner said: "Like a three-footed animal, it is only imagined—usually among homosexuals or pornography merchants."

Even homosexuality was taken as a fringe phenomenon. "There are so few open homosexuals in Paris that you can find all of them on any evening huddled together on one tiny strip of St.-Germain-des-Pres," a young Frenchman said. "They have had to become political lately, but not in order to receive advantages from society, just to gain acceptance. In France, the gay world is still a concealed subculture; homosexuals behave as guilty people. They make believe they are not homosexual or they play at it, pretending it is a game. They paint drawings on their faces and behave like women. They laugh at themselves, so heterosexuals laugh too. Then they can feel kindly to the gays, because they feel superior to them." But if their self-mockery were to end, he predicted, if homosexuals were to say to straight society, " 'We are not the wrong men, you are the wrong men,' then heterosexuals would become very rude to them, very threatening."

Charles Saint-Clair, a strikingly attractive Frenchman with international business connections, a shock of white curls, and a wide, sensual mouth that, in another face, might have seemed feminine, refused to discuss Gallic homosexuality. A bachelor all his life, he claimed three non-legal marriages, all presumably heterosexual, all now ended. Then he steered the conversation toward American bisexuality, a subject which seemed to amuse and absorb him. "It is still the 'hot topic' in the States, is it not?" he inquired, his round turquoise eyes widening. "But come, tell me, how common is it really?" As did so many Europeans, he inferred that our words spoke louder than our actions.

On the Continent, the subject of bisexuality was broached only in West Germany, where Americanization had reached a high-water mark. "Yes, it has become much more apparent here in recent years. So has group sex," said a Munich psychologist, classifying both phenomena as "abnormal." He was a kind of Germanic Alfred Kinsey, thanks to his books about sexual behavior in the German-speaking countries. "But what seems more than the average rate of abnormal sex activities may be a sort of experimental or temporary fashion," he added. "For instance, proportionate to the population, there are no more genuine homosexuals or lesbians in West Germany than there were twenty years ago."

So even in Germany, both East and West, it was still largely a matter of We and They. Few observers in Europe were suggesting that both worlds, the straight and the gay (as well as the omnisexual), could merge without rupturing the stability of society. According to the psychologist, "Sexual behavior in the D.D.R. [the German Democratic Republic] does not differ substantially in any way from that in the B.R.D. [the Federal Republic of Germany]. Since the beginning of the new era, after Ulbricht, the sexual revolution is progressing noticeably even in the East," he said. In his writing, he delighted in making that phrase the "sexual (r)evolution."

Nevertheless, a summer visitor to East Berlin could discern no revolution and little evolution. Instead, there was the strong sense of traditional family life among East Germans in the busy afternoon streets and, later in the day, in the outdoor cafés. Parents sipped brandy and coffee as the sun went down, with small children in tow who lingered over their Preiselbeere-and-ice-cream desserts.

The transvestite nightclubs that flourished throughout West Germany were nonexistent in the D.D.R. And on an all-day walking tour of East Berlin, there was virtually no sign of overt homosexuals of either sex. But in West Berlin, Cologne, and Munich, marceled young men with bleached hair and polished fingernails, engrossed in each other's company, were never absent from the restaurants and theaters. On Kurfürstendamm, West Berlin's main stem, lesbians embraced openly on street corners, and after midnight, female strollers were almost as likely to be sexually solicited by women as by men.

Connections between men and women often seemed familiarly short-circuited. In a nightclub in Munich, couples drooped over their beers, staring into the smoky distance—stone silent, unsmiling, and irretrievably remote from one another. Sexual apathy bred sexual decadence. Those who no longer excited each other sought more exotic varieties of stimulation: the drag show, the impotent pornography of the transvestite, hairy-chested homosexuals impersonating movie queens. Wolfgang Roth said of the Germany of the twenties, "The times were desperate and everybody knew it, and catastrophes were just around the corner, and everybody knew that too . . ." More than a half century later, those words seemed relevant again and with a shock of recognition, one was reminded of home.

In countries such as the Netherlands, Italy, and Greece, prostitution appeared an exclusively heterosexual commerce. In Athens, on Constitution Square, a woman could be loudly accosted several times in the same hour by smiling and genial young men. "You want man?" "You want friend?" "You want room?" But they accepted rejection with the same extroverted good nature with which they offered invitations. Homosexual advances, if they occurred, occurred more surreptitiously.

In the socialist countries, love among those of the same sex was viewed (along with transvestite supper shows, group-sex orgies, and so on) as a symptom of "corrupt and decadent capitalism," an affront to society because it threatened the life of society's main cell, the family.

In Greece and Italy, where macho was still king, the radicalized young and their imitators might express masculinity in new ways, outside the orbit of wife-and-family, but the expression itself was as lively and as heterosexual as ever. "In this beautiful country, one must only make love; other pleasures of the soul are cramped here. Love here is delicious," Stendhal once said about Italy. In the opinion of some American women, it was also uncontaminated by the sexual venality that they often found at home.

Francesco Alvieri of Verona and Milan saw women neither as competitors for male turf nor as counters on a sexual abacus. For him, the heterosexual relationship had not deteriorated into a power struggle, or an acting out of non-sexual needs, or a medium of exchange, or a political statement. It was, indeed, a pleasure of the soul.

Blond, robust, spirited, and sensual, Alvieri was an architect and graphic designer with offices in two cities. Asked why he was not married at thirty-four, Ceccho, as he called himself, returned the kind of sunny smile that mysteriously threatens rain. "I embrace the whole world," he said, speaking with eloquence in a language that unreasonably intimidated him. "For a wife, such a rival, it would not be fair." But for one long day, he stopped the world on behalf of an initially cynical young American student who had learned distrust of men at an early age. And at the end of it, he embraced her only lightly.

Weaned on the American custom of the sexual payoff, she was suspicious of the young Italian's invitation to stop over for a day in Verona on her return from Venice. They had met on the train from Milan. But Alvieri beguiled her with the promise of Verona's beauty, which, he said, "mixed Florence and Rome" with an intimacy unknown in either city. "Any American guy who puts himself out for a girl he never expects to see again usually has one thing on his mind: What's in it for me? And he damn well expects her to deliver the goods," the student said. "By cocktail time, this dude will want his pound of flesh, I thought, and when I don't fork over, he'll get ugly with me for leading him on."

Her internal warning system flashed red lights, she said, until Ceccho, "who didn't look like a cradle robber and was good at mind reading," reassured her of his intentions—or lack of them. "It is for nothing," he promised, speaking to her silent doubts. "It is only because the weather is beautiful and Verona is beautiful and you are beautiful."

The student sighed, remembering. "From your average American, it would have sounded like a send-up. From Ceccho it sounded . . . heartfelt. Well, by then he had just about used up his English vocabulary—or his self-confidence. So for the rest of those lovely twenty-four hours, we communicated through sign language, picture language, and the Grosset & Dunlap phrase book. When he wanted to tell me something for which he absolutely needed words, he would shout, 'The book! The book!' Ceccho made it rhyme with spook," she added, as if that were an achievement in itself. "When you have no common language, knowledge of each other is very direct. Feelings too." Words, she mused, could sometimes confuse things.

The young Veronese was just then working sixteen hours a day on a newspaper campaign for an exhibition of medieval art in Venice. "Can you imagine any ad man on Madison Avenue walking out on that kind of job at 10 A.M. on Monday to give me the keys to the city?" the young woman asked. But Ceccho appeared promptly at her hotel, she said, dressed like *la dolce vita:* mocassins on his bare feet, an African medal on his bare chest, a lacy white crocheted shirt, and "a smile that stretched from Verona to Milan. 'My office will be there tomorrow. But you, where will you be?' he said."

Over lunch in the country, the designer's pictograms began to appear. "He drew the big lake at Garda and two tiny people floating in it: me and him. I said I had no swimsuit with me, and we were twenty miles away from my hotel. It didn't matter. We would buy *costumas* on the way." His easy male authority, the student said, bewitched her.

At the beach, "a rocky, wild place" that opened out on the widest part of the lake, "we threw away the phrase book and talked about everything, even European politics. I talked English, he talked Italian. We understood each other perfectly. I don't know how."

Later that evening, Alvieri and the American girl drove high up in the hills over Verona with the city spread out like a carpet of light beneath them. Toward morning, they were eating sausages and drinking beer at a café in Dante Square. "We had met a bunch of Ceccho's friends in a restaurant halfway down the mountain." There he drew his final sketch. "A train, joined by a dotted line to an automobile; a man and a woman in the front seat. He was planning to take me to the railway station in the morning." She paused, remembering again. "By then, I was half hoping that when we drove back to my hotel he would ask to come upstairs. But he didn't. If I asked him, he would have been insulted. And it wasn't because we didn't feel it for each other. It was because we did."

The next morning, when the young man did not appear, the American girl took a taxi to the station, crying all the way. "As the train pulled in from one side, there was Ceccho running toward me from the other. He held me in his arms—for five whole seconds." He was wearing dark glasses, she remembered, that he had not worn the day before, and a gauzy shirt that smelled of flowers. "He must have washed and dried it in his goddamn garden." She pulled on her own dark glasses, she said, so that he should not see her wet eyes.

Months later, the student received a case of wine from Verona. "It came in the middle of that Italian postal strike. The card, with his name on it, nothing else, was smeared by rain. I sent him an art book from Rizzoli's. But I found out later that, all over Italy, it was one of those weeks they were dumping mail into the sea."

Would she and Ceccho ever meet again? That was not the issue, the student insisted rather haughtily. She illuminated the issue with another question: "Why did I have to go so far away from home to find out what this whole thing between a man and a woman could be?"

8 | The Americanization of Europe

"In Britain and Europe generally, we seem to have achieved a better balance—possibly a better separation—than you Americans between the poles of sexuality and materialism. For us, the two don't quite mingle," said Colin Scott, a correspondent for a left-wing British publication. "Money and power simply mean less here. Everyone cares less about them. So relationships between men and women have not gone bad. It gives us more time—psychological as well as real time—to be interested in each other."

As a study in contrast, he recalled his former life in Thailand. "In Southeast Asia, in places like Bangkok, for instance, the struggle for power does not exist at all." Libido had not become displaced into channels of acquisitiveness, either among men or women. "Instead, one finds an overwhelming indolence and sensuality," Scott said. A world without clocks, without daily reminders of schedules to complete and business appointments to keep—there was no more fertile ground for romance. "But to most Americans," such a world would be "unimaginable when not utterly awful," he thought. "The social environment of the United States seems more hospitable to making a fortune than to making love."

Nevertheless, most Europeans—Colin Scott among them—believed that whatever was American, including the social environment, must eventually influence not only Europe's future but the world's. "We say we disapprove of things in the United States, but really we are much attracted to the life there. Whatever is true in your country now, five years later, it will be true here," said a Frenchman in Lyons. "Europe finally follows behavior in the States—with appreciable differences," said an Italian in Rome. "We go in more or less the same directions, but with what differing undertones it is sometimes difficult to foresee. Considering our political chaos and our Communists, and the feminist campaigns and the abortion demonstrations, who knows what can happen next—and how soon?" A Viennese sociologist, just returned from a teaching assignment in the United States, summed up: "It's a world system. It's a global world," she said, emphasizing the growing similarities of sexual patterns in all societies, whether capitalist or socialist, planned or unplanned, underdeveloped, overdeveloped, or somewhere in between. "There's not much in any country any more, especially in the sexual sphere, that's unique."

In Paris, the first American-style sex-therapy center was an omen of the future. It filled many Frenchmen with apprehension and regret. Soon there might be sex-counseling services on every other street corner. "What is it for? Who is it for? The American tourists?" one Parisian asked, making no secret of his agitation. "We did not even know of the existence of this thing until my wife read about it in an obscure women's magazine. Nobody in France needs help in such matters," he said.

But by then, the capital of whole-grain sexuality was already contaminated by other American additives that might signify creeping sexual malaise. Not only pornography shops, but the X-rated motion picture, made in France for the first time, had already opened in Paris. In that film, homosexuality and masturbation were raised to heights of eroticism once reserved—at least in the City of Love—for connections between men and women.

The Americanization of Europeans was also taking place in other contexts and in other countries besides France. In Rome, a young Italian married to an English girl confessed that he had begun to wash the dishes after dinner. "Well, my wife insists on it," he admitted, almost turning "henpecked" into an Italian adjective. "But later, when I answer the door for my friends, I have put away my apron. Otherwise, my friends will laugh at me." He put his finger against his nose. "Yet it won't be long until my friends are up to the same thing themselves. Believe me, Italian women will make it their business to keep in tune with the world."

Within the feminist orthodoxy, however, the "ugly, enslaving macho" of Italian men was still a worldwide scandal. Avant-garde Europeans fueled the fire, supporting the feminist view of male assertiveness as essentially spurious and always damaging to women. "They *are* naturally very weak," Gilles du Vivier had said, of Italians. "They still consider women as mother or whore. Those are the sole dimensions. On the outside, they appear very proud, but on the inside, Italian men are uncertain and soft. They do not have a high opinion of themselves, nor is their behavior toward women very lofty." Yet he admitted admiring Rome more than Paris, and he spent as much time there as he could.

Italians in general smiled at such aspersions on the caliber of their masculinity. If they did not "like" women, in the asexual sense that one likes a comrade, at least they still remembered how to love them. Neither advancing age nor lack of conventional beauty seemed to quell their ardor. Italian women could be seductive, adoring, old, and ugly at once. On a cruise ship in the Adriatic, an unkempt, out-of-shape Sicilian matron with hot black eyes and long black hair threw her lumpy feet into her lover's lap. They shared a big juicy peach, passing it back and forth, exchanging bite for bite. He caressed her toes with his damp, hairy fingers. She scorched him with her eyes. Then the matron shifted her position, the better to stroke the old man's back. He purred like a sleepy cat, loud enough to arouse the interest, or the envy, of some nearby fellow travelers.

Later that night, on a deck chair under the half light of the moon, she lifted up her long skirt and, purring louder, he pulled down her pants. Although all the passengers had not yet gone to sleep, nothing could stop these old lovers. In the wisdom of their years, they preferred the sea air to their cramped cabin quarters near the engine room. Eros did not always seem so vigorous among the young in the U.S.A.

Mutterings of macho and economic strife, rising prices and rising blood pressure, the falling lira and falling teeth—nothing, it appeared, could daunt the spirit or the sexuality of the garden-variety, unself-conscious Italian male. On the island of Murano, a handsome man of sixty or so pushed his glasses up to his smooth, high, olive-skinned forehead and tapped underneath his right eye. "We know women!" he said, squinting before eons of that keen observation of the other sex which, for most Italians, remained a labor of love. He pointed to two American tourists visiting the island. One was plain, earnest, and fortyish. The other was laughing, coquettish, and fashionable—a Daisy Miller of this century. He took a fancy to the serious, plain one. "She has a fine, sympathetic character," the Italian breathed discerningly. But he shook his head over the coquette. "That one . . . be careful! Her husband, if she gets one . . . Ow! Behind that smile, he will find a prison warden with a heart of ice." Then this connoisseur of women returned his attention to the quiet one. "But, ah, that friend of hers! So serious and thoughtful . . . Those soulful eyes, those thick, full lips. *She* understands the subtleties of love." The man from Murano relished his appraisals of women, whether they were accurate or not. He felt stimulated by them. His eyes gleamed. The years weighed lightly.

And yet . . . these zesty, direct, self-assured Continentals who embraced life—and women—with such relish could be the last of a vanishing tribe. Not only in Europe, but throughout the world from Stockholm to New Delhi, the collapse of marriage, the rise of divorce, and the breakdown of the family underlined the widening gulf between male and female. "The curse of the twentieth century is communications and newspapers," a Turkish mayor said. "People cannot wait for half a century to attain what they see in the papers. We are all becoming America—rush, rush, rush."

Eastern Europe was both likely and unlikely as the site of some of the first serious storm warnings. Even under socialism, the rush to "become America" was well begun. Some believed that its long-range consequences could be calamitous. A young Yugoslavian journalist spoke with unexpected frankness about the new "upheaval in values" in Marshal Tito's land. It was largely provoked, she said, by the drive for sexual equality and the new competitive spirit among women.

"As the French say, we have all 'lost North.'" The social compass had gone awry. "Traditions are disappearing. Marriage is in peril. Our divorce rate is alarmingly high, second only to the United States." She took a kind of rueful pride in that idea. "And at the center of the crisis is the new status of women, their new demands and expectations. Perhaps we have deprived ourselves of more than we have won."

The journalist spoke with hesitation, wary of easy answers to complex questions. "Of course, men appear to accept our ambitions," she reflected. "They must give that appearance, otherwise they are afraid of seeming old-fashioned. But Yugoslavs and others in the East are really no more enthusiastic over self-ambitious women than men anywhere. After all, what are they getting for what they are asked to give up? Where are the rewards? Yes, they are socialists. But before that, they are men. They value their male dominance and power as much as anyone."

She related this dilemma to her own life. "My husband and I divorced after a disagreement over the size of our family. How could I know before we married that one child would be good but two would be a burden? Even with one, it is hard for me to travel in my work. My mother cares for my daughter, but I am among the fortunate few. Well, my husband wanted male heirs. Who can blame him?"

Miro A. Mihovilovic, a Croatian sociologist, did not deny socialist resistance to female emancipation. "Oh, men here accept women's new role formally," he said. "But when it happens to one of them that he must give up his own privileges

. . ." He pulled down his mouth into a grimace. "Is there anyone on earth who happily gives up his own privileges? On the other hand, circumstances are forcing all of us into cooperation with women." The primary coercive factor was urbanization, he said, with other observers in other countries. "Rural and agricultural life has faded away. In the cities, there are no more grannies, no more sisters, no more household help."

"Granny service" was the way Yugoslavian working women referred to the once-common practice of grandmothers taking over the care of their grandchildren, so that their daughters could take jobs. But in most parts of the world, including Eastern Europe, the extended family had shrunk with the countryside. Even grannies now sought their own liberation.

"So today, in the absence of these former helpers," Mihovilovic said, "the mother and father of the family must use each other more than ever." Yugoslavia was still too poor a country to meet even minimal demands for day-care centers; therefore, when wives entered the labor market, the mutual dependency of parents increased. "Together and alone, they must care for the children and the home. When the wife works outside, the husband not only lends a hand, he gives two hands, whether he likes it or not. For myself, I don't know many who like it." His tone mixed resignation and regret. "Then why do it? Because the family is the basic unit of society. Above all, it must survive."

Yet seldom before in civilized society had the family been called on to survive in the continuing absence of the mother. In some places, such as India, it remained alive on the strength of an ancient custom, the joint family, where several "part-time" mothers pooled resources. Jeremy Sotandi, an Indian in his late twenties from Bangalore, was learning Chinese at the Sorbonne in Paris. After finishing his studies, he planned to return to his native land with his wife, a UNESCO secretary, and their child. The young husband hoped to become an interpreter for the Indian government or a journalist specializing in Asian affairs.

His Indian wife, now learning French, wanted to teach that language in India.

"But it will take me up to a year to find a job when I return, and it may take my wife at least that long. So the joint family that we reenter when we return, it is like social insurance for us," he explained. Sharing a house with his sister and brother, their spouses, his nephews and nieces, and his mother afforded financial and psychological support as well as a built-in system of child care. Of course it afforded little privacy, but to them, at their time of life, privacy was a small sacrifice.

Yet Sotandi foresaw that even in India, joint-family time was running out. Here, too, urbanization took its toll. "In the old days, these large units were based on land ownership. Land was held in common. We all tilled the soil together. But when brothers and sisters seek jobs in different places, as often they must, the system breaks down. It is breaking down already everywhere in India," Sotandi said. "We have more than forty million unemployed and, among these, there are at least fourteen million university graduates. To find work, a man must go to where the projects are, where the dams are, where the big steel mills are being built." His black eyes softened as he thought of the past. "Today, nobody can stay home any more. That is a privilege of another time."

The young Indian made the same complaint that came up wherever social stability deteriorated. "Things are changing too fast. My own great-grandfather didn't even know that the English ruled India. But they were there for three hundred years."

In Eastern Europe, the joint family was hardly more than a memory. Working mothers were commonplace. And just as elsewhere in the world, husbands and fathers were plunged into silence by guilt, ambivalent feelings . . . and the need for a second salary check. But a small vanguard of educated Eastern European women, most of them working mothers themselves, had started openly to reassess the meaning of female autonomy and sexual equality in domestic life. Earlier than many others, they were confronting the agonies and ambiguities of the egalitarian role. Katja Boh, a young professor with a talent for Western fashion and straight talk, taught at the Institute of Sociology and Philosophy in Yugoslavia's University of Ljubljana. "In this society in transition, the price paid for our independence is sometimes so high, it is questionable whether the benefits derived from it are proportional," she said. She spoke of lacerating inner conflicts and the burdens of self-doubt. "Are the rewards commensurate with the pain? How much is too much to invest—physically, intellectually, and emotionally—in improving our social positions?"

Few feminists in other countries had begun to publicly ask such questions about the pain and the price of trying to be equal. "Think of the new tasks and responsibilities we have taken on, and the amount of energy we have given to them," Dr. Boh said. She ran down an incomplete list. "We have become highly educated and efficient in order to compete with men for work in the community. We are always pressed for time. There is no leisure left for ourselves. Our new duties outside the home make a staggering impact on family relations. Yet as mothers and housewives, we still do most of the work inside the home. There is great uncertainty. Among the parents and the children too, resentment spreads."

Professor Boh spoke of the work of another sociologist, Vera Ehrlich, who was then studying "the varieties of destruction and perplexity" that the transformation of sex roles bred. "The general and most striking phenomenon . . . is family discord that all of a sudden grows out of hand. Family quarrels become so regular, as though following a natural law." She told of a friend in Yugoslavia, a lawyer with a husband and five-year-old daughter who, on the surface, seemed to epitomize female success. "But in truth my friend was weighed down with more problems than she could manage. Not only the mechanical ones of day-to-day living, but the more complicated ones of maternity and wifehood." This young attorney wished for a larger family. " 'But a second child is out of the question, although I want it so badly,' she said. 'I cannot afford to stay home. My colleagues would take it as a betrayal. They would blame me for doing housework, when I have been educated to the law.' " Instead of offering men and women more options and more liberty, adhering to the letter of social equality often negated its spirit and narrowed the possibilities of free choice, Professor Boh said. "The obligation to achieve" could cheat women of their primary fulfillment and stunt the emotional life.

Boh asked for "a revaluation of the biological function, and the work stemming from it, from the point of view of its social importance." That might seem elementary, but its implications were momentous: how to give motherhood back the honor and sense of worthwhileness it had lost? It was a curious irony, in a way, that rising female materialism could rankle the idealistic socialist dream. Perhaps it was not the fault of women, the professor suggested, but a failing that must be remedied within socialism itself. "Childbearing and -rearing and the satisfactions of the psychological needs of the family are responsible social functions which also call for knowledge; that is to say, qualifications," she declared. "If those who perform these functions have no status, then this may be due to the fact that we have never given credit for them."

In Eastern Europe, some of the world's leading advocates of equality were among the first to reexamine the term. Insofar as the doctrine of sexual parity withheld dignity and self-esteem from traditional feminine pursuits, it could mitigate against the "equality" of wives who might not want sexual love, marriage, and motherhood to take second place in their lives, said Olivera Buric of the Institute for Social Policy in Belgrade. Assuming roles which were "the domain of men" often generated "dissatisfaction among women with what is achieved," she found. For many wives, the psychological and emotional liabilities of living two lives were devastating. "But it is a historical fact that women have joined the general work army and it is a historical inevitability that they will remain within it. So how to reconcile woman's biologic destiny with her demand for social position?" Dr. Buric asked.

Maybe, she suggested, shaking some carefully rationalized feminist structures, women should "seek employment that most easily harmonizes with their procreative and family functions; with the inescapable burdens of their manifold roles." In the socialist seventies, that was a daring idea. Were some kinds of work more suitable for women after all? Buric asked. Was the wish to live like a man, in men's domain, self-defeating—and the quest for autonomy, in the last analysis, unnatural to most women?

Tamara Hareven, another young socialist, pursued this inquiry to its logical end. She broached the long-dormant issue of "domestic feminism." Wives were once "the custodians of purity," the arbiters of morals, the wellspring of family life, Hareven recalled. In a world where moral values grew more tainted every day, what more positive and catholic use of power could one imagine?

Of course, for any wife to return to domesticity without anxiety, the family's financial burden could not be such that two incomes were necessary for sheer survival. It was up to socialism itself to provide the economic foundation for stable family life. But many feminist philosophers, with their insistence on women as victims, seemed unable or unwilling to distinguish the oppression of poverty from oppression by man. Millions of women in the world were subjugated by illiteracy, ignorance, and obscenely inferior living standards. Yet a peasant mother, working in the fields, pregnant with her seventh child, was not a sound paradigm for all mothers. Indeed, the father of those children was just as deprived, beaten, and humiliated as she. Both needed freedom from the yoke of poverty, not from each other or from the often saving bonds of family.

In France, Simone de Beauvoir swept past even the consideration of "domestic feminism" as a tool of power. Having babies and bringing up children were never among her main concerns. Instead, she spoke in praise of powerlessness and even offered it as a feminist strategy. "Many women think they should not play the game, not the game in its present structure," she said, startling those American feminists for whom "the game in its present structure" was the only one. "Women don't have to have the leading jobs . . . They don't have to be presidents of universities. They can be simple schoolteachers . . ." It was not the female labor force de Beauvoir questioned, but the female attitude toward labor. "One can have an education but refuse to use it in order to be amongst the 'elite' of a society we reject . . . What interests me is the work that certain feminist movements can do—to sap the regime but *not* play the game. Their politics is not to take part in politics."

The perniciousness of power and powermongers among both sexes—and the strategy of gaining strength by declining to compete for it—intrigued de Beauvoir. Belgrade's Buric went further. Many women were repelled by the power syndrome, she said. "They do not show an interest in authoritarian positions and even refuse them. They show no affinity for positions of power—not because they are not enough interested in social events and have no wish to influence them—but because they are not interested in the system of social power under which this influence is exerted. To go further, they are *against* it . . . Therefore, the answer to the final emancipation of women should be sought not in competing with men over powerful positions in society but rather on the opposite side, which could be defined as antipower positions."

The false values of materialism bred false emotions, Dr. Buric said. It was the goal of socialism to free personal ties, and so the emotional life, from corrosive and corrupting economic pressures. When that happened, Buric predicted, the family would come into its own as "the only institution that can preserve and confirm the values of life and individual happiness." This crucial transformation was already underway, she declared. In her country, organizations and factories belonged to the men and women who labored within them. Power bosses did not exist. Through Workers' Councils, workers had direct decision-making power and participated in profits and losses. "So the basic needs of working people cease to be private. They are taken over by the state . . ." Buric said. "And the social status of the father no longer defines the status of the family."

Released from its commodity value, freed from its bondage to drachma, dinar, lira, mark, franc, and pound, "with all extraneous motivation removed, and with the economic motifs removed from the husband-and-wife relationship," marriage would cease to be an intrinsically economic contract, Buric emphasized. "Emancipated and defunctionalized," the family would become "a true union of individuals based exclusively on feelings of affection, closeness, and connection." It would thrive, not as an aspect of community or as the basic productive unit of society, but "as a *communionship* in which only emotions exist. Children, freely planned and wanted, are the central value," Buric said. *Dominus*, no longer thwarted by social artifices or shattered by financial pressures, would find its natural expression.

Around the world, monogamy was floundering like a mighty, but mighty sick, whale. In of all places, Eastern Europe, could it rise above utilitarianism and be saved? Even under socialism, deep schisms separated the public wish and the private act. Men and women might extol marriage as the communionship of the future and children as its best blessing. Yet for the present many socialists—especially those well educated and Westernized—were almost as susceptible to certain common forms of "capitalist decadence" as anyone in Washington or Chicago.

In Belgrade, too, social equality implied sexual availability. "Liberated women" were easy picking, like those cans of Campbell's soup and tubes of Colgate toothpaste displayed on the supermarket shelves of every country. Remaining aloof, or merely selective, they became the discarded merchandise of sexual consumerism. On both sides of the ideological fence, male maneuvers were just about identical.

"You are a very beautiful woman, may I take the liberty of making a proposal?" said an Eastern European socialist to a rather ordinary-looking American woman not long after they were introduced at a party in Dubrovnik. The proposal was made before permission was granted. She cordially rejected it with a flash of her wedding band. The socialist returned the gesture with a flash of his own. "So what?" his glance asked in the Esperanto of the assignation. He refused to take no for an answer. At two o'clock in the morning, a call to the married woman's hotel room did not convince him she was sleeping alone. But by the next day, he had given up the chase, either out of wounded pride, fatigue, or because—East and West—those women who were not at once accessible were ignored. In the overstocked egalitarian supermarket of sex, why try harder?

Even among some people who had never heard of women's liberation or the sexual revolution and to whom America was only a distant fairy tale, new Western mores were moving in to unsettle old ways of life. "A change is always coming from Europe," said a farmer who had just migrated to Izmir from his rural birthplace deep in Anatolia. "Only God knows what is going to happen to the younger generation." Meanwhile, his wife still covered her face when she ventured into Izmir's streets, which was seldom, and when at home, did not look at television. "You never know what comes on the screen. There are things that a wife should not see, and she does not want to take the risk," her husband explained. But veils were dropping all the way from Izmir to Iran—and once she dared that decisive flick of the knob, she would never be innocent again.

Even in underdeveloped Africa, men and women were torn from the sleep of centuries. In Lagos, the editor of a Nigerian women's magazine remarked in *The New York Times* of her African sisters, "Today, they are being buffeted both by their own ethnic background and by news from around the world." African men were repudiating the polygamy of their ancestors to "take only one wife (like the Westerner), who looks good in an evening dress and can talk all the pretty nonsense of the cocktail parties." But as in many other places, monogamy was only a protective facade. "Nigerian men remain polygamous in practice . . . and [women] have not yet reconciled themselves to this fact."

One intensely life-oriented society, Israel, after decades of experiment, was already abandoning its insistence on sexual equality with the same enthusiasm that it had at first courted it. Men and women were reverting to their former roles—as men and women— anthropologist Lionel Tiger reported. In the Israeli kibbutzim, "despite basic social change" and identical sexual privileges, "nothing could finally jar the intractability of sex roles," he said.

Whether one was male or female had no political significance; nevertheless, it remained determining—indeed, more so than ever. "Major innovations in kibbutz women's lives have failed to stimulate the expected new social patterns," Tiger said. He observed "a strong, general, and cumulative tendency of men and women to become less, rather than more, similar in what they do and evidently want to do. We do not know which social realities relate to the biology of gender, or whether changing attitudes or even laws will induce people to act in ways that controvene, contradict, or distort what may be natural mammalian patterns."

Even in Kibbutz Harel, a radical-social settlement in the foothills of the Jordan mountains, these old patterns had acquired new life. "In the one place where feminists thought their ideal existed, the feminine mystique is ripening as fast as the corn in the fields," *The New York Times* reported.

"Kibbutz women aren't interested in equality. They're interested in children," one of their number explained without apology. Said another, with undisguised relief, "We are enjoying the privileges of being female."

9 | Power Drive: Managerial Men

Power to all the people, regardless of sex, race, age, and previous condition of servitude: as a rallying cry, it sang. As a practical program, it assumed a symmetry of needs and aims that, we were finding out, might not exist in human nature. And power had many faces, none without flaw. It could make hard, sometimes ugly, demands on the powerful. It could lead to ignoble acts. Having it and using it, especially for women, were as often as not mixed blessings.

Yet, since time began, women had coveted male power: indeed, many had mistaken it for the only kind. Two thousand years ago, Ovid, in his *Metamorphoses*, told of the strong and handsome son of Hermes and Aphrodite, called Hermaphroditus. It was the young god's misfortune to be courted by Salmacis, a beautiful nymph who envied him his manhood. She lured him into the springs which bore her name and, clinging to him "as if their flesh were one," raped him there. Robbed of his virility and force, "tamed Hermaphroditus" beseeched his stricken parents to take revenge: Make all who swim in these waters impotent, half man, half woman!" The gods agreed to that "weird magic." And forever after, each man who surrendered to Salmacis gave up his strength, his nerve, and his male energy. He conspired in his own castration—without a struggle.

Despite the millennia that separated today's feminist from Salmacis, they were hardly strangers to one another. But the tie that linked these women was not hatred of men. The sheer naiveté of that idea would have amused Ovid. It was quite the opposite: adoration of men, raised to the highest level. For, of course, Salmacis did not hate Hermaphroditus at all—except in the sense that envy (from *invidia*, hatred) sometimes seems "a monster begot upon itself." Indeed, she loved the god so much that she could not love herself enough. Jealous of his maleness and the special power that it gave him, blinded by it to her own abundant possibilities and resources, she longed only to possess it.

The nymph had none of the male talents of her time, as Ovid tells us. She was not "skilled in hunting, or practiced in the art of drawing a bow, nor yet a swift runner." But instead of cultivating her own garden, she let it go to seed.

Salmacis lacked creative self-appreciation, in any era and for every sex the essential condition of human liberty. Believing herself worthless, she sucked the spirit out of Hermes' son. So dazzled was she by his manhood that, when at last she lured him into her fountain, she exclaimed, "If you are not a god, then you should be one!"

Today as yesterday, woman's real calamity was frequently her deep conviction of inferiority. Too often, she was driven, not by her high opinion of herself, but by the belief that she had been born lowly and deprived by nature. This brought on defensive claims of superior worth and outrageous compensations which could only further injure, not repair. Her plight was nowhere more stunningly reflected for the ages than in Salmacis's pool. Calling Hermaphroditus her "darling stranger," the adoring but conflicted nymph grasped him "in a deathlock like the cuttlefish at deep sea's bottom captures its enemy." She wanted, literally, to love the life out of him.

Many a modern feminist was just as infatuated by manhood as her mythical predecessor. She, too, deified man as the custodian of all the influential magic she thought she lacked—and at the same time wanted to divest him of it. It was sometimes tempting to interpret her contemporary struggle for control and mastery as a kind of cosmic mugging in which the prize was male potency. One radical woman acted out the plot's intention in a graphic way: surgically releasing her clitoris from the surrounding tissues, she wore it on the outside, like a penis. Others took other means of male assertion—less metaphoric, more active. They were earnest but unpracticed muggers, often clumsy on the attack.

Sometimes their self-defeat in the world of men seemed almost willful, their ill-conceived tactics and strategy almost deliberately devised to fail. Victory would force them to face the perhaps unresolved conflict about exercising power and assuming its onerous responsibilities. Did they *really* want all that trouble? If they succeeded in succeeding, would they lose their reason to be? For the passion for protest notwithstanding, they sometimes thrived on second-class citizenship. It was, after all, what made them so touching, tragic, and important. It was also what smote the consciences of men. So it might have been almost intentional, that, in many personal skirmishes on male turf, they managed to lose the round and weaken their cause.

Feminist forays into the theater, for instance, need not have been doomed. What better place to play out the human drama of transition and change? But more than once, they were grossly mishandled.

As part of his annual festival of new plays, Anthony Morris, a prize-winning artistic director of one of America's most esteemed regional theaters, mounted an innovative drama by, with, and about women. Although the furor for liberation was then at its height, he had never received a viable playscript about women's contemporary struggle, he said, and he was eager to explore the theme.

Some months before the festival began, a director with an impressive reputation in improvisational theater proposed to create such a play out of the real lives of real women. The director—a man—would conduct intensive workshops in improvisation and technique; the women would share their private awakenings; the play would emerge out of ten weeks of mutual exploration and encounter.

One hundred women responded to an advertisement for non-professional performers. Morris and his workshop director wanted twelve women whose own search for self-awareness was, so to speak, a work in progress. They would express the new, exciting, often traumatic transformations of the sex no longer satisfied with second place.

"We preferred to work with women who had not yet arrived at final answers to their lives, rather than those who had already been radicalized and knew exactly where they were going. They had more questions to ask. That provides more and better drama than what comes out of certainty," Morris explained. The play evolved as the personal tales of eight women emerging from the women themselves. They ranged in age from the early twenties to the middle forties, and in occupation from an unmarried airline stewardess to a recently divorced mother of eight children. The true stories they told of their lives were gently structured and loosely scripted by a young woman writer-in-residence. "None were professional actresses," Morris emphasized. "They all trained themselves to perform."

He had thought of the improvisational play as an interesting but modest experiment, a kind of coffeehouse production that would give a limited number of performances (as eventually happened), not in the theater proper, but in the basement of a nearby church. He was, understandably, unprepared for the bitter storm that the play set off within the feminist camp.

To an onlooker, the work was immaculately well-intended—feminist in spirit almost to a fault. It took swipes at all the obvious targets: unfeeling, insensitive men with "rough laughter and stubby fingers" who brutalized women by their lack of compassion and caring; the oppression of mothers, daughters, and airline stewardesses; the intellectual impoverishment of the theories of Sigmund Freud. It even attended to the solaces of masturbation.

Nevertheless, for accountable and unaccountable reasons, the feminists raised hell. It was not that they really disliked the stage work they were attacking. "The funny part of it is that most of the women who protested loudest never even saw the play," Anthony Morris said. "They had no way of knowing firsthand how feminist or antifeminist or anything else it was." They seized on it as a *cause célèbre*, he believed, at a moment when militant women were "desperately eager to enhance their visibility." One feminist leader had recently announced to the newspapers that she was on the lookout for more direct-action, high-visibility projects to carry the meaning of the struggle for equality to her as yet unradicalized sisters. Her organization was one of those that later spearheaded the coalition which took action against the play and Anthony Morris's theater.

He himself—a popular culture hero in a city full of strivers—was no slouch at community visibility. When the affluent aristocracy gave fund-raising parties to help support his lively theater, they were likely to send invitations that read simply "Tony!" It was enough. It also might have been enough to irritate some feminists who saw male talent and male charm as a combination subversive to women in its potential power; therefore, as a subtle sexual conspiracy against them.

Before the play opened, Morris said, he began to "receive telephone calls and angry letters from feminist groups in the region, making certain explicit demands of us." In effect, they demanded to control his casting and to censor, if not create, his script. One local feminist organization wrote to him, in part: "We would like to register our displeasure at your reactionary sexist practices . . . it has come to our attention that recently you hired [male director's name, spelled phonetically and incorrectly] to create a women's theater piece . . ." Another letter complained, "A man is not the appropriate person to direct a play using material culled from the raw souls of women. Secondly, we understand that these women are to be paid only [fee stated]. This is outrageous exploitation, whether these women are professional actresses or not. Further, [male director, name again spelled wrong] gets the credit for the women's creativity and energy . . . If you think this project involving women is going to placate individual and organized feminists . . . you are far from correct."

In a letter, Anthony Morris set the record straight. There were, he replied, "women in virtually every capacity in this theater since its creation—administrators, directors, stage managers, producers, literary personnel, actors (meaning actor-persons), lighting designers, costume designers, composers . . ." He defended his artistic independence. "I do not accept the premise that you as a group have the right to tell me that any person is not appropriate to direct any play which I choose to present; that's my choice, not yours." He explained his rates of pay. "Everyone gets the same, regardless of sex, age, race of the people involved in our Laboratory (developmental) projects . . . If you feel it's exploitation, it joins the category of *artists in general*, of which we are society's victims."

But the feminists rattled their swords louder. Within weeks, a coalition of eleven community and other women's groups, some national in scope, had joined the protest. Insult had been added to injury, they said. "Despite the extreme concern of women's groups" regarding its content, a local television channel had filmed the play-in-progress, photographing auditions, rehearsals, and staging. The feminists tried to suppress the screening. ("It was no longer just our theater they were attacking. They went after that educational station with hammer and tongs," Morris said.)

A well-known feminist lawyer, threatening "to move nationally on this issue," requested from Anthony Morris "(1) a working script of the play; (2) formats, outlines, creative processes, transcriptions or otherwise, written or visual, relevant to the creation of the play; (3) descriptions of hiring practices, promotions, upgradings, etc., regarding the production and creative staff of the theater; (4) a description of the method of selecting material for the group; (5) a financial breakdown of the funding, salaries, decision-making practices of the theater" . . . and so on . . . and on. The lawyer demanded that

Morris send copies of all such materials to her offices on both coasts.

He met with the coalition the following week. The women appeared in black robes, as if in mourning for their lives. During a long confrontation, they pulled out all the stops—again accusing the controversial play of "regressive implications" and Anthony Morris's theater of having "no built-in balance of feminist-initiated and controlled programming to provide alternatives." About the projected television show, they said, "the reactionary elements who exercise such efficient censorship in television . . . do not wish the American people to know the truth about their lives." The truth about American lives, the feminists implied, was their property.

Although much newsprint was consumed by this dispute, reason won out. The television channel showed its documentary. The feminists ceased their attacks on Morris and his theater. But the women had taken a giant step backward. They had forfeited the support of a man of far-ranging influence and intelligence who had started out as a well-intentioned friend of their movement.

"Now I have come to believe that the militant feminist is her own worst enemy," Morris said. Getting to know her only too well, the artistic director had lost sympathy with her tactics, and also with her view of life. "Her position is shallow, thin, and one-dimensional—a simplistic interpretation of our sociosexual life. Once stated, there are no more mysteries," he said. "It doesn't pry into the secrets of human existence. It doesn't examine the intricacies of human affairs." But the irony was enormous. By attempting to suppress the free will of the artist and to impose on his work the bias of the censor, it violated feminism's first principle, that of individual autonomy.

In an Eastern city, another feminist confronted another prominent theatrical producer in the lobby of his theater. "When are you going to put on my play?" she barked. It was already under option by him. "It's something of a masterpiece, you know. What's taking you so long? Why did you bother to produce that piece of shit before you got around to me?" she cried, of the current work of a young male playwright.

Like Anthony Morris, the producer was full of deference and good manners. Feminists, feeling wronged, could call forth the gallantry, as well as the guilt, of men. Withdrawing a little from the playwright's tongue-lashing, the producer spoke of his "loyalty and responsibility" to the young man whose earlier work he had also staged. "What about your loyalty and responsibility to me?" she cried. "I'm better than he is. I'm a lot more talented. It's just that you like him more!"

The producer remained calm and conciliatory. But beneath his surface affability, male forces gathered to protect his power. With a smile and a handshake, but no promises for the future, he hurried off into the theater's auditorium.

Outside, trembling with rage, the playwright accused the producer of latent homosexuality and a secret hatred of women. His many wives were proof, she pointed out to a feminist friend, of his real preference for his own sex. Her friend was fairly indifferent to the specific circumstances of the producer's marital life, but not to the sexual dynamics of the scene in the lobby. "You were absolutely craven in there," she told the playwright. "He made you eat shit!" she said. "Why didn't you stand up for yourself? Why didn't you tell him where to get off?"

The playwright's anger brought tears to her eyes. "Yes, I was craven," she said. "Why was I such a fool? Next time I won't be. Next time I'll tell him where to get off!"

It was probably the producer's sense of social justice, rather than his sense of theater, that led him eventually to put on her play. He did not seem susceptible to intimidation. His whole career was a testimony to his creative courage. The feminist's work, for all her own faith in it, turned out to be something less than the masterpiece she promised. Despite its sporadic eloquence, it was scarred by self-pity and feverish propaganda. She blamed its tepid critical reception on the fatuity of men in high places and its short run on the shortsightedness of her producer. He himself grew wary and weary of female playwrights and female directors (with one of whom he suffered through a similar confrontation). His next successful play was written by a man, directed by a man, and portrayed by an all-male cast.

So did some gifted and energetic women snatch defeat from the jaws of victory—and not only in the arts. High-handed demands to "include us in" often ricocheted, setting the stage for their exclusion. But if they sometimes seemed determined to court failure, maybe it was easier that way. One could not bemoan success, delegate blame for it, or claim persecution in its name. To the feminist who sometimes nurtured her own "oppression" as if it were a crippled child, defeat could be more congenial. At least it renewed her obligation to protest.

The way women dealt with their power drives often depended on how their male colleagues dealt with them. David Thorp, senior editor of trade books for a prestigious publishing house, had worked on the manuscripts—and inadvertently on the psyches—of some of the most formidable feminists in the U.S.A. His editorial touch was light, but its impact was great. When he was at the peak of his powers, practically all his female authors were militant women, aggrieved by men. His diplomacy, if one could call it that, was simple and disarming. He did not smooth their ruffled feathers. He did not dissemble. He did not appease. He treated his feminist writers as human beings, rather than as heroines or harridans. He was stabilizing, straight, and evenhanded in an era that, largely because of women's social evolution, bred more than its fair share of shaky, double-dealing men.

In short, David Thorp was an unusual man for the times. Women admired him, whatever their politics. He was sexual without stressing it, but never merely flirtatious. He seemed unafflicted by the common male maladies—free-floating misogyny, vagina envy, the machismo that so often disguised gender discomfort. Thorp's long, reasonably happy marriage might have accounted for the antibodies he was able to build up against these viruses that were so widespread. He spoke of "the old values" of stability, continuity, and fidelity as if they still mattered. His wife was a college graduate and former magazine copywriter who lived a non-conformist life. She kept house with good humor and more than ordinary grace. She did not look forward to returning to the copy room or to the campus to study for an advanced degree. Their children attended parochial schools, never smoked pot, and were polite to their parents. It was an unusual family in a world where almost any authentic kind of family was fast becoming an anomaly—or so it had begun to seem.

And in his way, David Thorp was an unusual, if admittedly anachronistic man. In some deep-seated way, he still took *dominus* for granted. He called himself "a dinosaur" with only half a smile. He wore his hair short and his ties narrow when his colleagues wore theirs long and wide. Thorp distrusted social and literary fashion too.

It was quite telling that this traditionalist—the sort that, in theory, feminists admired least—should have worked out more congenial relationships with them than many others who catered to their politics. Indeed, the men who bent like grass in the wind were often suspect among militant women themselves. "Hanging on the coattails of the movement," "exploiting us for their own ends," they would say of the Johnny-come-latelies to feminism. Wives were warned against their "liberated" husbands by the very women who had heralded the liberation of men: "Watch out he doesn't make you his little slavey and live off your salary check and your hard work."

But even these distrustful women trusted David Thorp. In his easy, warm, honest way, he seemed to bring out the best in them and, not by accident, in their work. Although never manipulative, he filtered out the sediment, dumped a lot of the debris, and substantially improved the prose of more than one literary feminist afflicted with, as he said, "a tendency to ramble. Why is it so hard for women to keep to the point?" Thorp asked. More prudent men had learned to steer clear of such "sexist" generalizations, at least around the sex at which they were aimed. But he said what he meant and, if there were consequences, he survived them.

Under Thorp's guidance, one of his most famous clients—her reputation for intractability was international—became almost as docile as a child. Most men feared or resented her. They toadied, were terrified, or put up defenses. Thorp just told her what he thought. Their relationship was comfortably (for both of them) in the classic mode. The editor functioned as the father-mentor to whom the feminist brought her work. He revised, reconstructed, passed judgments. She accepted and appreciated his advice, gradually shedding the tough shell of the polemicist for the softer, more human woman she had long repressed.

But without meaning to, probably without knowing it, men like David Thorp created emotional havoc in some female lives. Where *dominus* thrived, deep feelings could be stirred that set off subterranean battles between the worker and the woman.

"There are shades and grades of femininity," Thorp said. "Dealing with certain women in work situations is very much like dealing with another man. They set themselves deliberately to eliminate sexual feelings and sexual gains in an office context. That doesn't mean they're dykey. But sometimes it's a relief." Men more often felt grateful than deprived when the promptings of libido did not overheat the day-to-day affairs of business.

"Then again, there are women whose most human female qualities make them impossible as colleagues," Thorp went on. He spoke of one—she had left the company—whose old, aggravating (to her) need for dependence clashed with her new desire for authority. It was the perennial conflict of the woman in power. With one hand, Thorp's co-editor clung to him for advice and guidance; with the other, she rejected what he gave her. She flirted with him on Thursday and fumed at him on Friday. He liked and disliked her; was simultaneously attracted and outraged. "There was a lot of hand wringing, as well as real tears," he remembered without much affection. "Everything was off balance. It was no atmosphere for an office." He could still recall her potent charm. But, Thorp admitted, he was glad when she took off for "more creative" but more solitary territories where the only authority she needed to exercise was over her own work.

A department-store executive said of a female co-worker, also saddled with more autonomy than she could coolly handle, "I spent an awful lot of time in the store hoping Nancy wouldn't come unglued in front of my eyes. I got so I hated to go into her office, she was so desperately uneasy. In a few months, she had fired everyone in her department she sensed would be a threat to her and filled the positions with friends. She got rid of some of our best personnel that way, including several women sharper and tougher than she was. She surrounded herself with people she knew she could keep in line. And she had a tremendous fondness for hiring gays." Because they deviated just enough from maleness, homosexual men were often the most congenial associates for such women. They could vent their power drives on them without the doubts, dilemmas, and self-questioning that other men incurred.

An older man in another profession, corporate law, acknowledged that there had been moments when the unbusinesslike atmosphere provided by a new senior partner beguiled him. "I went to lunch with Belle the first time thinking I was Brian Aherne and she was Roz Russell and we were reenacting one of those old late-night movies. 'Boss Lady,' I thought of calling her." He did not suppress a smile. "I had all I could do to deal with her insecurity, her indecisiveness, her quicksilver nature. Every brief she wrote was a dramatic struggle. If I pointed out difficulties, contradictions, non sequiturs, she would shrink up and say, 'I just don't want to talk about it any more. I don't want to face it. Tell me tomorrow.'"

When this female attorney left the concern, she joined a feminist law firm committed to "direct democracy." Leadership was outlawed as immoral and all decisions were made by the group. The feminists ruled by committee; no one had to take control. Perhaps it was the best way out of the female power quandary.

Of course most of these male executives agreed that many working women were neither so volatile, so irresolute, nor so torn by criticism as the ones they chose to gently censure. Certain men, possessing similar qualities of personality, said David Thorp, "could make office life equally impossible." Yet many women, insofar as they were still women (and excluding the exceptional few), might never feel entirely comfortable as bold, decisive, self-directed organization people. To make the office seem more like home sweet home, they would carry into it their vulnerable and diffuse emotions, their need to nurture, their desire for support and courtship and, not in the least, their sexuality.

Drawn together with men in their business lives, they would often act out, willy-nilly, one version or another of office marriage. There were buddy marriages, based on professional partnership rather than on sexual magnetism; mother-son and father-daughter marriages, based on Oedipus and Electra bonds; as well as those more dangerous, high-velocity unions founded on mutual attraction (imperfectly suppressed) and intimations of the erotic. Perhaps it was unrealistic to expect the sexes to behave asexually—even at the office. In the corporate pool as in the springs of Salmacis, the thirst for male power could not prevent women from acting like women . . . or men from responding like men.

10 | The Old Boys and the New Woman

"Women describe themselves as waiting to be chosen—discovered, invited, persuaded, asked to accept a promotion . . . as hesitant, as waiting to be told what to do . . . as reluctant to take risks," a recent book, *The Managerial Woman,* reported.

Nevertheless, some men said that, at her highest level of accomplishment, the new managerial woman was unsurpassable —bringing all her legendary gifts of warmth and caring, discretion and tact, gentleness and grace to bear on cold business. Once in a while, with tenderness that might have been just as well directed toward a mistress or a mother, a grateful young man described a female employer as "the finest boss I ever had." This potent combination of lover, tutor, mentor, and parent did not necessarily detract from her real capacity to command.

A salesman of children's toys and books remembered his first employer: "She brought me up within the company. She encouraged me, cared about me, forgave me when I made mistakes, congratulated me when I didn't. When I left, I was making twice as much money as when I started. But all in all, Mrs. Morton had a bad effect on me," he added ruefully. "Because I've never been happy working for a man. I miss all that . . . stroking."

Other men who worked for women owned up to even more complicated feelings. "I'm trapped and stereotyped in my role with my female boss," one complained. "Mothers give you more 'smother love' than fathers, don't they? So you might imagine you'd be more fearful of a male boss. But you're really more fearful of being smothered and patronized by a woman.

| 155

You have a tendency to say okay to everything she asks, even when you don't understand what the devil she's telling you to do. It's easier to show another man your inadequacies. You don't have to worry about losing your self-respect." *Dominus* was at stake in the workplace too—fiercely protected or bitterly lost on every rung of the ladder.

Here and there, one still heard some vestigial talk, left over from past generations, about those old-fashioned women who took the bedrooms of men in power as steppingstones to their ultimate destination, the board room. But in the new epoch such women were, by and large, anachronisms. For one thing, the prevailing female ideology frowned on such crass exploitation of sexuality. For another, the high availability of no-strings-attached sexual partners, coupled with the curious downgrading of the act itself, mitigated against the use of femininity as commodity or currency. Few ambitious women could depend on looks and charm alone to get them where they wanted to go.

Most insisted that they wouldn't take that route to success, even if they could. They deprecated other women who "use their sex aura to move their work through the office and get preferential treatment," as one executive secretary in a Washington government bureau put it. But even more, she said, she disapproved of "the old boys who insist on making everything a sex issue. They refuse to take me seriously because I'm twenty-eight years old and I like to wear short skirts and sweaters. There are specific work requests I need answered every day," she explained, "but I'm always getting derailed. 'Pretty blue eyes,' the guys say to me, 'why are you working at all?' " The besieged young woman heaved a heavy sigh. "Lunches, travel, drinks after work—everything becomes a sex situation. At the cocktail hour, you'd rather pay for your martini or your glass of wine. It's one way of reminding them that you really are your own person." Another sigh, a frown, a pucker. "It's not even proprietous" (she probably meant judicious) "to travel on assignment with your boss. All in all, you take an awful lot of flak in the course of the business day. You flirt your way out or you serious your way out. One way or the other, it's exhausting."

Almost no one dared suggest that, given two genders, sex in the office, field, and factory was not only inevitable but could even soften the edge of a hard day's work. In the grayed-out, genderless new world of "persons," sexuality itself—the very smell of male and female—was in danger of becoming déclassé. One middle-aged company president said that, actually, it had been swallowed up in the maw of high management. "We've been so accustomed all our lives to seeing women in a totally sexual focus that capability and intelligence on our own plane of achievement just seems to desex them," he explained.

But Herbert Stockton, chairman of the board of a coast-to-coast chain of consumer-service centers, refused to be inveigled into the discussion at all. "I'm not interested in talking about the problems of women in upper-management positions," he declared. "That stuff bores me." His voice dropped and his steel-gray eyes grew confidential. "What's really interesting is male *sex-u-al-ity*. Men know less about that than they know about anything else." Stockton had a habit of drawing out certain words that meant a lot to him. His evident desire to appear more open than other men might have meant that he was really more closed. "The mystery of male sex life *ob-sesses* them—although of course they won't admit it to you," he said.

In point of fact, many did. American men often admitted that, in paying such undivided attention to the sexual mysteries of women, they had neglected to decipher their own natures and were therefore, throughout life, puzzles to themselves. But self-puzzlement was by far the more prevalent attitude. Whether old boys or young, what perplexed men most about their own sexuality was its devilish precariousness. They seldom got over feeling frustrated that, even while they might be in perfect command of their corporate lives, they could not always rely on their copulative organs to behave as they wished. Although articles on the American "impotence epidemic" had long been appearing in medical and lay publications, from the *Archives of General Psychiatry* to the staid *Wall Street Journal* and the lubricious *Forum*, in two hours of talk, Herbert Stockton never brought himself to utter that fraught word. But in carefully constructed euphemisms, he implied over and over again that the liberation of female sexuality—by some inevitable process of intimidation—was strangling normally "exuberant" male sexuality.

"Enormous, *vi-o-lent* change is in the works, more so in men's lives than in women's," he said in hushed tones, as if telling me a secret. But magazine articles as well as the media in general, Stockton cautioned, were "very remiss in disseminating among women misinformation and miscalculations" about maleness. Most men were not sexually indiscriminate, he insisted. Exuberant, yes; but selective and, above all, sensitive. "How did the idea ever get started that, for most of us, only the physiology of the thing matters? We care more about the emotional and psychological aspects of sex than you do." It pleased this Old Boy to turn conventional wisdom outside out. He seemed to view the overthrow of accepted ideas as a moral imperative. "The screwing, the orgasm, is only a minuscule part of the whole male episode," he said. Whereas for women, it was the world and all. That was the gist of his not-so-unusual sermon.

The text was far less original than he supposed. He was by no means the first man to observe that women were adopting male behaviors and assuming male prerogatives in many other places than the world of business. But as they asserted their right to discard the straitjacket of sentiment and behave "like men" in their sexual lives, men were asserting that they had never really behaved that way at all. Each sex was repudiating its own legends with a vengeance. ("The hardest thing to live with now," a female college student said, "is that you don't know *what* to believe about *whom*. Nothing is sure any more.")

Unlike most men of power, Herbert Stockton could not be

easily cajoled into talking about women in power. Each time I brought up the topic, this man, who presented candor as if it were his calling card, tossed it off with a few bland words and swung right back around into sex. It seemed not to occur to him that one of the keys to the big "mystery" that so confounded him might lie at the door of the executive suite.

"Tell me how a woman behaves in the office and I'll tell you how she behaves in bed," one company president said. Endearing or officious behind the desk, endearing or officious between the sheets: it was a perfectly plausible rule of thumb. Men as well as women revealed the secrets of their sexual selves in nonsexual situations—across a conference table, a tennis court, a classroom. Erotic interest was never first awakened in the bedroom; it only culminated there. No one really changed his colors when he changed into his pajamas.

But such speculations would have seemed mere diversions to Herbert Stockton. He wanted to talk about female prodigality ("Only after brain surgery that separates mind from body" could men become as sexually prolific as women, he declared) and about how "infinitely *frag-ile*" male sexuality had begun to appear in contrast. He spun out the last syllable, rhyming "fragile" with guile. "To record what's happening to women today that's bringing out this . . . *frag-il-it-y* in men, that's your most important task," he admonished. "Because it's a symptom, not a cause. It's a symptom of the times."

He told of two love affairs that ended badly: one his own and one his friend's. "My friend's girl was never completely satisfied, never sated," he said. "For him, she was enough. But she needed to be made love to by five or six men. Well, it undermined his ego, feeling like a face in the crowd."

His own incipient affair collapsed, he confided, when "the attractive, tasteful Vassar graduate" he was wooing (although, he maintained, he loved his wife) told him that "all I want to do is screw." Stockton was one of many high-echelon men to put on the record that, in choosing women, he never reached below his class. Only lesser men, it was frequently intimated, sought out women who were "less" than they.

"Of course it was her perfect right to want straight sex from me," he continued, of the Vassar woman. "But she should have kept it to herself. She should have let me believe she cared more about me than that." Social equality did not faze him. Yet when it came to making love, Herbert Stockton had to be, as it was aptly said, "top dog."

But he was as misled by the old mythology of the sexually insatiable female as woman ever was by the old mythology of the sexually insatiable male. Gullibility about the Other often verged on the astounding. Among most women, it was already an open secret that the experience of intercourse ranged from disappointing to disastrous when, reckless with their new freedom, they undertook it solely for its own sake.

"Love is the real aphrodisiac," said one of America's foremost sex therapists, Helen Singer Kaplan, M.D., at the risk of sounding outdated. For ordinary people, emotion had to catalyze desire. But many men still held the notion that they could learn to be good lovers without really loving. True, they might learn to be good technicians. They might learn to manipulate "the tit and the clit," as another sex therapist said, fanning flickers of sensation that appeased an itch or moistened a part. Yet if the performance was all pyrotechnics and no real feeling, it could arouse without touching the heart or the mind.

"How come millions of men buy every joy-of-sex book that comes down the pike?" Stockton was asking. "Because we're *myst-i-fied* about how to give women everything they want." As a specialist in consumer expectations, he saw all of us as consumers of sexual experience whose expectations—for our partners and for ourselves—had gone right through the roof. "The big sell these sex manuals get just expresses our anxiety, our generalized hope of finding out more about the thing."

If the sexual mystery deepened as sexual information mounted and men grew old, wondering, wondering, the implicit irony might have been so flagrant that it was overlooked. Maybe emotional falsity, making love lovelessly—by the book, as it were—explained many human enigmas, including the one Herbert Stockton called "fragility." Men could lie to themselves, but not forever.

After unloading his anxieties and airing his grievances, at last Stockton turned his attention to the woman in the workplace—middle-management woman. The stellar positions in his company were all held by men. Traditional patterns of domination and control prevailed. Rank was preserved. Male ego was unchallenged. The aura, at least, of potency was intact. So he could say blithely, because it was not—yet—happening to him, "I like what's happening in business today. I regard it as positive and participatory, getting women up there into the higher echelons with men. Equal pay for equal work, the opportunity for them to climb the executive ladder . . ." He nodded approvingly. "It's nice to watch. It's interesting to talk about." As long as that essential hierarchy endured. As long as, within the company, Herbert Stockton was still top dog.

Many other men, from bank presidents to department-store owners, had come to a meeting of minds about the women who courted power. These Old Boys put out the welcome mat in front of executive suites across the country, even in the once laggard South. Then they laid down the law: The price—or the penalty—for success in a man's world was, in effect, to become one. At least for the length of the office day. And as so many of the Old Boys pointed out, in their velvety-carpeted corner suites, the office day never really ended. You lived it even while you slept. If his career was always a top man's true mistress, it would have to be a top woman's true lover. Good old-fashioned female *sex-u-al-ity* was bad form in business. One could not hope to have the cake of power and eat it too.

Oh, once in a while, a top man and a near-the-top woman, flouting the new customs, might duck into a midtown hotel at high noon and pull down the shades. But by the time she overtook him on the upward climb within the organization, he was already gazing down the ladder at the younger girls on the lower rungs. *Amour* and equality did not usually go hand in hand.

Secretaries, clerks, and other underlings, by remaining subordinate, were exempt from these rules of the Top Woman game. For them, light flirting on company time was, as ever, permissible; so was the decorous display of fecundity. But making heavy, if hasty, love behind the file cabinets was now off limits at every level. Female consciousness, if not female rates of pay, had been raised across the board. Tractable, trusting, trustworthy, illicit sexual partners were almost as hard to find as girls who would fetch coffee. By and large, they too had turned into upward-bound women, no more fun and games. They meant, in a word, business.

"Bring 'em on, bring 'em on! We don't have enough of 'em!" Hiram Clark cried, in the best Old Boy style, about "females with leadership potential," whether in politics, publishing, or retailing, it was all the same to him. Rich, rotund, "content as a cow and disgustingly healthy" in late middle age, he was the mayor of a sizable Southern city and the president of its foremost chain of tobacco shops. "It goes back to nature, back to territorial imperatives," Mayor Clark said, explaining his own enthusiasm in throwing wide to women the portals of male-only conference rooms. "Take the animals. They have their territorial rights. Well, the ladies should have their rights too. They're just beginning to claim them in every phase of life—in jobs, schools, at home. And what's it really all about? Why, they're claiming territory that's rightfully theirs, just like the animals." Behind his huge desk, rubbing his hands across his high belly, he looked happy for both species.

"Feminism? It's here. It's a fact," he said. "What's the use of negative feelings?" He emphasized the positive, glowing with good will. "It's your whole society that's changing, your whole

American philosophy, and you just got to adjust on things. I mean, my goodness, everything is adjustment, isn't it?" Southern men, he said, were past masters of that art. "We're open-minded about events like feminism. It's no surprise whatsoever that you have fewer male chauvinists down here. There's charm, there's chivalry, there's brains. Look at Jimmy Carter! Southerners are willing for everyone to make their own way—and that includes the ladies."

Mayor Clark blew his nose, hiding his face in a flag-sized white linen handkerchief. "Why, I know one man, right in my own company, who travels with his wife. Wherever she goes, whenever she's promoted, he just changes his spot. By now, he's worked in three different locations for us. Just follows that woman around. Yessir, there's a great deal of change going on." He offered a trenchant insight. "That's the main trouble some people have with female independence. They got to tear it down because they just can't adjust to change."

Finally, Mayor Clark broached the first person singular. "Say, I got a wife of my own who's a judge! Now that's considered a male occupation. The girl was a judge for years before I ever set eyes on her. I says, 'Listen, little girl, I never had a date until I bumped into you!' " By the time of that first encounter, Clark was more than fifty; his wife was about thirty-five.

The mayor beamed as he spoke of their new baby daughter. Her birth had made necessary a major adjustment in his wife's life, territorial imperatives notwithstanding. "Of course, she did not run for election a year ago. She was expecting by then," he explained. By Old Boy standards, one did not become pregnant and cling to power at the same time. When you started to behave like a woman, you had to give up living like a man.

"We got married when I was already mayor. I reckon that was helpful to her," he said, alluding to the solace that even vicarious power thrills may provide. "But now she's busy with her child. You see, she was elected to office even before I was. So she already had a certain amount of satisfaction competing in the outside world. She was mature enough to appreciate the value of accomplishment—and mature enough to put it aside. She earned her stars. Proved to herself she could. Yet . . . she's a *female*." He gave that word the same weight that Herbert Stockton had given *sex-u-al-ity*. When all was said and done, to many a man—and not merely the Old Boys—being female still explained everything, from emotional jags to the descent of judges from bench to bassinet. "Now she's content to let nature take over . . . to the full extent of nurturing her young," Hiram Clark said. "She's like any other proud mother with her baby, just as happy as she can be. Matter of fact, I'm asking for minority rights in my own house now. I'm the only male in it!"

He was twinkling all over. "Not many mayors have married a judge, but I'm the only damn mayor who ever got a judge pregnant! There's been lots of jokes about that around here." Probably not for the first time, he appreciated them with such relish that he laughed until he wheezed. Feminists might accuse Hiram Clark of arrant sexism. Yet he came just about as close as almost any man to welcoming women with unfeigned cordiality into the managerial world of men.

The South was one of the last bastions of what many Old Boys, without batting an eye, still called "the male tradition." With no sacrifice to that tradition, they often seemed more capable than some others of coping with the female drive toward power. Their method was to more or less ignore it.

In Georgia, one corporate vice president of aeronautics said, "I've had a lot of women, I like a lot of women—and some of them are ardent feminists. But as I see it, they're still women all through." He let them know it too, he claimed. "There's enough of the old South left in me to want to open doors for them, to light cigarettes for them, and to buy them flowers. I am hopelessly chivalrous, you might say. But retaining a few Southern graces has never been a handicap to me as far as women go, my feminist friends included."

He recalled the "most hard-hitting professional woman I have ever known," whom, he implied, he had bedded more than once or twice. "It all began when I got so impressed with her ability to get the job done that I sent her three perfect roses. Betsy adored those roses and she let me know it. She kept all her aggressiveness on the professional level. Now certain female executives up North," he said, "might have crammed those roses down my throat. But Betsy's commitment to her job ended at the threshold to her bedroom. A lot of women could learn from her. Of course," he added, "she came from a Southern family, seven generations old."

In the Carolinas, a prominent management consultant who had written some books on the subject agreed, with Old Boy pride, that "the male tradition has not yet been erased from the Southern subconscious. Down here, we sure do open doors for women, literally and figuratively. But the one with her eye on the door of the executive john does not disturb us either. We see her as a woman—with a chip on her shoulder and a fixed idea—but a woman nonetheless. We treat her accordingly. It usually works," he said, with that particular brand of male assurance that could bring fire to the eye of feminists.

Conceding Southern management's initial "psychotic response" to the black movement of the sixties, he said, "Well, we weren't going to be stupid enough to make the same mistakes twice. So a decade later, when the women demanded power, we just sat back and smiled. We put up and shut up. In the South today, only rampant female extremists and obvious incompetents get any static from business and industry."

Then this Old Boy grew almost mournful. His attempted grin came out a grimace. He made a compulsive confession. The "homogenization of the sexes" did not appeal to him personally, he said. "But hell, it's not just me. I guess there's hardly a man alive who's stopped believing that he's gonna wake up one of these mornings and things will be set straight again and it will all be gone away."

Some Southerners said "it" was here to stay. Some said "it"

was a social fad, of not much more lasting significance than skateboards and hula hoops. And some said "it" was a kind of excrescence on the body female—nothing that most women ever really wanted in the first place. Andrew Bancroft, a smooth-talking, young-looking, illustrious Old Boy in his early forties, was eclectic enough to borrow an inch or so from each point of view. His father had been governor of the state for many years before his death. Now Andrew Bancroft was president of its leading textile company. His *curriculum vitae*—which he called his "bio" and gave out like free passes to the circus—suggested that one day he might become governor himself. He had already run for political office more than once. He was consistently a near winner.

Bancroft's relationship with his attractive, efficient, and unmarried secretary resembled that of other such dynamo executives with their office wives. Whether or not it was sporadically sexual was rather beside the point. No more total fealty ever existed between vassals and their feudal lords. The corporate lord could still elicit from his female staff the unconditional loyalty and fidelity that was less and less forthcoming from his at-home wife. "Most women in business are concerned with ideas so obvious that they have become trite," the textile-company president said. "Ideas like pride and professional status and how-do-you-get-beyond-being-a-secretary?" He preferred the finer feelings of his own administrative assistant. "In Diane's case," he explained, "she doesn't *want* to go beyond. She doesn't *want* to be totally detached. But all that has got to be the condition of a woman of determination on her way up."

His office was hung with the abstract paintings of his at-home wife. They were importantly framed for such unimportant work. "I've seen it happen so many times," Andrew Bancroft said. "These executive secretaries who have their own real place in the company but want to get into administration . . . They know they do your job," he admitted gracefully. "So if you're paid a hundred thousand dollars, naturally they don't understand why they're worth only ten." Yet when at last they rose to the executive level, with a commensurate rise in income, they found no silver lining in those clouds, Bancroft asserted. In fact, it was worse than that. "My God, they're miserable up there! There's no more emotional attachment to the job, no more working hand-in-glove with a man they care about, whose future really concerns them. It's all intellectual and grim determination up there. It's a tough, hard life." No life for a lady, as it used to be said.

He had a few choice words for those single-minded (and often single) women who had made the "me-first" decision. "Those great workhorses," he called them, "with education, ability, and willingness to struggle who, starting from Day One, wanted to be in a career." He reiterated that theme which, among the Old Boys, had been worn thin by constant use. "In my view, there's no difference between them and any man. We treat them that way within this organization. And we yearn for more!" Bancroft said.

Then he struck a warning note. "But even for the Thelmas of this world, it's going to take at least another generation before anything *really* happens." Thelma, the current young female success story in the company, was local shorthand for woman-on-the-make. "By definition, she comes on too strong to suit some people. Thelma's trying harder than she has to and that puts a lot of people off. "But within another generation, maybe that won't be a problem for women. Maybe they'll learn to relax with executive responsibility." Gazing out of his ceiling-high window, through which all he could see was blue sky, Andrew Bancroft looked doubtful. "Even the Thelmas will find out," he predicted, "that there's no way anyone can be the president of a demanding, successful business and be happy at home too. That goes for males as well as females. It's impossible to have a good home life, spend time with children, and also remain sufficiently dedicated to your work. There are not enough hours in the day. There is not enough energy in the person. Women don't realize that yet. But if these 'other values' of home and children are actually more important to them than to men, then they ought to . . ." He sucked his teeth and started the sentence all over again. "Well, women ought to realize when they're around thirty that, at forty, after ten years on the climb, they may deeply regret all the sacrifices they made for a seat on the board of directors."

Worse yet, after a decade of striving, they might never realize the dream, he said. "Well, heck, it even happens to *us*. There are plenty of successful kids in college. But at forty, damn few bright guys are left in the race. They burn out. They get lazy. They lose the stamina, once the going gets rough. They discover they're not as smart as they thought . . . or that they're really not willing to put in what it takes. It's a question of priorities—for female and male. Life is a trade-off," he said.

Bancroft told of a distant friend, "the director of one of the largest mills in the country—it's a sad comment—everyone liked him so much—but he was . . . sort of let go." The fabric-company president made a glum face, contemplating this man's trade-off: success for, apparently, sex. "He had just remarried and he was happy for the first time. He wanted to go home at night to see his new wife. He was working 100 percent of the time and he was a very good man." Bancroft drew the moral of his tale: "*But to be president of that kind of company takes 150 percent of your time.* There can really be nothing else in your life. So the chairman had to get rid of his director because he was not quite as dedicated to the business as he once had been." Love, sexual or otherwise, was always disruptive to the company and almost never in its best interests, displacing as it did the first allegiance of employees.

When women moved up within the company, some male personnel, Bancroft admitted now, began to grumble about "sex discrimination in reverse." It was a topic on the minds of many middle-class men. A. H. Raskin, of *The New York Times*, reported male response to a recent lawsuit in which 2 million dollars was settled on female employees charging sex bias in hiring and promotions. "Look what those pushy women are getting away with now," one man said. "Here they walk away with this fistful of loot, when everybody knows all the big companies are on their bellies welcoming them into top jobs they aren't equipped to fill. It's us men who should be suing; we're the ones getting stepped on." Raskin called this "a dreary conviction"; nevertheless, it was widely held.

"When we automatically make a number of women officers of the corporation, it's bound to knock a few noses out of joint," Andrew Bancroft said. "But we've got to make up that way for the sins of the past. While our people may respect the intention, they don't really respect some of the women. They think they're just flukes of history. On the other hand, they do work side by side quite nicely with several female vice presidents who are really very good. When a woman's really good," he emphasized again, "there's not an iota of difference between her and any man."

In the South, almost none of the Old Boys spoke about the condition of women without, in the next breath, bringing up the condition of blacks. "The black question's about the same. The key word there is 'qualified.' I hate to put it that way," Bancroft apologized. "Blacks hate for you to use the term 'qualified black' because to them *that's* a form of discrimination." His tone grew firmer and stronger. "But we have sitting out there a vice president of this company who is black and who has earned his title the hard way. Now it's a shame that there is only one. Be that as it may, all of us are delighted, just delighted, that there *is* one! He has earned our respect, just as certain women in this company have earned our respect. What our people don't like to see is discrimination in reverse—the practice of rewarding somebody just *because* he's black or female." It was a thought as common to Old Boys as gold cuff links, long cigars, and the eighteen-hour workday.

Andrew Bancroft pulled out a plum to show what a good Old Boy he really was. "Just yesterday—and if I may say so, primarily because of me—this company elected to its board the first woman on the general board of directors in any company in the state." He mentioned the name of the recently anointed Old Girl and ran down the list of her solid-gold credentials: "Vice president of the university here. Full professor of economics in the School of Business Administration. On the board of the Stock Exchange . . . and also on the board of the largest chain of department stores in the South . . ." He seemed to have run out of breath, if not out of titles. "All in all, she is one of the foremost female businessmen in the country."

Jack Calhoun, director of corporate communications at the same company, was Thelma's immediate superior. He introduced himself provocatively. "Remember, I'm a Gemini," he said. "I can give you two answers to anything you ask." He was one of those men who could be for and against the same issue simultaneously, seeming not devious but open-minded—able to see both sides of knotty questions. We were talking after office hours at his club.

He began by expounding the rationale for the working woman which seemed to permeate the company's male personnel. "Most secretaries, in their heart of hearts, really don't want to be any more than secretaries," he asserted with as much assurance as Andrew Bancroft. "They may like the idea of moving up, but not the actuality. I discovered that through sad experience. I have never yet promoted a secretary where I didn't court trouble." Jack Calhoun recollected one young woman whose existence he had unbearably complicated by his good deed. "I made her office manager. It was a favor to her, so I thought. She just had to do all the purchasing, the vending, the book work, and so on. Well, it overwhelmed the poor thing. The responsibility was more than she could handle. She was miserably unhappy and so was everybody else in the office.

What was worse, she started to make as much money as her husband. Neither of them could handle that either. So her marriage got messed up, too. They were already in the throes of a legal separation when she found out she was pregnant. Well, I practically ruined her life with my good intentions. But as my secretary, she had been happy as a clam."

He then turned to Thelma Kane, who he himself had hired to create a new corporate-identity program. "Now there's a different breed of cat," he said. "I continue to cheer the Thelmas of this world." Within the company, her name had become a generic term, representing the new genus of ambitious, independent woman. "They believe in themselves. They fear nobody. Nothing's too tough for them. There are some men around here who need to be shook up," Calhoun declared. "And Thelma knows just what she's doing. She can stand the gaff. I support her against the opposition in this place every way I can."

In a kind of undeclared class warfare, he and Thelma and the black vice president had formed a coalition against the people in power. It was not that they intended to make a revolution, but they did enjoy rattling the throne. And although she was then an activist in the feminist army, Thelma accepted Calhoun's help gratefully—as her ally and her guide, he said. "You can't compare her to one of those ordinary knee-jerk feminists: hit the nerve, get the stock reaction," he pointed out with a certain paternal pride in the house radical. "I challenge her on every point she makes. I goad her into thinking logically, instead of coming up with number forty-seven on the party line. She respects me for it. She depends on me to keep her honest."

He expanded his encomium to take in all her kind. "The greatest women are the strongest, hardest women. Regardless of which of the fifty states she comes from, the Southern belle is a vanishing species," he said. "Oh, you still run into an occasional magnolia blossom around here, but they're very few and far between."

Jack Calhoun's wife, an airlines secretary, soon came to pick him up at his private club. A soft, glossy magnolia blossom of a Southern woman with a melting smile and a steady gaze, she did not speak until she was spoken to. Before she sat down, he dispatched her to make two telephone calls for him. "Don't get me wrong." He laughed, as he watched his pretty wife disappear into the dim reaches of the cocktail lounge. "I love feminists. But for most men," he added, "the Thelmas of this world are the first step to a castration complex—regardless of how smart and necessary they may be."

11 | Male-Order Feminists

Who, then, would marry Thelma? What kind of man had the guts and the nerve—or harbored the wish to be gelded? Benjamin Kane, like many of his peers, had embarked on this union of equals with his eyes wide open. No man married a feminist by accident. "When I first started to date her," Kane said, "Thelma was already very assertive, very independent. Even at twenty, the passive, conservative, push-the-husband type Thelma was not. She was right in there pushing herself. For me, that was the source of the attraction. I have always admired female strength." Some men still divided women into two strict categories: those they respected intellectually and those with whom they formed emotional attachments. But for the Benjamin Kanes of this world, intellect subsumed emotion.

He was "fed up to the teeth," he said, "with rigid role definitions." He was as impatient as Thelma herself with yesterday's view of female and male, and just as committed to radical change. Both saw themselves as members of a vanguard society which would sweep aside the cramped, categorical family system that, they believed, had soured their parents' marriages and circumscribed their lives. Both were proud of their courage, their bold vision, their apartness from the common herd. They felt enlisted in a new crusade. It lightened days that otherwise might have been ordinary, drab, and empty.

"My father wanted sons," Thelma said at once. "That's where I became a feminist—in the delivery room. He called the hospital, and when they told him I was born, he said, 'Oh no, you must be wrong. I'm having a boy!' and hung up." She was thirty-two years old, but resentment still smoldered.

Thelma was square and her hair was short. Benjamin was round and his hair was long. Her hips were narrow and her shoulders were broad; his hips were broad and his shoulders were narrow. Yet they looked like brother and sister with their full, pouty mouths, and blunt brown eyes under high, domed foreheads.

Thelma took Benjamin's name in marriage, she explained, "only because I relate to Anglo-Saxon, one-syllable labels." Her own father's name, Thelma explained, "was very ethnic, as long as a dirt road. I never related to it." Of a married friend, she exclaimed, "For Christmas, her husband's going to give Margie her name back. That's neat."

Benjamin filled in his own early history. "In my background, the women were all well above average, and like Thelma, just as strong," he said. "I never called my mother 'mother' because I never thought of her that way. I thought of her as a rock." He thought of his eighty-six-year-old grandmother the same way. "She sold housewares all her life, drove her own car until last year, and never looked back." He thought of his sister as "ballsy. She's divorced, with four kids, goes to college, and holds two jobs. In her spare time, she's a member of the school board in Brookline, Massachusetts. Thelma is like those women. She can take care of herself." Like so many of the men in his generation, if there was anything he didn't want, it was a wife who needed care. Marrying a feminist, you got a built-in guarantee of self-sufficiency.

"My husband does not approve of dependency," Thelma pointed out, although it could not have been more apparent. "Ben doesn't want anyone to lean on him. If I ever ask for advice, he says, 'You make that decision.' So I've had to be completely independent. Not that I would have liked it any other way."

Many of these hard-headed new unions of equals were separatist at the core and founded on unabashed materialism. They pooled their resources, like small businesses, for the greater profit of each. "We're both high achievers," Benjamin said. "We have a common game plan and the same view of the future. We agree on all the central issues, such as making early, wise investments and going where the best jobs are. My company offered me a promotion. I could have gone anywhere in America, but the most promising opportunities were here. San Antonio was our second choice. But these great golf and tennis facilities sold us."

"Of course, we're very competitive people," Thelma admitted, "in large things and small. Frankly, sometimes I don't understand how the marriage works. Last night, Ben started supper. He had the meat on too high. I turned it down. Ben got angry. We had words about it. Each of us wants to dominate, even at the stove. But we're open about it, anyway." She patted her husband's hand.

Benjamin smiled. He appreciated her openness as much as her independence. Encouraged by Thelma's candor, he explored "the competitive factor." "It isn't always easy," he confided. "You go out into the hard, cruel world and you rely on the family unit as your basic strength." He spoke of Thelma as his "family unit." But while applauding her self-sufficiency, he did not enjoy all of its fruits. "If too much competition enters into that family unit, if a man fails to find the sympathy and comfort and moral support he needs . . ."

"What about a woman?" Thelma snapped, her tone suddenly less mellow. She had her role conflicts too.

Benjamin swallowed the rest of his thought and started out on another tack, aimed at lauding his wife's capabilities. Safety first. "This is a transient town. It's a regional sales center for national companies. Not many people are willing to give of themselves to the community, because they come and go so fast. When we arrived, nobody was really getting it together for women. So Thelma assumed the leadership role right away. Her dedication is a constant delight." He patted his wife's hand. "She speaks on the ERA at local schools and clubs. She's waist-

deep into politics. The only thing . . ." His unblinking eyes
grew wider. "Thelma's giving more and more time, emotional
and spiritual, to public causes." It left their private lives somewhat bereft, he implied.

However, she still found the hours for their favorite recrea-
tion: buying stocks and corporate bonds. "We're financially
astute," Thelma said, brown eyes gleaming. "We don't have
piles of money, but we've learned how to make a little go a long
way. Our stocks are held separately—although we both went
into one stock deal together and it worked out fine. Each of us
contributed half."

Shrewd investments had enabled them to purchase a large,
slightly used Cadillac car before they were thirty. They also
kept two Siamese cats gifted with almost unnatural calm. One
lay quietly in Thelma's lap and Benjamin stroked the other as
they spoke warmly of "ZPG," a friendly abbreviation for zero
population growth. "The freedom of the post-nuclear family
not to parent" was dear to them. "But we don't want to glorify
the fact that we don't want children." Thelma made that plain.
"There's nothing wrong with children. It's just that they have
no place in our particular lives."

"Having children can't be an emotional, frivolous, conformist
thing," Benjamin warned, stroking his cat. He offered cautionary advice to couples in doubt. "Either do it seriously or don't
do it."

The erotic life that Thelma and Benjamin shared (if they
did) seemed of no great moment to them. It was talk of money,
rather than talk of sex, that made their dark eyes shine and
brought a lilt to their voices.

"Sexuality is not the key to marriage," Thelma said, as soon
as the subject came up. It was an idea she held in common with
others of her self-contained generation.

"Sexuality, frankly, still seems to hang up a lot of people,"
Benjamin chimed in. "They can't get beyond it. Let's say it's
been semi-imposed on them." He advanced a more rational, less

stressful alternative: "For men to be friends with women, for women to be friends with men—to interrelate in human ways, not necessarily sexually—that's what we all need now."

Thelma summed up. "Marriage has got to be more than going to bed. The true relationship lies elsewhere. Sexual fidelity . . . ?" She shrugged, gently belittling it. "Ben and I don't believe in authoritarian situations, in laying down rules. So what if you feel an infatuation for someone else? Finally it's over and the marriage remains—that wonderful security, that mutuality, that concrete edifice you built together over years."

"I don't know much about infidelity," Benjamin said. "But I was a bachelor for a long time. I know that relationships based on physicality don't last. Sure, there's a strong possibility that Thelma or I may become attracted to someone else. But if there's enough maturity, if the growth level of individuals can adjust, why should that destroy a successful marriage partnership?" In certain young marriages, sex-in-the-head had been replaced by success-in-the-head.

Thelma's thoughts broke through. "American women have got to get their asses in gear!" she cried. "It hasn't really happened, after all this time. We've been bred to believe we can achieve our own success by being nice, sweet ladies. Well, we can't. The blacks threw a lot of bricks and other things before anyone noticed *them*." Then she exclaimed, as if spitting out a bone: "The women's movement was bought off! I'll say that to any feminist in this country. It could have turned the tide for us, but it was bought off! A few women in New York and Washington went through the doors of business and government and got their fancy titles. A few others wrote their books and made a lot of money. But in the rank and file, in terms of real achievement, what's happened? Bloody nothing." She offered herself as a case in point. "In the company, I'm the butt of plenty of resentment. I'm called pushy and obnoxious and worse names I won't repeat. It's been hell for me, but what have I accomplished? Bloody little. By Eastern standards my salary is ridiculous. I'm not well liked, so I'll never get the promotion I deserve." Her mouth narrowed into a thin, hard line. "What's the matter with women in this country? Do they like their rotten lives? Why don't they get their asses in gear?"

Benjamin went on stroking his cat. It was whispered by some townspeople that he was a "closet chauvinist," motivated in his marriage by personal opportunism. "It's not the old-fashioned, two-can-live-cheaper-than-one thing. It's the Cadillac car and the joint savings account and all those smart investments," said one man who knew the Kanes quite well. But others insisted with just as much certainty that he and Thelma were made for each other, linked by ties stronger than love.

Of course, not every union of equals was dominated by stock certificates and money in the bank. Earl Atwood, the middle-executive manager of a paper mill in one of the Carolinas, described his marriage as "revolutionary." He wore a red knit shirt, a long, auburn mustache, and a solemn but not unattractive frown. He strove for sex blindness as other men, studiously ignoring skin pigment, strove for color blindness. Ignoring gender might allay sexual panic—up to a point. But it probably could not resolve the sexual dilemma. As Thelma had pointed out, the resolution of the race issue depended, first of all, on acknowledging that black was black.

Like Thelma and Benjamin, Earl and his wife seemed in more intellectual accord with each other than many couples not bound by their belief in feminism. Yet they could cause one to wonder whether matrimony might not be turning into an abstract state. "Seven years ago, we set it right out in our contract that nothing in the marriage would be determined by sex. Not child-rearing, if we were to have children (they had none as yet), not division of labor, or working patterns, or domestic responsibility. If Ruth were to become pregnant and desire to terminate the pregnancy, I would have no recourse. I view pregnancy as an arduous task—painful and potentially dangerous," he explained. "Our marriage contract stipulates that, in the event of conception, I can argue with Ruth about the abortion. But if she still doesn't see it my way, that's it."

If Earl Atwood saw pregnancy as a form of pathology, he saw child-rearing as a form of punishment for adults. "It's much too limiting for the things we would like to do. What about day care? What about babysitters?" He looked alarmed. They could have been problems as insurmountable as the Himalayas. "Ruth and I see other people, friends of ours, feeling too tied down and depressed. We're curious, though, about the whole concept of having children," Atwood added. Turning parenthood into another abstraction drained it of urgency. "Maybe in five years or so, we'll begin to think about it seriously," he said. By then, each of them would be almost forty.

As for Benjamin and Thelma, sexual fidelity was also "no big deal" for Earl and Ruth. Their marriage contract took little notice of it. "For the moment, we both seem to believe in monogamy," Earl Atwood said. "But I think I believe in exclusivity more than Ruth. According to her, it's the males, primarily, who support monogamous relationships, because we had more opportunity to play around before we got married. 'I never had a chance to do that,' Ruth says, 'and I want the chance. It may make us a better marriage.'"

Earl Atwood was a tall, thin, slow-moving man whose air of languor, while characteristically Southern, seemed at odds with his insurgency. His brow was furrowed into a dozen creases now. "Ruth believes that, if the sex urge strikes you, you've got to follow it to find out if it's a strong lead. She tells me, 'If you're pushing a grocery cart around the supermarket and you see something better than you've got at home, I want you to go after it.'" She herself, Ruth assured him, would do the same. The supermarket, overflowing with merchandise, was perhaps the country's favorite metaphor for itself: a place of endlessly prolific rating alternatives, unlimited choice, with the possibility of something better, at a lower price, at the end of every aisle.

Although he did not sympathize with Ruth's mental-health view of "playing around," neither did he dispute her right to it. That would have been domineering. "But most radicals are extreme sexual conservatives," he remarked in his own defense. "Look at Marx, Lenin—and Stalin, too, although I don't put him in their class. Revolutionaries don't dissipate their energies with a lot of meaningless encounters with women."

Issues that seemed less momentous to couples less radicalized, such as the naming of the wife, remained sources of intense debate within many feminist households. Ruth had made it plain before the wedding, Earl went on, "that of course she didn't want to change her name to mine. Well, why should she?" he asked in the magnanimous, accepting way common to such husbands. "I didn't mind. Traditional heritage means nothing to me," the manager-revolutionary declared. " 'I'm not even sure I want *my* name,' Ruth said. 'After all, it's really just the name of some other man—my father!' Well, I understand that too." Empathy for his wife's situation pulled another earnest frown. "Her mother's maiden name is no good either. It actually belongs to Ruth's grandfather. Names are a drag for women," he said, sighing.

Meanwhile, with no children of their own and no reason to stay put, Earl and Ruth were taking their two names, as inadequate as they might be, and moving on quite soon. It sometimes took a lot of effort to catch up with the life of ease. In seven years of marriage, they had already sampled three American cities, one North, one West, one South. In this rolling-stone society, there was a supermarket of dwelling places too.

Within the year, Earl said, they planned to settle in Chapel Hill or Washington, D.C., where he would study for his master's degree in political science. Ruth was a remedial-reading teacher. Such was the functional illiteracy of Americans, he said, that she could get work anywhere. The pay for her specialty was excellent. It would cover the two or three years that he would have to spend on campus. "Earning ratios are still weighted in the male's favor," Atwood declared, "so he's usually forced to be the major wage earner. But give a girl the greater earning power, and then a man can relax." Not that higher learning would relax him completely, of course. Going back to classes, he observed, meant "lots of hard work. Harder, intellectually, than what I'm doing now."

His forehead turned into a corrugated washboard. "I would like to become the first truly feminist male political candidate," he confessed. "In the late sixties, feminism became an intellectual principle for every thinking man. It's the most dynamic force to hit humanity yet. And it's ripened in the course of time. Feminism as a social program holds the greatest promise, maybe the final promise, for the whole world." Far from selling out, he thought, the international women's movement was just beginning to work up a good head of steam in other places than the U.S.A. "Everywhere, the new revolutionary class is made up of women. I'm a little bit jealous of that."

He was also, Earl Atwood said, "a little bit jealous of female intimacy. By and large, women have relationships with each other that transcend anything that happens between men." Once such jealousies might have stigmatized him as overidentified with the sex not his own. But now it could seem no more than enlightened for a man to "liberate the woman" within himself.

Considering his own attitudes toward feminism and his belief in the transcendent nature of female intimacy, Atwood was understandably perplexed by what he saw as the perverse conduct of some women with whom he worked. Their intramural "bitchiness" (his own word) upset him. "They have no concept of sisterhood," he lamented. "The most difficult part of my job is to ameliorate disputes among them. 'Can't you see how your sister feels about it? Can't you try to be more human?' I ask. But they're so envious of each other! And they quarrel over me. There's an ongoing fight for supremacy. It's disheartening." He stroked his mustache. "This incessant wrangling and courting of the boss . . . I guess these must be traits they've picked up from male management."

Recently, Atwood related, he had given each of the three clerk-secretaries on his personal staff a ceramic coffee mug lettered with Ms., the feminist honorific. Only one woman kept hers in the office, using the cup as a container for pencils. The second took hers home, pleased by the present but somewhat ambivalent about the inscription. The third, an older, unmarried woman, rejected the gift out of hand. "I'm *Miss* Brown, and I'm proud of it," she told Atwood. "Miss Brown idolizes me and holds that men are smarter than women," he said, with a worried look. "But none of the secretaries really identified with Ms. at first. It was I who insisted that we use it on all correspondence with women." Few of the other female workers at the plant, he added, felt "enough commitment to feminism to make it a primary interest in their lives. Kids, husband, family—all that stuff comes first." Why, he wondered aloud, did he feel more commitment than they?

However, Earl Atwood acknowledged, it had not been ever thus. "I have had my struggle," he said. Now it was over—and won. "There are lots of other men, though, still suffering through a very painful evolution. It shows up in their attitudes to their wives: 'Do anything you want, but be sure the house sparkles and my dinner's on the table on time.' In a more radical environment, even I might feel challenged and insecure." But in this small Southern city, surrounded by Masons, Elks, and members of the American Legion, it was easy to appear advanced. "Besides, I enjoy cooking and cleaning," Atwood finished. "And I just don't care to be dominant sexually. Most men are offended when their dominance is attacked. But I've progressed beyond that point. I'm cured!"

The "painful evolution" that other men went through when their dominance was attacked took more than one direction. Some pursued the horse of *dominus* knowing it had left the barn. "Polly will say, 'Well, I'm too tired, I don't want to do it.' I'll say, 'Well, I don't want to do it either.' So it just doesn't get done," Jordan Stern, a real-estate lawyer in New York, said. "It" could be anything from taking out the trash to laundering the bed linens. "If you're the kind of guy who wants to hold on to some male turf, you live in a chronic state of disorder. If I agreed to do more, more would get done," this husband confessed. Stern, whose wife was also a lawyer, held his ground at the expense of his well-being, a not unusual circumstance. "The constant mess is really too much. We both leave droppings everywhere. She says she's too busy to care, and I'm too obstinate. It's sort of undeclared war."

But salvaging male pride was not impossible, even among those who had given up the chase for *dominus*. They sometimes encouraged female independence as if they themselves had thought of it. By murmurings of revolution, acts of self-hypnosis, and impassioned assertions of support, they could feel convinced that the fight for social equality was their own idea.

Barry Cline was a member of Men for ERA, the National Organization of Women, and the League of Women Voters. Explaining his all-out identification with the female cause, he described himself as a sort of modern savior, only half in jest. "I'm just an egalitarian swell guy," he said. "For all their big talk, most women are humble and scared, just the way they have always been, right through history." Cline painted a picture of people so deprived, depressed, and beaten down by centuries of subjection that unless men fought their battles for them, they would continue to lose . . . and lose until the end of time.

Of course not all male-order feminists made themselves out angels of female justice. Many acknowledged their "shameless self-interest." A film producer said, speaking for many, "The sooner *you're* free, the sooner *I'll* be free." Free, as applied to women by men, was almost always a euphemism for "economically independent." The producer was still smarting from the alimony awards of his recent divorce. Yet at the same time that he supported "the women's revolution," he foresaw death for the ladies who fought in the front lines. "The troops that carry the revolution—the ones willing to go out and be sacrificed—they all get lost in the shuffle when the revolution succeeds. So the women who have manipulated this whole male-female upset . . ." He shook his head compassionately. "They're just killing themselves."

Another Man for ERA was frankly irate at one of those troops. "I'm getting sick and tired of my wife's complaints," he said. "I'm getting sick and tired of her grandiose ideas and her trivial life. She's all talk and no action. Flo's so anxious to live like a man? Well, then, she really deserves the chance." Honesty overcame him. "Maybe my reason for joining the movement was fundamentally selfish," he admitted. "I want to share this hell with women now."

For men like him, the best revenge was equality.

12 | Blue-Collar Men, White-Collar Blues

"More power to them, more power to the ladies," the blue-collar husband would say with the rest of his brothers, hoisting a glass at the neighborhood pub. Usually less affluent and often less educated than his middle-class counterpart, he was likely now to be just as sensitive and just as enlightened about matters of sexual justice. Nevertheless, his toast to woman power was freighted with a special wistfulness. Because by and large, for the working-class man, *dominus* dwelled at home. He was deprived of the perquisites of a professional career. He did not control other men's lives, make corporate decisions, or consummate six-figure business deals. When his command position within the family was challenged, so was his personal worth. More keenly even than for the upper-class male, more power for his wife had to mean less power for him.

Patrick MacGrath, a tall, lean construction worker in his early forties, said that, by nature, he was "no worrier." But when his wife decided to return to work after ten years at home rearing their four children, her imminent departure unnerved him. He began to wake up in the middle of the night, "thirsty for a belt of brandy." Like many white-collar men in the same situation, he blamed his consternation and his "mixed feelings" mainly on his children. "After school, they take care of each other," he explained regretfully. It was a current American pattern, permeating the society, that seemed to upset more men than women. "When they come home for lunch, their mother's not there. The twelve-year-old supervises the five-year-old and the seven-year-old with the assistance of the ten-year-old." Household help? MacGrath shook his head. "Out of the question. Too costly."

He spoke with a faint brogue and a clear recognition of social values that also cut across classes. "Well, my wife doesn't give me permission to go out to work. So why should she need my permission?" Women themselves, as well as the media, were potent educators. The cultural mythos of Archie Bunker, both reflecting and raising male consciousness, had hastened Archie Bunker's real-life demise.

MacGrath's liberal view of the liberated woman was widespread among blue-collar men, only partly because television was such an effective arbiter of conscience. The complexion of the hard-hat industries had also changed dramatically in the last decade. Many thoughtful younger men, rejecting middle-class mores and constricted, not just physically, by four-in-hand ties and fluorescent-lit office cells, chose the seemingly freer, more natural life of the laborer. "I'm a sucker," one said, "for outdoor light and a lunch pail." Many others, including some college graduates, turned to blue-collar jobs because they were available when other jobs were not. Sometimes, in an era grown somewhat soft and effete, unexpected values could accrue from remaining what more than one young woman called a "working-class hero."

"Long hair was once very challenging to the red-necks around here," MacGrath remembered. "But today, 50 percent of the fellows at the union meetings have let their hair grow and nobody thinks anything of it. Well, in lots of ways, their minds have grown too." His own prematurely silver thatch was short and bristly, Archie Bunker-style, but he was long on admiration for those others. "Their liberal orientation is amazing. Most all of us were chauvinists when we first married—even the college boys—and the women's movement was something of a thorn in the side. But that's changed too. We don't take 'pro' positions now. But we're not 'anti' either. Live and let live, that's the new spirit. There's a hell of a lot more tolerance for women's rights in most men than I once thought there was." Within the working class, as his conversation testified, there was a lot more male sophistication too.

Pat MacGrath emphasized his own toleration. "Labor has taken a strong position in favor of the ERA," he said, identifying himself with that set of mind. "In the suburbs where we live, women like my wife are moving right up there into important civic affairs. We've already got one woman trustee and a woman village clerk. My God, those girls are so good when they get going that one of the men said, 'For the next few sessions, *I'll* make the coffee!' "

The Irishman's tone of respect was resolute. "With this new independence trend, with a new job and a paycheck in her pocket, of course the wife expects to take on some new prerogatives too. It's been brewing for a long time among the girls in their group. There's a lot of soul-letting goes on there. And through that soul-letting, they've found out they're not in the boat by themselves. They all want to make their mark." This group was an informal network of about a dozen wives in the community. "A lot of water's gone under the bridge since their first weekly meetings. And as husbands and fathers, we're caught in the riptide, you might say."

It occurred to him, MacGrath went on, that "the men themselves might feel some relief in bringing their own situations out and to the surface. Even if we did not let ourselves down in the personal way that the women do, I figured that it would be an outlet we never had before." He feared, however, that his invitation to meet and talk, as their wives did, would elicit indifference, or resistance, if not outright contempt from the husbands. But to Pat MacGrath's surprise "every one of the thirteen men I asked said yes."

Their initial gathering, in his own living room, lasted from eight o'clock in the evening to one-thirty the next morning. "No one wanted to break it up. And the men were much less guarded than I thought they would be. The competitive situation was uppermost in their minds." Yet that preoccupation had spilled over from a man's work life to his home life, MacGrath said. Now that his wife was employed outside, or intending to be soon, would he be competing with her too?

" 'You spend sixteen hours a day in your job-oriented situation, counting overtime and coming and going,' one man pointed out. 'You're a cog in the wheel of industry. Well, you take it for granted. But when you leave the job, what you want most of all is to drop that competitive situation. You don't want to compete with your own wife or find yourself just a cog in the wheel at home too!'

"I brought out the topic of new prerogatives," MacGrath remarked. "Now that the women are cutting loose, do they have the option of utilizing sex as a political maneuver? When they're paying their own way, so to speak, is it their prerogative to say no? Let's agree that healthy sex relations take place about eight times a month. All of a sudden, there's a blanket rejection on the part of the wife, six out of those eight times. 'I'm too hot, I'm too cold, the baby will wake up.' What is the significance of that rejection? What does it really mean?"

He had his own opinion. Her refusal signified, he felt, that "the wife's come to believe she's being used eight times a month. She's just valuing things materialistically now—even sex. She adds up what she's getting against what she's putting out. The system does that to people," he said, careful not to blame his wife personally. "It turns them into calculating machines."

Nevertheless, most of the men were not worried about being "frozen out of bed," MacGrath reported. "But because I introduced the topic, everyone assumed that I was being cut off. 'What you can't get home, you get elsewhere. The market is free,' the men advised me. They said that sex was always a woman's commodity, from the very beginning, and that she had always traded it or not, depending on the return. Well, we found out that we had lots more to talk about together than we thought."

At the end of the first meeting, MacGrath suggested that the group convene again the following month. But the husbands were disappointed. Why not sooner? Why not the following week? "Nothing earthshaking has come out of our Tuesday-night talks so far. But the men are putting aside many important things to get together," he reported.

Patrick MacGrath returned to the conditions of his own marriage. "My wife became an activist during the Vietnam war and the civil-rights movement. To my discredit, I've always been more easygoing. She likes to have a certain say in things, more than me. Recently she blasted the local high-school administration for its all-male membership. You know that Virginia Woolf book, *A Room of Her Own*? [sic] Well, right out in public, at a PTA meeting, my wife stood up and said that it didn't have to be the woman's washroom, it could be the superintendent's board room! She told the high-school administration to get up off their asses and open up the *superintendent's* position to women! She said it, just like that, in the high-school auditorium, with practically the whole town gathered."

He took out a well-pressed handkerchief and, without unfolding it, mopped his face. "That's a whole lot of fireworks for a little community like ours. The local TV called up," MacGrath said. "They wanted my wife to talk some more on the evening news about the school-board issue. It's her kind of thing. She loved every minute. I made the crew some drinks and just stayed out of the way. Anyway, I was in the midst of putting a new roof on the house. But before they left, the men coaxed me to come down. Well, I didn't want to look like I was scared or something, so I came down. They asked me right on television, was it really tough having such an active, volcanic, outspoken wife?"

Pat MacGrath seemed to think the whole thing through again. "My answer was no. My wife's competent and capable and involved in the community, but she gets all the women's things done too, I said. She cooks the dinners, she makes the beds, she irons the clothes, she keeps up the back-yard vegetable garden . . ." He covered his mouth with his hand, ashamed. "Then, when I heard myself talking, I felt like a shitheel. Suddenly I saw what was really on my mind." MacGrath's light eyes were full of probity and self-deprecation. "How small can a man get?"

Which work was properly woman's and which man's? It was not the only issue, borrowed from the middle class, now raised by newly emergent blue-collar wives. They were also asserting their right to sexual freedom. Sometimes even women without independent incomes took that as their special franchise on liberation. Just as among white-collar couples, the price of such freedom was frequently divorce. But because the blue-collar divorcé often still cherished his offspring as his most precious form of wealth, his equity in the future, the family remained the main focus of his concern.

Nick Farmer, a wiry, buck-toothed garage mechanic with red-gold hair and a bouncy Adam's apple, had just been released from the hospital after spinal surgery. He had four young children, almost the same ages as MacGrath's—seven, nine, eleven, and thirteen. "I postponed my operation until the divorce was final, although I was in a lot of pain," he explained. "And I learned a lot while I was laid up. It gave me time to get my thoughts together. The last day in bed, I made a promise: I'm not going to kill myself any longer. My kids need a father more than ever now. They got a raw deal from their mother." He planned to open "a little tune-up shop," he said, devoted to a single, relaxed specialty: tuning up automobiles.

When he smiled, which he did rarely, Farmer was all front teeth and affability. "During all our married life, I was glad that I didn't need for Carol to work. An auto mechanic makes upward of three hundred bucks a week; trying hard, even more." But while he was working at the garage, trying very hard, his wife took it as her prerogative to spend several afternoons a week in other male company. "I blew seven thousand dollars in private-detective fees and eventually nailed her to the tree. All told, in a period of twelve months, that divorce cost me over nine thousand bucks. It was just about every cent I had in the world. But when it comes to the lives of your children, nothing's too much."

Farmer had grown up in the rural township near Schroon Lake in upper New York State where he still lived, but his marital woes were remarkably like those of the men in midtown Manhattan. He recounted the methods that the detective had used to "get the goods" on Carol Farmer. "This private eye took incriminating pictures and even made recordings of some bedroom conversations. He got a lot of the stuff in unethical ways. He parked a van disguised as a delivery truck outside the place of assignation. Then he sneaked his equipment into the building and made recordings in the van. You pay plenty for technology like that." His tone was harshly triumphant. "Today I look on that woman as I would a total stranger. She just had an illegitimate child with the guy and they aren't married yet."

Nick Farmer's moral indignation seemed to console him. "I got custody. The kids were bitter for a long time. Their mom made them believe I was going to put them in a foster home. But little by little, they're getting back their faith in me. Their mother has visitation rights just once a month. She can see her children from eight in the morning until six in the evening—and that's it!"

That seemed to him an excruciating punishment—and he was not sorry for his former wife. "She thought she was Vanessa Redgrave and Goldie Hawn rolled into one. But she wasn't either of them and this isn't Hollywood. This isn't even Schroon Lake!" He laughed, showing all his teeth.

Then, as he told of his brother—a truck driver in Florida, with a child of twenty months—Farmer's face fell back into sobriety. "My brother calls his wife one night from somewhere in the Keys and she says to him, out of the clear blue, 'Come get this kid of yours. I don't want to be tied down any more.' The next morning, she blows town and leaves him in a permanent bind. If he files for divorce, he'll have to fight her for custody of his son. And my brother's not a fighter like me. Besides, he hasn't got nine thousand bucks to deliver to detectives and divorce attorneys. I have nothing left to lend him. So what can the poor guy do? Some days he hires a babysitter, other days he takes his boy with him to ride on his truck. And the kid gets motion sickness! My brother goes in strictly for short hauls now."

Owing largely to the new self-perceptions of the working-class woman, some working-class men had become year-round "mothers," often with initial reluctance but eventual success.

For obvious reasons, however, these were among the least likely men in America to take a positive view of female emancipation—or even to pretend that they did. They felt unfairly tried by circumstance, innocent victims of an impractical ideology, anguished by the dropout mothers who had got away. For them, unlike for richer men, just hiring part-time household help or a regular babysitter was often an intolerable financial strain. They had been left holding the bag, not only emotionally, but economically too. Yet few felt lonely enough, stressed enough, or desperate enough to actively seek new marriages. Indeed, they shared a tendency to consider all women, militant or not, suspicious characters. Admitting that their sex lives were "inconclusive" or "irregular" or—dryly—"pending," they seemed somehow able to relegate that part of their lives to a back corner of their psyches. Instead, they pursued their commitment to their children with passion. This fathers' crusade was what kept them going. For many, it signified their last claim to *dominus*.

In Washington, D.C., a refrigerator repairman who looked older than his thirty-seven years said, "My wife ran away with my best friend. She left me with the twins, on my daughters' third birthday. Well, in a way, it was a good present. For a long time, although she lived with us, she was just not *there*. How can kids feel?" He answered the question with an agonized glance. "To make ends meet and pay the babysitter, I work for three companies at once. My budget emphatically does not include the luxury of another wedding. Anyway, marrying a woman to be a mother to your kids is like buying a bulldozer to get the snow off the lawn. Maybe it works—while there's snow on the lawn. But when summer comes, there's that piece of useless equipment sitting out there in the yard." No other reason for marrying again occurred to him.

A gray-haired assembler in a California leather-goods factory reflected, "You marry one of these liberated women and she doesn't *want* to be a mother to your kids." He related the experience of his fellow worker, a fifty-year-old widower. "Marvin's new wife got insulted when he asked her if she would sew the name tapes on his boys' school clothes. 'Did you marry me to fill your housekeeping needs?' she said. The poor guy was embarrassed enough to sew on the name tapes himself. Marvin also throws a load into the washing machine every morning before he leaves the house. His wife says to him, 'I wouldn't think of asking you to wash my clothes. Why should I wash your clothes and your kids'?' So he's the maid—and the mother too."

A television crewman in Hartford, Connecticut, turned down the possibility of second marriage with a wave of his hand and a thin laugh. "I've had enough misery in my life," he explained. "Anyhow kids brought up by their fathers get along better most of the time. Men are less emotional than women, but they care a lot. Where the mother's around, you spend more time calming her down than relating to your children. Sometimes I miss having regular sex. Other times, I think sex is the most overrated thing in the world. Anyhow, let's face it, how can a man be a make-out artist with three little kids in the house?"

A New York policeman, not yet forty, said, "I got married too young. My four kids were born before I was thirty. Maybe that's why I don't miss women a whole lot now. Plenty of girls will go to bed with you on a one-time basis, but that's not my way. I'm too old-fashioned . . . and they're too immature for real relationships. They don't enjoy the female responsibilities. Children irritate them, mine included. I'm a mature man. So the girls today don't leave me with too much sexual incentive. All that rolling in and out of bed just for the hell of it . . ." He pursed his mouth into a grimace of distaste.

In Providence, Rhode Island, a telephone-company lineman said, "In this situation, without a wife and all, everyone figures you're sleeping with someone, living it up. But you know you're not sleeping with anyone. And you're almost too busy to notice. You're strapped for money, you're running home to your kids every night. In two years I have hired and fired a half dozen babysitters. They were unreliable, or they made more of a mess than the kids did, or they just couldn't get along with young girls. Since their mother's gone, they're very high-strung. Now a woman of forty-three comes in every afternoon, and thank God, they really like her. She works for the telephone company too— on the night shift. I hotfoot it home after work without even a beer so she can get out to her job. It's been rough on the children. But we're closer to each other now than we ever would have been if my wife hadn't left us. I don't say it's an easy life. Yet I feel more like a man than I did when she was cheating on me and we both knew it."

All these blue-collar husbands who could have become casualties of women's new battle for freedom were discovering great compensations in fatherhood. That they could function effectively as single parents was their pride and their salvation. After divorcing wives who had filled them with self-doubt, they often felt more in control of themselves and their lives than before.

But more often, the new self-consciousness of working-class women could instill self-doubt in men, turning the struggle for *dominus* into an uphill battle. Manuel Rust, a fighter in that battle, was proud of his life as a man. Parenthood—and stepparenthood—was his first priority. The Rusts lived in a small Wisconsin town, where he worked eight hours a day in the local post office. On weekends, he dispensed gasoline at the local garage. "I put myself through school, almost right up to the diploma," he said. "Lumberjacking, farm work, anything I could get my hands on, that's what I did." But he was worried now that his fourteen-year-old stepson, Luke, who cut classes two days out of three, might not share his old-fashioned sense of industry.

"The boy is very smart, but he's a famous hooky player in these parts," his father said. Nevertheless, he would not exonerate himself from blame. "Well, I must figure into that somehow. Somewhere along the line I must have missed out on giving him the right idea of what it is to be a dependable, responsible *man*." Although he saw in Luke's truancy the shadow of his uneasy relationship with his wife, he was more critical of himself than her. *Dominus* lay, in part, in giving justice where justice was due. "She figures into it too, but only because she wants the best for all the kids. Luke is her child. So is our oldest daughter. We both been married before." Manuel Rust was a man of feeling, yet in several hours' conversation, he never once referred to either of his wives by her given name. Like many of his working-class peers, his awareness of woman's "role" predicament and her right to personal freedom had increased at a faster rate than his ability to assimilate them into his own life.

"While I was in the army, the first wife was running around with a flyboy. She got herself a job when I was in the service and thought that gave her the right to take off. Before we was married, I belonged to the Church of Christ, but they put me down for my divorce. According to the church, it was a mortal sin to marry again unless I could prove adultery." His eyes, a watery, transparent blue, looked pale as ice in the winter sunshine.

"So I guess I started out the second marriage a little bit

sore at women. I guess I had the wrong idea: 'What can I get out of it?' There was a little bit of revenge in my soul."

Manuel Rust admired the truth as much as some other men admired lies. He would have been handsome, with neat, even features, except that his teeth were jagged and discolored yellow, like a beat-up old player piano. And he never stopped smiling, even when he said, "Now it seems that the wife cares more for the kids than for me.

"If I say anything about them, especially the hooky player, she'll jump right down my throat. A man's not a man any more with her." He did not whine, just put it out the way it was. "I'm only good to pay the bills and come down on all the time. She used to try to be nicer to me, even when she didn't feel like it. She don't try much any more. Flew into her head some time back that women don't *owe* men. That's not true. We owe each other."

Studying the sere brown flatlands outside the window, he peeled the silvery paper from a stick of chewing gum and folded it between his fingers. Like many other husbands, he coud not leave the subject of his wife alone. "Let's divide our relationship into two equal parts," Rust suggested. "The first part we'll call home life: everyday activities, scouting with the kids, things like that. But what's the rest of our life? Nighttime, when we're in bed, our physical love . . ." The words were spoken with yearning. "Shall we say that, for some reason, the wife is not liberated in that respect? Or rather, she's liberated in the wrong direction. Sex ought to be a two-way street. I do for you, you do for me. Well, sometimes it's fine if I caress her, stroke her hair. But any sort of reciprocal thing?" Rust shrugged. "There isn't any."

Still he grinned. "Naturally, the wife knows that unless I get sex once in a while, I get uptight and owly. So I suggested, 'Let's draw a compromise. You give it to me once or twice a week, and I'll be as easy as you want on Luke.' 'Well,' she says, 'if that's the only way I can get you to act civil to him.' And I thought she was coming around. But no soap. She turned down the compromise flat." Sex might have meant even more to him than to some men of the middle class because, in its absence, there were far fewer compensations.

His smile dimmed again but did not go out. "She won't touch me," he said bluntly. "She was never very . . . touchy in the past, but she would always care for my needs. Sometimes she would even kiss me, providing I specifically suggested it. The wife didn't used to turn me down outright—except when I was drinking beer and came home pretty late. Well, maybe two-fifteen is a kind of weird time to wake somebody up to do *that*. But now I don't get sexual intercourse more than once a month." He sounded more regretful than resentful.

"Four weeks ago was the last time we slept together until this morning," Manuel Rust revealed. "It's not that I go around keeping a record. At least I never used to. But maybe I have started now and I just don't realize it." He dropped the gum into an ashtray, unchewed. "Well, this morning it was exactly the same as usual. She was stretched out, laying there, although I could definitely tell that she would just as soon not be. The wife was smoking a cigarette and I touched her left elbow this way." He demonstrated delicately with two fingers. " 'Do you always have to be so grabby?' she asked. "Oh, I understand that the woman has her rights," Rust added. It was a lesson well learned throughout the working class. "But the man should have his rights too."

He answered an unspoken question. "I don't go with other women . . . although I never been above looking at a pair of pretty legs going down the street. My father was a minister in Meredith township. He gave me a puritan feeling about the sacredness of marriage. I think it's morally wrong to get sex outside. So there have been only two women in my life."

For the first time, his smile disappeared. He seemed suddenly older. "See, I don't want to *use* nobody," Manuel Rust explained. "But using each other is part of married life." He rubbed his face with calloused hands. "One wife runs away from me and one wife turns away. Is that what being liberated's supposed to mean?"

For working-class men, stuck fast in their situations, negative assertions of female autonomy were often the hardest to bear. Women who opted out, sexually or otherwise, left a space at the center of these male lives that little else could fill.

13 | Superman and Wonder Woman

"Feminism is misused to justify the end of protectiveness between the sexes," wrote Dr. Herbert Hendin, a professor of psychiatry at Columbia University. "Feminists feel men protected women to infantilize them, or men wanted women who would mother and protect them. Women are increasingly not asking for protectiveness from men and not giving it, facts which make many men feel justified in abusing them even more. In a culture that is making caring synonymous with losing, we are forgetting how much mutual protectiveness is a part of love."

It was one more symptom of the times which was no respecter of class. Feminists (and their husbands) might have originated the equation—of protectiveness with childish dependency. But by "attitudinal seepage," as another social scientist put it, that idea was percolating through the whole society, from the top to the bottom. To want or need loving care was interpreted as weakness, and the weak were, per se, losers.

Yet absolute independence was as farfetched a fantasy as absolute power. In real life, regardless of social class, mutual dependency was the measure of love.

Wonder Woman and Superman—those eagles able to soar alone—were comic-strip figures that only fed our delusions of grandeur. As role models, they were delinquent. As man and wife, they were bizarre. Nevertheless, the idealists of female emancipation persisted in imaging a human paradise of autonomous, perfectly matched pairs. When self-realization rendered all of us truly adult and independent, so they reasoned, then the true marriage of equals could take place. But it was a fool's paradise . . . or an adolescent's. Only children saw maturity that way—as a flight from the clutches of dependency. Mature men and women acknowledged the child in themselves and, when the child clamored for attention, they listened.

"I would like her to baby me. I need a lot of care," said a man with a hawk's nose and a minor potentate's fortune, of the woman he loved but decided that he could not marry. Jacob Sandman was a New York physician in his fifties, a cardiac surgeon, divorced for years from a woman he considered "infantile." She had not been "motherly" enough to minister to his needs, he complained without embarrassment. Nor was his mistress a particularly maternal or nurturing woman. Although not infantile, she was "hopelessly self-involved, full of herself," the doctor said. To some observers, *his* self-interest would have been more insufferable than *her* self-involvement. Yet, in a way, it was a draw. For when Superman and Wonder Woman tried to get together, eventually the clash of interests had to grow deadly. Each one, absorbed in his own trip to the heights, was unable to give to the other.

"Actually, Katie's a talented, terrific person. But she's been taking care of herself too long ever to learn how to take care of me." Katherine Foster was an actress in her middle thirties, divorced for more than ten years. "She's sexy, amusing, and good-humored. That's a bonus these days. But I could never marry her." Sandman sounded wistful . . . and resigned. "She would make a terrible wife. The theater means everything to her. She wants to be a star. When she hasn't got a play or a television show, she's taking acting lessons, voice lessons, dance lessons, yoga." He sighed with a kind of vicarious fatigue before all that enterprise and ambition. "If it's important for Katie to stand on her head, she should stand on her head. But what's in it for me?" Sandman owned a house in Palm Springs, and one in Southampton, as well as a duplex apartment on Park Avenue. Wealth and distinction had made him haughty. He might have been no paragon of Supermanhood, but he was a proud house-holder who could still lay down the law.

"I like to entertain and I do it often. Would Katie plan my menus, shop for my parties, supervise my cook?" He smiled at the absurdity of it. "Usually she's too busy to eat. She slurps down some yogurt instead. She likes actors better than doctors. Doctors' wives bore her. I need a wife who has time for my friends and enjoys them. My houses need attention too." He spoke of them as sort of bright but naughty children. "The plumbing's full of temperament in Palm Springs. The roof leaks in Southampton. The wallpaper's a mess in New York . . ." Rounding up the plumber and picking out fabric samples, he observed, would hold no charm for the woman whose goal was to become her generation's Lynn Fontanne.

"I think Katie loves me. She says she wants to marry me." But their worlds were too distant, their needs would conflict. "Love," said the physician with the wisdom of his years, "is not enough. It ought to be, but it isn't." What he did not say was that, in his firmament, he had to be the brightest star. And he did not know then that, within a year, he would marry his new office nurse, for whom nurturing was a profession.

Superman and Wonder Woman always lived on planets of their own. It was the flair for enlightened egocentrism that gave them their extraordinary potency. Married to each other, as the physician recognized, they could only court disaster. Few house-holds were large enough to accommodate two such sizable, separate identities, with such hungers, such needs, so much ac-cumulated ambition and the talent to express it.

The exception, as one woman said, was that rare household in which the "killer couple" resided. She described a prime example. "Jerry has got to be crazy about Barbara to put up with her single-minded power needs," she declared. "Either he's so masochistic that it appeals to him to suffer; or he admires the same qualities in her that he admires in himself. That's why a lot of killer men marry killer women. They identify. They encourage each other's worst designs. Jerry's a fighter and Barbara's a fighter, so they goad each other on. We've got to watch out for these killer couples," she warned, half seriously, "lest they take over the world."

But more often than not, it was the supershlemiel that lurked within the superhero, in critic Leslie Fiedler's description, who eventually doomed these superpower marriages. For the other side of male pride was male paranoia. And the female social revolution had revived the old suspicion that most women, underneath the frilly bonnets they no longer wore, were really sexual mayhem artists, out to cut men down. Wonder Woman had the means at hand. Nothing was beyond her, with her sharp golden dagger and her long gleaming hair. That supershlemiel who cowered inside almost every Superman was deathly afraid of her potency. At three o'clock in the morning, the eternal question loomed (which history has so far failed to resolve): who's got the balls? And of course it was one of Wonder Woman's primary wonders that she was not without them. In the idealists' seventh heaven, two pairs would a perfect marriage make. But on earth, often even in those "killer" combinations, they just spelled double trouble.

Peter Reinhold, a communications superhero, sat near the pinnacle of one of the world's great television empires. His superwife, Jessica, an anthropologist, was a renowned authority on the animals of Africa and Asia. She spent some months every year trekking through the jungles and the plains with backpack, guide, and camera. Together with a faithful but harried housekeeper, Reinhold was left in charge of their six children. (Sometimes the ambition of these powerhouse people ran away with them. They could also see themselves as supermom and superdad, populating the planet with a race of superchildren.)

Peter Reinhold's stiff upper lip, his studied complaisance, and his husbandly discretion, were models for the genre. He admired Jessica's photographs but he had never met her jungle guide. And although he spoke with proper deference of her devotion to the leopard and giraffe, male anger glimmered through the cracks in his conversation. It was the counterpart of the female anger of the sixties. The rage of the oppressed, the frustrated, the conned and traduced was no longer the monopoly of women.

But he was desperate in his determination not to seem desperate. It would have been inelegant and *démodé* to object to the babysitter function that had been thrust upon him. It would have exposed the supershlemiel who lay, quivering, just beneath the skin. Uncouth! Instead, he too resorted to benign acceptance and modest self-congratulation. "No person like Jessica stays married for long without her husband's support. She depends on my good will," he explained, taking modest credit for her courage and her trips into the bush.

But the ego, like the elephant, needed to be fed. And seated near the window in the executive dining room—a symphony of browns and golds and beiges in his $600 custom-tailored suit— he did not really want to discuss his superwife's accomplishments; even less, his feelings toward her. He wanted to talk about his extramarital affairs. That was the joy of a liberated marriage, he was quick to suggest. There was always room for one more . . . affair. To Reinhold, it must have seemed that he was opening up fresh vistas of consciousness. "She lives her life, I live mine . . . Independence . . . Freedom . . . Mutual respect . . . Why be imprisoned by a dying reality?" But his words echoed a refrain that had already grown old.

"The kids have no problem with their mother," he explained. "They know where she is . . . [in Tibet], and why she's there . . . [to photograph the mating habits of the yak]. And they understand that it's her privilege, even the youngest." (He was then four years old.) They would never puzzle over the justice of equal rights for women (even if Reinhold himself, with his faulty conditioning, might).

But once this superdad had got them all tucked in, had told

them bedtime stories, had turned the night lights on, he could not ignore the pall of grownup loneliness that settled on his big suburban house. "You're fifty-one, loving life, and the woman you live with is a whole world away for months at a time . . ." His shoulders drooped under the expensive brown plaid cloth. "For a while, conversation becomes a substitute for sex. You make a lot of lunch dates, you have too many drinks. And it can be like making love, even if you don't make love." But eventually one thing could lead to another. He did not sort out the tangle of loneliness, lust, and retribution. "And liberation," Peter Reinhold reiterated, "means that both of us are *free*." It was a strange word on which to grit the teeth.

When Superman translated his ambivalence about Wonder Woman into awe rather than into extramarital affairs, sometimes self-mockery touched him with a special, melancholy charm. "I am Jane Sanger's husband, Henry Sanger's son, and Hugh Sanger's father," Louis Sanger said by way of introduction. He was also the president of a blue-chip family business in which his older brother was chairman of the board. But his gentle smile called to mind the woman (apocryphal or real) who, on her deathbed, was reported to have murmured, "Never for one moment to have been myself!"

Jane Sanger, a politician whose star was rising in their region of the Middle West, "was the first woman to campaign for and win public office in the entire state," her husband said. When he spoke of his wife, the superheroine, Louis Sanger gave glowing-with-pride the old school try. "Nearly a million and a half of the electorate voted for Jane. Her department has a $300 million annual budget and $1.3 billion at its disposal for projects in sanitation, flood control, and sewage. Over the years, that kind of money can stick to a lot of fingers, but not Jane's." She was not only smart, she was honorable, he asserted with fervor. "She feels extremely responsible to her huge constituency. She takes it as a mandate, as a holy charge."

He took her as something of a holy charge. Like many other husbands whose wives wore the seven-league boots in the family, Louis Sanger bolstered his self-esteem (or tried to) by kissing them in public. He was enough of a man, he wished to make clear, to show some regard for her achievement. "But of course I don't want Jane to run for senator or anything like that," he said. "I don't want her to go to Washington. It would make our lives even more complicated than they are now."

Sanger himself was not immune, so not unsympathetic, to the thirst for power. In his youth, he remembered he had had political aspirations of his own. "But that all seems so long ago." There was no irony in his smile. "We always knew that it had to be one of us. We just weren't sure which one it would be."

He accepted his fate with the grace of a superhero, side-tracked but still standing tall. "My mistake?" Pinpointing it, Louis Sanger quoted some unnamed personal god: " 'Make no small plans. They have not the power to stir the blood of men.' " He rubbed the gold band of his wristwatch reflectively, as if it were a talisman that failed. "Well, I guess I made small plans. Jane never did. 'As soon as the youngest starts kindergarten, I'm going to law school,' she said. And damn it, when the mayor called on her, she was already making out the applications."

Like Peter Reinhold, and other such superhusbands bent on salvaging *dominus*, he regarded his wife as his protégée. And in a way, she probably was. As women once did for their husbands, he had lovingly sacrificed his own ambitions for his wife's. "I not only encouraged her to run for office, I helped her to do it. She couldn't have done it without me. Now she needs my guidance on a day-to-day basis and she's frank to say so. She always comes to me for political advice. Jane has a great sense of public relations. She knows how to sell herself and she gets a good press. But I don't feel threatened by the publicity that keeps pouring in. I go on thinking up new ideas and she accepts them . . . gratefully." Sometimes it seemed that, behind every achieving woman in America, there stood a master puppeteer, usually married to her, intently pulling strings.

Other women in public life leaned on him too, Sanger confided. And he did not disappoint them. He mentioned one who was just then running for office. "I'm doing a lot of political things for René," he said. "Her husband always shows up, just tagging behind." "If you can't lick 'em, join 'em" was Louis Sanger's attitude toward the new supersex. Asking no fanfare, receiving none, he achieved his quiet victory by leading the conquering heroines on to theirs.

Sanger traced the genesis of Jane's career as a public servant. "We were both amateurs in politics for many years. Some months before the last election, a ballet for position on the ballot was developing. Jane said to the mayor and his slating committee, 'All your people are old, white, fat, and male. You've got to open up the party. There are women qualified to open up the party in this state.'" By implication, she gave him the names of some young, thin, black females. "But the next morning after breakfast, her call came. It was the mayor for Jane," her husband said. "'I almost dropped the telephone into the dishwasher,' Jane says when she tells about it now. 'We want you,' the mayor told her. 'Let us know in half an hour.' 'I have to call my husband,' she replied. Well, of course, I said go." If he had not said go, Sanger implied, Jane would have stayed. Sometimes a man could wield power over a woman simply by refusing to do so.

Louis Sanger thought of himself as a "late bloomer." He had not quite given up his own dream of glory, although its precise details had grown blurry. But Jane was a perennial—blooming, as he said, from the first day they met. "When I bumped into her on the ski slopes, she was going to college. But even at that early age, she was busy organizing foreign students' trips for the Institute of International Education."

He told a story that foreshadowed the course of their long marriage. "It was the day we got back from our honeymoon.

We had spent three weeks in Paris. I was looking forward to the first night in our own little nest. Well, Jane hadn't told me, but she was committed to meeting some foreign students after dinner. Ninety-two Japanese were arriving and she had taken on complete responsibility for housing, feeding, and programming them. I didn't see her for the next three days." At the very onset of her life with Superman, Wonder Woman often gave fair warning that sometimes he would have to play second fiddle to such larger concerns as ninety-two Japanese.

Decades later, that had not changed. Soon, Sanger said, he hoped to take a business-and-pleasure trip to Europe. "But my wife's got her own travel schedule and I wouldn't dream of going without her. If Jane can't make it, I'll just cancel out. I'll let my brother go." He seemed as determined as women once were to hold on to their marriage and keep it alive.

"I want Jane to be happy," he said with an ardor and simplicity many a wife would have envied. "All our lives depend on her being happy. So how can I do less than help?" He sounded so full of fine resolve. But in the last analysis, this upright, attractive, intelligent man was—not uniquely—an enigma to himself. "I have either an overdose of male security or an overdose of male insecurity." He smiled. "I am either completely self-confident or so frightened of Jane that I don't dare object to her. Frankly, I haven't yet worked out which."

Louis Sanger filled his short-stemmed pipe, meditating on those alternatives. "But what's the next act?" he asked. "What happens, I wonder, when I hit sixty? I'm a late bloomer," he repeated. "If I'm a late bloomer, maybe my time is still to come." Anxiety mingled with anticipation. "*Quo vadis?* Where am I going?" He tapped down the tobacco leaves. "I hadn't thought about that." But his wife knew where she was going . . . and she was more than halfway there.

The troubled husband lit his pipe with a gadget that looked like a midget torch. He watched the flame die down. "Lately, the lives around us have been riddled with divorce. We've been spending lots of energy getting dates for girls whose marriages break up, often when the last kid goes off to school. Some of these girls adapt, some don't. But the men?" He inhaled deeply on his pipe. "The men survive."

"Not one upright figure which she could respect," Max Beerbohm mused of his famous superheroine, Zuleika Dobson. "Though she herself, womanly, would utterly abase herself before her ideal, [she could] love no man who fell prone before her . . . To be able to love once—would that not be better than all the homage in the world? But would she ever meet whom, looking up to him, she could love—she, the omnisubjugant? Would she ever, ever meet him?"

The language might be archaic, but the sentiment endured. Human nature had not changed strikingly across the years. It was a rare woman who could love while looking down, and a rare man who could love while kneeling.

But if to be omnisubjugant, all-controlling, was the neo-feminist dream, so far, it was largely lily-white. The black man as superhero felt almost none of its effects. When the Wonder Woman of his own race could lean on her husband, instead of being leaned upon, she thanked her lucky stars. It was like coming in from the cold of seven generations.

"Oh, the man has got to be supreme," said one black superwife who was raising three children with her right hand and teaching college-level sociology with her left. "If Robert wasn't so good at taking charge, I wouldn't have the peace of mind to think straight," she said of her husband. "My brains are functioning because he takes that big load off my back."

The pursuit of power, wealth, or fame might make sense for those "who have made up their minds to do without men," another black wife conceded. "They have that need for personal prominence that drives them. But I'm just an ordinary woman. My need is the ordinary kind." "Ordinary" hardly described her. She was a talented fabric designer who turned down as many freelance assignments as she accepted, not out of any careless disregard for money or prestige but because, as so many black women agreed, family "came first." She valued her artistic gift, the designer added without false humility. "But I consider it something of an adornment. Work is secondary, at least until the children grow up. It used to be a white woman's privilege, putting her family first."

Other black superwives with the same set of priorities might fade in and out of the job market casually enough to distress some inflexible, old-guard bosses. But the Supermen they married agreed that it was healthy for their home lives. If male prerogatives were not to die, more than one black husband suggested, perhaps sporadic or part-time employment had to be the prerogative of women. Without upsetting the balance of power, it added spice to life and, now and then, provided a second income. "Anyhow, you don't get too attached to that extra cash if it's only a sometime thing," said one in-again-out-again legal clerk who was the mother of two teenagers. "I never had a boss who wasn't sorry to see me leave. And I never had one who didn't sympathize with my going." If, as Marshall McLuhan proposed, there were two American consciousnesses —one structured, tight, and goal-oriented; the other loose, intuitive, and life-affirming—it was clear which of them these black women possessed.

Their husbands' consciousness, however, was often more mixed. Clayton Hooper was the deputy mayor of a large Southern city. A short, round, genial man, he looked incipiently airborne even while sitting still. He unfolded his "success story," as he called it, with an engaging air of satisfaction. In his middle twenties, after managing a nightclub in an adjacent city, he had gone to work for the state department of labor. "It was my job to convince employers to hire minority people. Today *everybody* ought to have a chicken bone or a chick, I used to say." A little later, at City Hall, he was appointed administrative assistant for human resources. From there, it was just a few steps down the hall to the mayor's office.

As goal-oriented as Hooper had become, adopting the attitudes of the larger society, he encouraged his working wife to feel free to take her career *and* leave it. The births of the children, the state of family finances, her own mood' determined the ebb and flow of her dual existence. He was not deprived of *dominus*. She was not worried by the obligation to "achieve." In an imperfect world, it seemed a sane enough interim solution. It was quite common in the black community.

"It's an in-between-the-children kind of thing. Most all of the wives work intermittently," Clayton Cooper said. "For Fran, it's 60 percent economic and 40 percent change of scene. But it's no percent power drive. I've got the monopoly on power drive for my whole family."

Business and industry would accommodate only with reluctance to a widespread pattern of seemingly "erratic" female employment, Cooper acknowledged. "But it's not so much erratic as obeying natural rhythms. Anyway, if this society wants to save the family—and save men's jobs—maybe it has no other choice," said the former administrator of human resources.

Nevertheless, some black women, like some of their husbands, were falling into white patterns of response. Cooper spoke of two married neighbors. "She has a degree, he doesn't. She got that degree in the first place to assist in the family situation. Now she's a little bit uptight about her advanced education. 'Are you looking for a guy with a title and a tie?' I asked her. 'Are you looking for a guy drowning in his own status who takes out his secretary three times a week? Or are you looking for a *man*? It's not what he does, it's what he is!' I reminded her about her husband. Well, she told him she had to go away for a month to think things out. 'Then take everything with you. I won't be here when you get back,' her husband said. "I kind of support that," Clayton Cooper admitted. "A man has got to stand for something in his own home."

The deputy mayor was skeptical of "liberated" marriages. "I'm not going to be judgmental about it. Cheating can be good, bad, or indifferent. Sometimes a friendly persuasion just sort of develops . . . and dies. But you get hung up too long on a thing like that, your success story can go right down the drain," Cooper said. "Just on GP, that stands for general principles, it's not my life style. For me, marriage is a yes-or-no kind of thing." He sat up straighter in his straight-backed chair. "If I found my wife stepping out, maybe I wouldn't pack my bag—the first time. But if it were to happen twice, then she don't need me any more. A man's no man who rolls over and lets people walk on him, even if that person happens to be his wife."

If the black husband felt more urgently than other men the need to "wear the pants" in the family, it could have been because he could not forget that his ancestors wore chains.

Toward the end of the Civil War, a former slave said, "I's want to be a free man, cum when I please, and nobody say nuffin' to me or order me aroun'." Wearing a white collar now, and university-educated, that slave's great-grandson was listening more attentively than ever to his inner voices. It was understandable that the white man sometimes envied him his certainty. For his own inner voices had grown increasingly confused, largely through his good intentions. Often he was trying so hard to be a *super* superhusband, that he submitted to his own subjection, and even to his sons, as passively as women (and slaves) were once said to have done.

Jeremy Brandt, a writer transplanted from Chicago to California, told of one friend, the president of a small but thriving advertising agency, married to a woman who not only wore the pants in the family but put her sons in skirts. "Jeanne's extremism hardened as the years went by. Her husband was a reasonable man who didn't want to veto ideas that meant so much to her. He tried to be sympathetic, even when she dressed their two sons in girls' clothes, so that they should not grow up contemptuous of women." The boys were then about five and seven years old. "They wore girls' blouses, girls' shoes, girls' underwear. If Jeanne could shop for herself in the men's department, why shouldn't she shop for her boys in the girls' department?"

Finally she prevailed upon her ever reasonable husband to sell his advertising agency. "Now he stays home and takes care of the kids while his wife does her thing." Jeanne taught high-school French. She was also writing a semiautobiographical book about married feminists. "But it'll never sell because it's so full of rage," Brandt predicted.

Jeanne was as wary of him, the writer revealed, as he was wary of Jeanne. "My cardinal sin in her eyes is that I *gave* Rachel our babies. Worse than that, I hired a 'slave' to take care of them, while systematically avoiding my duties as a father."

Jeremy Brandt's wife had recently become a graduate student, pursuing a doctoral degree that would take four or five years to complete. "The only way I could support Rachel's habit," he said, "was to hire a housekeeper and buy time that way to finish my book. But Jeanne insists that I'm a cad, shirking my parental role, and angry at Rachel for going back to school."

With his bright-blue eyes, butter-colored corduroy jacket, and blue jeans, he looked more like a graduate student himself than a cad. "The other day I said to Jeanne's husband, 'How can you go on living with her? Don't you know she hates men?' He reminded me of his wife's early history. 'Jeanne's family came out of concentration camps. She was born in Europe. The big man in her life was Hitler. She sees Hitler as a metaphor for man: Hitler/man, man/Hitler. Yes, she hates men,' her husband said. 'But you see, it's really not her fault.'"

The French teacher's househusband was no longer very remarkable. He was one of a fast-growing company of men, often but not always moved by pure compassion. Beneath the headline How Men Are Changing, a member of his tribe appeared on the cover of *Newsweek* magazine, wearing a ruffled gingham apron and a look of chagrin. "I did it because it was the right thing to do. I have a very strong sense of justice, and I realized how totally unjust I'd been," said one contrite man in James A. Levine's book about full-time fathers in America, *Who Will Raise the Children?* For many like him, to take over as the primary homemaker was an act of personal conviction. "Doing the right thing" meant everything. The motives of others were political. They wished to "revise the norms of manliness" and "expand the possibilities of male choice." Still others were openly adventurous; like radical women, eager to find out where throwing off the last constraints of gender could lead.

After all, many psychologists and psychiatrists had begun to treat masculinity and femininity as indications of neurosis, "our species' pathology," as one put it. Serious books appeared, such as Dorothy Dinnerstein's *The Mermaid and the Minotaur: Sexual Arrangements and Human Malaise*, which made the case for "loosening and restructuring the rigid forms of symbiosis, of fixed psychological complementarity, which have so far dominated relationships between men and women . . . Until we grow strong enough to renounce the pernicious, prevailing forms of collaboration between the sexes, both men and women will remain semi-human, monstrous," Dinnerstein wrote.

A female economist added that, to help man grow strong enough and less monstrous, we ought drastically to revise our social policies. "If we tax the earnings of men more heavily than those of women, we will increase the *relative* attractiveness of work at home for men, and the *relative* attractiveness of work outside the home for women . . ." This, said Carolyn Shaw Bell, "would make men consider, more seriously, employment at home as an alternative occupation." Such radical restructuring of the sexual mores was usually advanced by female analysts.

Meanwhile, some women took more flagrant forms of protest against "rigid forms of symbiosis" than simply reversing domestic roles. Jeremy Brandt told of a female friend "who wants to promote more real intimacy among males. She's unhappy that we're not really brothers. She wants to see more brotherly love."

She also wanted to see more sisterly love, regarding lesbianism as a necessary step in the continuing evolution of women away from "fixed complementarity" toward loosening up and liberty. "Looking Rachel deep in the eyes, she asks, 'If you really care about women as much as you say, how can you deprive your sisters of your love, your tenderness, your caresses?' "

Not unexpectedly, she had also "opened her husband up to homosexuality," Brandt reported. "Now he says, without even lowering his voice, 'I'd like to make it with a man. I just haven't found one yet who attracts me enough.' " During this no longer extraordinary conversation, his friend gave Jeremy Brandt a long, appraising glance. " 'Well, it couldn't be you,' he said. 'You're too old a friend and too good a friend. But it couldn't be a hustler either. That would be too crass, too venal.' "

Why did such husbands acquiesce to—and sometimes even adopt—the extremist ideology of their wives? "Men may be essentially more conservative than women. But they don't want to look like they're behind the times . . . or God forbid, *reactionary* . . . enemies of progress," Brandt speculated. Nevertheless, he confessed to some misgivings about "ideological sex. If you decide to sample gay relationships because it seems politically appropriate, how much does that really have to do with personal liberty?" he asked. "Or is it only another form of tyranny?

"But all these new definitions of freedom are in the air today," he said. And they did not merely influence matters of sexual politics, like converting homosexual from a noun to an adjective. ("There's no such thing as a homosexual," one young ideologue insisted, intent on eliminating sexual categories. "There's only homosexual activity on the part of human beings." Although she made it sound like a fresh insight, it was hardly a new idea. She was, in fact, paraphrasing Gore Vidal, who had written some years earlier: "There is of course no such thing as a homosexual. Despite current usage, the word is an adjective describing a sexual action, not a noun describing a recognizable type.")

Unorthodox definitions of freedom, whether actually new or just now gaining currency, also influenced matters like child-rearing and the continuance of family life, Brandt said. "In another time, Rachel would be staying home most of the day, helping the kids grow up. But these outrageous people, these crazed, well-meaning friends of ours"—his smile was sad, not mischievous—"sanction another kind of behavior for my wife. They permit her to do something more wild," he maintained. "It's pretty wild for the mother of three kids, all under five, to start work on a doctorate in Latin American literature. It's also damned expensive. We're into nursery schools, car pools, live-in housekeepers . . ."

Yet he too deferred. He was cooperative, conciliatory, and compassionate, beyond his better judgment and their financial means. "I have a very bright wife," he explained. "It wouldn't be fair otherwise. It would be unjust to Rachel to be swallowed up in the world of a middle-aged writer with no outlet for her ability. I wouldn't like to be responsible for a woman whose Bryn Mawr education had gone to waste."

So he was trying to keep the ship of family, and his inherent good nature, afloat against difficult but (he said then) not insurmountable odds. "A little while ago, Rachel became involved in Latin America week at the university," Brandt recalled. "There were lectures, workshops, seminars. It was hard for me not to feel left out and bored. For a whole week, Rachel was talking Spanish and I was Rachel Brandt's husband." When that sort of stuff is a gesture of assertion or hostility, it's just got to tear the marriage apart. But for his wife, he said, "it was a positive, not a negative thing."

Brandt added another thought. "Even so, it sometimes destroys the guy, if not the marriage." He reviewed the situation of another couple. "The husband, a philosophy professor, turned down appointments at Harvard and Yale. He accepted a job at a third-rate college in Ohio because this backwoods place would also hire his wife, an instructor in history. He was bending over backward to do the right thing. But he drank an awful lot after that. 'At Harvard you would have had to teach only four hours a week,' I said to him. 'You would have had more time for your writing.'" The compromising (or compromised) professor replied, "'So I won't become famous. Who cares?' Well, by then he was hitting the bottle in a big way. His own survival had begun to seem unimportant to him."

Married to Wonder Woman, how did man survive as man? "Maybe he doesn't," Brandt replied. "Maybe there's no way. It's not easy under any circumstances to be masculine now in the old-fashioned sense. We aren't hunters any more. Even in my father's time, men lived very differently. There was still the small business—his to command, dominate, struggle over, fight for—although it might be only a corner newsstand. But now a guy works for IBM, he wears a uniform, and someone tells him what to do. He's got to be passive to the man ahead of him. He learns passivity. It permeates every corner of his life. He can never assert himself in the world. And now, with what's happened to women, he can never assert himself at home either—even in a sexual sense. This fellow who works for IBM, you know, he can't pull his wife to bed by the hair. It would make both of them feel ridiculous."

Jeremy Brandt came back to where he had begun. He spoke, as did so many other men, of male surrender. Husbands submitted to their wives, he said, "with the best, the most honorable intentions in the world. But the surrender turns out to be antithetical to the marriage. Finally, these men have to get out . . . or they're wiped out. Deliberately or not, their wives turn them into miserable, cowed creatures."

Some time later, perhaps to avoid a similar fate, Jeremy Brandt divorced Rachel. For men of every class, almost the only assertions of *dominus* left seemed to be negative ones.

An East Coast gynecologist, having witnessed the sexual evolution of women during more than thirty years of practice, said that he could perceive the crisis in heterosexual relations—of which Brandt's divorce was only one small symptom—in his own consulting room. "The best of women are deballing the best of men," the doctor declared. "They're winning political races, they're fixing their own cars, they're focused on their careers now, the way they used to be focused on their families. They're making men feel superfluous. That's fatal." What could be more annihilating, more anaphrodisiac, he asked, than the conviction of expendability? Today's active new breed of educated, self-realizing Wonder Women, "with their own incomes and their own ambitions, really don't need husbands any more, they need studs," the gynecologist went on bluntly. "Men are getting wind of that. I see them walking out every day in a desperate attempt to save what's left of their balls."

A soft-spoken, middle-aged psychiatrist on the West Coast agreed that "the hotbed of high-powered women" could seem to many men no fit place to make love. "Yet female power is an old, old story. Human nature hasn't changed," he insisted. "I myself never believed in the myth of the passive woman, even when it was popular." He recalled Alex's de Tocqueville, who, more than a hundred years ago, wrote about the pioneer woman, self-reliant and aggressive, who dominates men and shoots Indians. "This domineering, take-charge kind of wife has been around a long, long time," the psychiatrist said, "and she's still here. What's new today is that, between her and her man, the bedroom's become the biggest field of conflict." He stroked his short white beard, reflecting. "After you ask who washes the dishes and who takes out the garbage, it's only a short step to ask who fucks who. Who's the dominant party in the act of sex? The husband with the strong, self-determining wife is apt to take the obvious way out. Little by little, at least at home, he begins to direct his energies into spheres other than the erotic."

Another psychiatrist in New England, whose wife taught a college-level course in women's rights, was also keenly aware of the uneasy relationship between the new ideology of sexual equality and the old necessities of the sexual life. Some wives might now want husbands more than they actually needed them as providers and protectors; his own wife was one of them, Dr. Charles Gladstone acknowledged. Nevertheless, he was not convinced that this implicit challenge to *dominus* inhibited Eros. "I don't go for the implication that the new aggressivity in women can bring on perpetual impotence in men," Dr. Gladstone said. "It's a bald attempt to discredit the women's movement by making spurious claims that female activity is destructive to men . . . and especially to male sexuality." Gladstone was distressed by this idea. "It's a resurgence of witches and the witch hunt, a return to the Dark Ages when it was believed that women actually did take potency away from men. Hence they were witches who should be burned at the stake."

The psychiatrist referred to *The Handbook for the Persecution of Witches*, which, he said, examines "the phenomenon of the female who casts a spell on male potency. She was accused of having slept with the devil," he explained. "In the Middle Ages, midwives were called white witches. They were the only ones who could administer in childbirth. In fact, by Church edict, women weren't good enough or important enough to be seen by doctors at all. But as these white witches gained power in the community, they came into conflict with the Church. And finally they were burned for robbing men of their virility."

Today, Dr. Gladstone said, liberated women were once more being charged with just such witchcraft—if not by the Church, then by some of those new priests themselves, the psychotherapists. Describing psychiatry as "a male-serving profession," he suggested that the "impotence effect" of women's new assertiveness actually signified a bold and desperate maneuver to undercut female militancy.

In a remarkable display of inverted logic, Gladstone saw sexual impotence not as a result of the female plot against men but as a strategy in the male plot to oppress women. "It may be men's answer to the question 'How can we intimidate women into being submissive again?' " he speculated. "Because what could be more effective than threatening women with the loss of their heterosexual lives? It's the thing they still value most; in fact, maybe more than ever, since women have just recently become aware of the full force of their own eroticism."

Indeed, to Dr. Gladstone, the potency issue—like *dominus* itself—seemed something less than urgent. "Usually, it's nothing." He shrugged. "It's just a way of saying goodbye. A man wants to break off the relationship, but he can't or won't verbalize his feeling." In this time of swiftly shifting sexual values, he said, more men than ever were 'saying goodbye.' "But if he's impotent in marriage, he doesn't want to be brought back alive," the psychiatrist warned. "It's a flaccid way of saying no to his wife on a permanent basis."

For most men, he believed, the primary fulfillment was not in the primal act itself but in its spin-off, so to speak. "The afterplay," Gladstone said, "is where men's real gratification lies." For most women, *afterplay* signified the post-coital swooning and rapture that, in the best of times, occurred. But Gladstone meant by afterplay, "When a woman gets up and makes the coffee and the breakfast," affirming that, at least in some crude and imperfect way, the spirit of *dominus* did indeed survive.

The psychiatrist told of a female patient engaged in a long-term love affair with a lawyer in New York. She flew nearly halfway across the country to spend each weekend with him. "But before she left on Monday morning she cooked a lavish breakfast for him, complete with fresh-squeezed orange juice, and cleaned up his apartment."

The lawyer's very potency seemed to reside in the sense of power stirred by his lady's acknowledgment that the sexual pleasure he gave was intense enough to enslave her (symbolically at least). Finally, however, her raised consciousness began to raise doubts in her mind about her real place in her lover's life. Dr. Gladstone advised that she "stop doing the Monday chores, just to see what happens."

On the following week, the psychiatrist reported, "instead of making breakfast, she made a lot of personal telephone calls. Then she left the rugs unvacuumed and the bed all rumpled up." The apartment owner telephoned his mistress, outraged. "The place is a mess! You didn't clean up!" he shouted, thereby precipitating the end of the affair. "My patient decided this guy needed a weekend housekeeper more than he needed her," Gladstone said. To the lawyer, housekeeping symbolized "the idea of having a woman submissive to him and sensitive to his needs." That provided his deepest pleasure, not sex itself.

The psychiatrist made one more point about the erotic life of the American superhusband and its place in the constellation of male values. Even in these traumatic days, sex was not the "presenting problem" of any of his male patients, the doctor said. "There's only one real problem for men: how successful are they? Why aren't they more successful? Physicists come to see me because they haven't won the Nobel Prize. Writers come to see me because they haven't won the Pulitzer. Their deepest preoccupations have very little to do with sex or with women." It was the power drive, not the sex drive, that moved men most, he said.

But these two drives were not always mutually exclusive. Just as some women still did, some men now used sex as the springboard to power. For instance, certain superhusbands married to *super* superwives—the stars, the heavy earners, "the big-timers," as one said—turned their seeming surrender into concrete, dollars-and-cents advantage. It was yet another way to nourish the illusion of control.

In the past man had worshipped woman as the embodiment of the erotic and the divine. She had stood for purity and passion, for the spirit and the senses. But very seldom had she stood for Mammon. Very seldom had she been the object of man's cupidity, the target for his greed. It was perhaps the most startling transformation: woman displaced from the realm of the erotic, where man gave vent to his best instincts, to the realm of the pornographic, where he gave vent to his worst.

Yet, as women moved up . . . and up, and men moved over, female earning capacity became entangled with Eros in the pantheon of male success. Looking into his wife's eyes, like as not, he saw dollar signs. Her turn-on was her purchasing power. Now she was *really* ripe for exploitation. She was available for use not in the old picayune ways, such as baking bread, making beds, and lying in them, but for the main event, making money.

As the number of husbands whom wives could lean on diminished, the number of wives whom husbands could bank on grew. "I keep the wolves away from her door, the ones who feed on notoriety," one such gentleman explained. He was tall and bushy-haired, and the tip of his nose wiggled when he talked. In white flannel trousers and a shirt to match, he looked something like a wolf in sheep's clothing. "I brush off the hangers-on. I invest her money. I pick out her clothes. I tell her how to dress and what to buy. When she can't sleep, I hold her on my lap all night and rock her like a baby. I have known plenty of women in my life, but I have never known another one so totally vulnerable, so totally dependent." His wife, only a minor heroine of the media, was his career, his commodity, and, to put it coarsely, his wage slave.

Other such consorts—most of whom lacked the drive and vibrancy of the women that they courted—spoke in the same general vein. "She isn't the big-time publishing whiz to me," another gentleman-in-waiting said, not without affection. "I knew her as a college kid. I knew her *when*. She used to take in proofreading for a couple of dollars an hour, the way laundresses take in wash. On Saturdays, she sold brassières at Saks Fifth Avenue. Then she used the money she earned to buy herself one nifty outfit at the employee's discount. She came from poor Jewish people and graduated from Brooklyn College.

But when she went job hunting, she looked like a job was the last thing she needed. That was part of her game." His tone, typically, mixed respect with envy. "Even in those days, she was itchy. She always had that itch to make it. Getting there was half the fun. I knew I had to help her. Otherwise, the marriage would have failed." He spoke only of his forbearance and his cooperation, not of his fringe benefits: the summer house on ten acres in the country, the trips to Europe twice a year, the BMW in which he moved around town.

"She has the glamour, he has the gimmes," a female colleague of this superwife's remarked. "But of course guys like him are a dime a dozen these days." She mentioned four women she knew, all of whom virtually supported "big, healthy, lazy men. One girl runs a beauty shop, one's a lawyer, one has her own public-relations firm, and one's a fashion director. But, you see, all of them really believe they're in love. So maybe it's a fair trade-off."

Inevitably, such men sometimes harbored resentment toward their superwives that was bound to spill over into bed. In the course of time, they became sadistic or dispirited as lovers. They either acted out their hostility in cruel and hurtful ways or they became impotent. The same man could veer between those two poles, a demon one day, dysfunctional the next.

In Hollywood, a stage-and-movie star of the second constellation said of her two former husbands, "In the end, I had to get divorced to save my life. These were fine, well-meaning men who had lost their balance, and somehow I got blamed. But it wasn't actually *my* success that spoiled the marriages," she declared. One man had been a millionaire; the other had been something of a star himself. "*Their* maleness was undermined. I bore the brunt of that."

No doubt she did. Yet among some husbands content to be kept, there seemed less of the male discontent inherent in so many superpower marriages. These men were not necessarily weaklings, one psychiatrist said. It took a "tremendous amount of ego strength" to be "always the bridesmaid and never the bride," he explained, neglecting to revise the gender to "usher" and "groom." Often, this ego strength was so prodigious that such a husband could enjoy his retainer role without feeling subordinated. For by "trading up," in marriage, as ambitious women still did, Superman demonstrated (at least to his own satisfaction) that he was even more wonderful than Wonder Woman herself.

14 | The Deepest Part of the Tunnel

"Fucking used to prove a lot to men about their masculinity. It was very easy to cope with women in positions of dependency. But now women have gotten so emancipated that even sex is not a simple matter any more. Men are giving up on themselves. They've lost their pep. They complain that they can't meet female expectations . . . and the whole damn thing goes too deep to resolve." So said one East Coast psychiatrist, echoing others.

Arnold Josephson, a clinical psychologist in a Middle Western city, practiced what he called "liberation therapy." He was one of those therapists who declared that, as men lost their pep, he was losing his male clients. "Men are just not coming in much any more—except reluctantly, as adjuncts to their wives," he said. "And I'm not getting male referrals from my colleagues either. They treat depression. I treat social causes. That threatens everyone, doctors and patients." (Some other psychologists testified that their rosters of male clients were lengthening. But men's motives for coming in were substantially the same as their motives for staying away: apathy and despair.)

Josephson was a soft, ruddy man with wavy hair and sleepy, hooded brown eyes. His face was moist. He looked like he was running a slight fever. "Today, most marital problems have liberation issues at their base. Women with their new self-interest are saying to men, 'You're inept. You're a shlepp in bed.' But political issues are almost always involved in poor sexual relationships." Josephson saw the lives of men with women as composed of endlessly debated "issues." It could make for some contentious unions. His own was one of them.

"Ineptitude on the part of men is not indifference," the liberation therapist explained. "And it's not sexual skill either that's really at issue. Usually it's repressed anger . . . a deep desire *not* to make love, because one doesn't feel loving." Some men no longer felt loving, he said, because some women were no longer lovable.

Once in a while, even feminists caught a clear glimpse of that hard truth. One wrote, in a published fragment of her diary, "Maybe I've become something unlovable. Maybe men and women are now on such divergent paths that we will never manage again without maiming ourselves irrevocably . . ."

But many such couples on divergent paths were already maiming each other. "If a man can't satisfy his wife sexually, she's miserable. Then he becomes intensely dissatisfied with himself," said Josephson. "At the same time, he won't accept the blame for her unhappiness. When she drags him to her therapist, he takes the attitude that 'I am here because she's sick.' "

"But of course she's not sick," said Lois Brill, Josephson's second wife, with some impatience. She sat beside him, looking as wan as she was pretty. Brill was also a successful psychologist. She and her husband often worked as a team. She wore as much makeup as a photographer's model and retained her maiden name. "How would *you* like to wash floors and cook three meals a day for some ungrateful lout? And do nothing else for the rest of your life?" Her tone of empathy was perhaps excessive, like a millionaire president pouring out compassion for the poor.

"If that's her life, it's her own fault," said Arnold Josephson, of the hypothetical wife. "She's talking feminism, so why does she go on living like her mother? 'Stay home, make dinner, care for the kids, and you'll go to heaven when you die.' "

"Because she's got some new ideas, but no new behavior to go with them," his wife said. "She's still afraid to assert herself. She's afraid of losing him. It's a common conflict among women, even some of the young women in my courses." She taught at the local college.

Josephson groaned over such obtuseness. "Meanwhile, dinner doesn't even interest this guy. He would like her to be the sexy chick, whore, mother, and superstimulator all at the same time. By nature, he's a dyed-in-the-wool chauvinist. But he's picked up the freedom jargon too. He's learned to say the acceptable things, while acting in the same old ways." Borrowing the rhetoric of female emancipation was part of the new diplomacy of marriage, the liberation therapist said. "Men adopt the language, just as women do. They mouth the right words and give up the wrong ones. They carefully refrain from talking about 'chicks,' 'broads' and 'screwing around.' But it's like smiling with the teeth—completely phony."

Lois Brill shot a dark glance at her husband, then turned away. At that moment, a dispassionate observer might have accused him of smiling with his teeth. "The false, trumped-up respect for women's issues all over the campus" aggravated her a lot, she said. She mimicked the prevailing male atmosphere, talking through her nose. " 'Ah, yes! Women should move up.' 'Ah, certainly! We need many more of them in top administrative positions.' The big brass has been saying so for years. But somehow or other, we haven't moved up in large numbers. That's why all the polls and surveys about what's going on in men's minds are worthless. They don't record real attitudes at all, only what people profess their attitudes to be." Lip-service liberation, she declared, was a chronic disease among male administrators.

Once in a while, Lois Brill continued, someone showed his "true reactionary colors," falling into what she called "the old sex-object trap. After all this time, we aren't rid of it. The other day, a colleague actually said to me, 'You've got nice legs, so why can't I admire them? Why don't you take it as a compliment?' Would he take it as a compliment if I said, 'My, what a nice big cock you have'?"

A pause fell upon the conversation. The new female explicitness distressed some men, who felt deprived even of their own language. At last Dr. Josephson responded, "Not all of us are equally regressive. There *is* a new kind of guy—gentle, tender, open, honest." The sort, he implied, who had passed beyond all the old, unworthy preoccupations, such as the curve of a female calf. "He's the one who's really susceptible to change. But he's still on the fringes of society, an isolate, estranged from the mainstream. He feels as out of it as he ever did. He was never into football games. He never made it with the boys. He felt drawn toward women's things . . ." Josephson said. "Now he's getting some support from men's groups, such as the one that I facilitate, but . . ."

Lois Brill looked up sharply. "You give too much of yourself to that group," she said.

"I know there's a time-and-energy issue," her husband admitted. His handsome face had become ruddier and more moist. "Those sessions are so strenuous that I feel as if I'm driving a team of horses. But the problems are immense. If things are going bad for someone, we've all got to be there. Yet the sort of unliberated men who would benefit most never appear. And when the homosexual in the group starts to talk about gut male issues, he terrifies the others out of their minds."

"You're not terrified," his wife said. A silence descended. They both seemed absorbed in private thoughts.

"All of them are experiencing less and less rapport with women all the time," Josephson remarked. Why is it, he asked, that "lesbianism doesn't threaten men? But when men experiment with homosexuality in a fairly casual way, women go bananas?" He did not wait for her reply. "I guess they're afraid once men open themselves to a homosexual relationship, they won't turn back. They'll just go on . . . and on."

Lois Brill blinked her eyes, as if caught by too much light. "Some will," she said. "Won't they? Once they open themselves?"

A good friend of theirs, a psychiatrist, found himself in precisely that predicament, Arnold Josephson conceded. "After a whole long life as straight as an arrow, he came to see me one night. Jack threw himself down on a chair in our living room with a terrible look on his face. 'I'm dying,' he said. The locked-in pattern of his life was suffocating him. 'The house, the lawn, the dog, the kids. They just don't mean enough.' "

"You left out his wife," said Lois Brill.

"He left out his wife," the psychologist replied. "Well, there were tears in Jack's eyes that night. I figured, 'He wants to tell me there's another woman, but he can't bring himself to it.' So I asked him, 'Jack, is there another woman?' He shook his head. By then I knew. He always had that delicate, tender quality . . . It didn't surprise me a bit. I said, 'Jack, is there another man?' He nodded. A little while later, my friend gave up his wife, his kids, his hundred-thousand-dollar practice, and the two men ran away. "It was very unfortunate," Arnold Josephson said. "They should not have had to run away."

Under her mask of porcelain makeup, a flush like sudden fever turned his wife's face pink.

Quite soon now male couples, such as Arnold Josephson's friends, might no longer need to run away in order to live happily ever after. In one state, Colorado, they could already marry one another with the consent of the law. In one popular magazine, *People*, the straitlaced intention of two male lovers (both ruggedly handsome, heavily bearded, muscular) to enjoy "the same kinds of lives our parents did" was sympathetically recorded. "Sexually distinct we may be, but most of us are surprisingly like you," one of these homosexual men reminded heterosexual society. It was inconsequential, he maintained, that their erotic feeling was prompted by those of their own gender.

Another said, "There are lots of gays who have stable relationships and simply do not go through the great traumas, the anonymous promiscuity, the one-night stands you always hear about." Today promiscuity and one-night stands were just as likely—perhaps more likely—to appear as symptoms of the heterosexual funk. Indeed, some people believed that the gay community showed signs of becoming the last outpost of true love. "We are discovering the potential for human warmth and feeling that seems so absent in modern society," one member of that community said. "I can understand why one of my straight friends told me that he envies me . . ."

The popular arts in America were among the gays' best friends. It was already a cinematic cliché that most of the real love affairs in American movies, whether overtly homosexual or not, were between two men. On national prime-time television, male homosexuals were portrayed as agreeable, emotionally honest, often endearing people. Their "stable relationships" extended deep into the straight world, where they were greeted in affectionate, if sometimes perplexed, embrace.

Considering the mood of the day, it was hardly surprising that so many heteros flirted with the idea of emulating them. Not only feathery young men, but air force officers and star athletes confessed their sexual proclivities to the world. It was rather more confounding when husbands and fathers, with sexual histories as straight as sticks, were swept up in the mounting gay tide.

In life as well as art, "male bonding" had become a new American romance. Women of all ages were whispering to each other about a shared trauma: a husband or boyfriend who confided, quite without warning, that he had turned gay. It was perhaps the pivotal private drama of the times; more dismaying than the conventional old triangle, because the match was so uneven when one's rival was a man. Yet we were almost getting used to it . . . or at least resigned. A divorcée in her early forties, confronted by admissions of "gaiety" from her two favorite dinner companions, decided to introduce them to each other. They had both complained of difficulties in "meeting the right man." "Well, I still like them both so much," she explained, looking only a little unstrung. "They're really sweet guys. And who knows? Maybe they were made for each other."

In the heartland of America, "the tender bunch of men" in Arnold Josephson's male-liberation group—grandsons of pioneers, husbands, fathers, professionals all—did not openly court the homosexual life. Yet they made no secret of the fact that their interest in women *qua* women was waning fast. They were engaged in reviewing male commitments in preparation for abandoning them. The rewards of traditional marriage, with its old rigors and egalitarian injunctions, seemed more uncertain than ever. The institution itself had come to seem like a prison, drained of spirit and devoid of charm. What good was cultivating *dominus*, with all the sacrifices it imposed, in a world in which it was so grossly undervalued?

These Middle Western family men were just now beginning to face that question and others like it, in the light of day. Or more precisely, in the half light of the group. This morning, in their expansive, expensive conference room, the drapes were closed and the blinds were drawn although it was high noon and sunny. The warm but sullen light intensified the intimacy of the occasion. And intimacy with each other—a thaw in the spreading heterosexual chill—was what they sought. At the session's start, some dispute arose about admitting a female journalist into the all-male gathering. But after a hasty closed meeting, the men agreed to let me stay.

In the conference room, the guest guru, hailed as "a leader of male liberation" and a theoretician of the men's movement, had already plunged into his autobiography. It seemed designed to exhibit the ritual compassion for women that such men often expressed. Watching his mother "fade in and out of mental depression as she faded in and out of part-time jobs," the leader said, had opened his eyes to "how deeply identity and paid employment are related . . ."

But the men in his audience were already restless. By now, they had had a bellyful of woman's plight. It was their least favorite subject. Long ago, their complaisance had turned to complaint, and complaint had turned to contentiousness. "The great unexpected dividend of the feminist movement has been to elevate an ordinary status—woman, housewife—to the level of drama," as Tom Wolfe had written. "One's very existence as a woman . . . becomes something the whole world analyzes, agonizes over, draws cosmic conclusions from or, in any event, takes seriously . . ." Enough already!

The guru smelled their impatience. He shut up and listened while little pellets of discontent exploded here and there around the room. Taken one by one, these outbursts ranged from trivial to petty. Taken together, they seethed like a restless volcano. The classic "housekeeping issue," as Arnold Josephson called it, erupted first. He and most of the other men were part-time househusbands. Since most of their wives worked, the etiquette of social equality dictated that they should help with domestic chores and the care of children. "Not help, *share*," the guru intoned piously.

"Share, my eye," was the group appraisal of their situation. Accepting domestication with good will and in good faith, most had found themselves "relegated to the floor waxing, the toilet cleaning, and the yard work." It was not quite what they had bargained for.

"Maybe it's a mistake to make waves," Josephson ruminated. In the absence of his wife, his complexion was notably paler, as if his blood pressure had gone down. He seemed more relaxed—and oddly, more male. But whether helping out or sharing in domesticity, he was having extensive second thoughts. "When I offer assistance, Lois says, 'Go do.' But in reality, she's still doing it all. She's boss. I'm staff. I shop the supermarkets, but Lois makes up the lists of what to buy. She won't even let me throw the laundry into the machine without orders about which buttons to push. She refuses to give up control."

They saw control as the key to the "household issue." (Josephson was one of many men who spoke of private matters now as if they were political enterprises. On the way to liberation, they seemed to have mislaid a personal language.) Their wives did not want to relinquish kitchen power, these husbands believed; they only wanted to extend it—beyond the front door and out into the world. Just the day before, Josephson had been twitting women who still lived by the old precept: "Cook dinner every night and you'll go to heaven when you die." But now he was insinuating that, in their heart of hearts, they liked it better that way.

The other men agreed. Instead of resolving the "equality issue," taking on domestic tasks had seemed to exacerbate the struggle for power. The experiment in "sharing," they told the guru, had failed. "You can't win. Whatever you do, it's wrong or it's not enough," said one husband, now absorbed in inventing stratagems to avoid the chores for which he had once volunteered. "I fuck up as a subtle way of getting rid of those stupid jobs," he confessed, not shamefacedly. "But of course my wife knows that I really feel better with the abstract bullshit thing than with a dust mop and a dish towel." His "abstract bullshit thing" was sociology. Asked to dress his children, this sociologist put on their sweaters backward; asked to clear the table, he broke a plate or two. His wife shook her head, called him "Butterfingers" once or twice, and went back to doing it herself. The silliness of it all was less dismaying than the familiar anger that glimmered behind his account of weaseling out.

The men were applauding each other's escape from house-husbandry. "I just plain forget," another one revealed. "That's the easiest way. I was asked to make dinner preparations last night. It's amazing how it slipped my mind. We were in the middle of an office crisis. I couldn't remember anything but what I had to do to get ready for an early-morning meeting."

The group was a lot looser now. Discovering that they were not alone in their acts of domestic disobedience had thawed the atmosphere. Where the men had been resentful, they were now laughing, lapsed into a little gang of mischief-makers pulling a fast one on Big Mama. They drew closer together, buoyed by the laughter and the sense of brotherhood, as in the age-old game of The Boys Against the Girls.

The guru was pleased. He sat on the thickly carpeted floor—shoes off, legs folded yoga-fashion—cheered by these confessions of grown men goofing off. "It reassures us that we weren't made for that trivia, after all." "Trivia" was his term for what was once called "women's work."

But one of the men was not content with the general levity. It had not assuaged his indignation. "She holds on with her teeth to the goddamn house," he exclaimed of his wife, who sold real estate on a part-time basis for a local broker. "I tell her she's a lousy housekeeper. I offer to pay for help. 'Go out and hire someone to clean up this incredible mess,' I tell her. Then I threaten to hire someone myself to get the place in shape. 'The hell you will. I won't let her in!' my wife screams at me.

"Yet at the same time, we practice emotional blackmail." Arnold Josephson was looking contrite. "I say to Lois, 'If you don't take care of the kids, you're a shit. If you don't feed me well, you're rotten. If you don't clean the house, you're a slob.' On the other hand, I resent her for wanting control and throwing her weight around. Women are in a double bind—damned if they do and damned if they don't. It's a lot harder for them to move toward freedom than us." Josephson saw freedom as a concrete entity. It had everything but a street address.

The men were drawn into a discussion of that emblem of freedom, the spouse's salary check. "I sort of like Edna making her own money," one said. "It relieves some of the pressure. But I won't stand still any more for the crap in the house that I don't want to do." He borrowed the guru's good word. "I'm not ready to take on the trivia. It makes me feel . . . trivial. It *is* part of a power issue," he said.

" 'Who's in control' defines the backbone of the marriage," the husband next to him observed. "But who drives the car is actually more important than who's bringing in the bread. Money in the bank, it boils down to some impersonal numbers on a check. But who's behind the wheel, that's intensely personal. That answers the question, who's *really* in control."

In the kitchen, the car, even in the nursery, there was almost always the ruler and the ruled. It concerned husbands everywhere. "My wife was always letting me know that I handled our baby like a clod. Finally I realized that, even while she demanded my participation, she was afraid I would take over her function . . . and improve on it," one young father said.

The men in Arnold Josephson's group were torn between their sense of social justice and their sense of self. They might regret the loss of *dominus,* yet there seemed no diplomatic way to retrieve it, no honorable way to reassert themselves and renegotiate the terms of power.

It was tempting to put the blame on economic circumstances. "If we were all very rich, and we did not have to work at anything at all, would that solve everything?" a man in his late thirties asked. "Solving everything" seemed as real a possibility to him as freedom did to Arnold Josephson.

"Not really," the guru replied. He would admit no such easy resolutions. Only "changing the whole setup" could solve everything, he intimated. "Wealth does not free a man from the pressure of producing more wealth. Money may seem to make you free, but it can also lock you in. Nelson Rockefeller's career became Happy's career, and they were both imprisoned by it."

Although none of them were "very rich," all were solid wage earners. Yet small success did not solace them. They felt no more in control of their work lives than their home lives. "I wish I had been stronger," one said regretfully, about accepting his current job. "I wish I had known the shit I would have to go through. I wouldn't have wanted the fucking position in the first place. I was seduced by the title and the promise of big bucks."

"I'm worse than you," another added. "I knew it was a crock.

I knew that I would have to knuckle under. But I went for it anyhow."

The guru seized the moment. Fomenting dissatisfaction was his current mission in life. He was an artist at catching disturbance at its crest. He presented a scenario for the future. "By the time you're forty or forty-five, you've experienced all the male bribes—power, prestige, status, money. You've sweated all your life for those you love . . . and you end up alienating them. According to your family, you played the absent father, absent husband, absent lover, absent handyman. Now they hate you for it." Confronting that idea, Arnold Josephson's blood pressure went up again. His face grew red as he listened to the leader's words. "For all your hard work and self-sacrifice, you've won only defeat. You're a loser! But what to do about it? How do you liberate yourself at age forty-five?"

Most of these men had about ten years to go before they reached that crucial crossroads, forty-five. Yet it screeched with the immediacy of tomorrow morning. Liberation now!

The guru's preparations were complete. His orchestration of these male emotions was approaching its climax: a pencil-and-paper game. Softly, as one might pacify a schoolroom full of agitated children, he passed around lined yellow strips, torn from a legal pad. "Is this going to be the length of our penis?" one asked. It relieved the tension that the glimpse into the next decade had produced.

"What would you change about yourself, if you could?" The leader coaxed them into revelations about their most private fantasies. "If you could start again, what new career would you choose? If you could choose a new life style, what would it be?"

Ten minutes later, they were shyly exposing their dreams. They would be sailboat skippers, greenhouse owners, potters, innkeepers, islanders, archeologists. They conjured up visions of blue water, white boats, silent earth, wilderness, warmth, tranquility. But the complaint was always the same: commitment to those enchaining others limited the freedom to act. How would their families survive? The guru was gleeful. The group had not disappointed him.

Only one man exploded, "Am I the only money hound here? If I gave up my job for some fantasy life on an island, I couldn't exist. I wouldn't know what the hell to do. I need my job—and not just for the dough. I need it to prove what I've got between my legs."

The guru was also accomplished at ignoring what displeased him. He plunged on with his sermon. Male choices for change were always "escapist, humanist, ideal," he confided. But female choices tended in the opposite direction—materialist, grand, this-worldly. If women could choose, they would be United States senators, Supreme Court justices, Nobel Prize laureates. He spoke of both sexes generically, admitting less variation than nature gave to daisies. "So perhaps we should be changing places for a while?"

While the air still rustled with disturbance, he invited the men to join him on the floor. They were to form a circle and hold each other's hands, the way they used to do in kindergarten when the class sang songs. "Observe how the atmosphere changes," the guru advised as, obediently, they slipped off their shoes and slipped down to the ground. "I'm so cold, I'd rather hug than hold hands," one of them said.

The quiet that came down on the circle seemed louder than the laughter at that gentle joke. Not a word was spoken for quite a long time. The leader broke the trance. His voice had dropped another octave. He was whispering very softly now. He would refuse, he whispered, to be the first to speak out. Finally one of the husbands said, "I don't want to give up my wife."

No one stirred or seemed surprised. "But I do want to find out what it's like to live with a man. I want that very much. I want to know how it feels, living with and caring for a man. I want to explore homosexual relationships."

No one raised his eyes toward the speaker. Once more, the

guru broke the trance. "How about your wife?" he whispered. "Would you want the same thing for her?"

In the half light of the conference room, the silence lengthened. "I don't know," the speaker said at last. "I don't think so. That would be very hard for me. We've already talked about it a little."

Another voice rose up from the circle, stronger than the first. "I can love men," this husband said, "with warmth and tenderness." He began the steep descent into jargon that often characterized such conversation in such groups. Once more, abstractions lessened the threat. "But it's degenitalized, wholly emotional. Maybe my roles are so thick that I can't begin to shed them. I can't dredge up what I assume is there."

The guru tried to reassure him. Daring to touch one another, he promised, would help dredge up what was there. The circle was unbroken. The men were still holding hands.

"I don't want anything to make any real difference between me and my wife," the first speaker murmured. "I want to go on loving her. It's just that I don't want anything, any other loves, excluded from my life." He was not alone among men these days in anticipating a life from which nothing was excluded.

"Coming into this group has been very good for me," another husband said. His tone was almost vigorous. "It's really got me in touch with my potential homosexuality." Then he amended that to "bisexuality." He was the father of three young children.

These confessions were quickly incorporated by the men. Now the circle rippled with new animation. "I have the same yen for exploring masculine closeness as you do," another man said to those who had already testified. "But I do see genital sexuality as a component . . . if only to get it out of the way as a barrier."

His peers approved. "Even in heterosexual relationships, there are times when genital sexuality has to be gotten out of the way as a barrier," one observed.

The leader had the last words. He turned to the man who

had first disclosed his homosexual desires and whispered to him, eyes alight with empathy and excitement, "I was hoping you would get more support." It was difficult to imagine how much more support he could have gotten—short of an outright invitation to sodomy.

A couple of days later, Arnold Josephson's group convened for a "post-mortem" at the offices of one of the members. By then, the euphoria of release from previously unacknowledged feelings had worn off like heavy anesthetic, leaving dull, depressed, disgruntled men, deep in the throes of anticlimax. Coming down from that high of the circle, they had run into a collective, jangling hangover.

It was siphoned off in rage against the guru. The angriest men of all were those who had been prompted to reveal their suppressed desires. "Manipulated," they called it now. "The little fucker didn't meet any of my expectations," one of them said. "I didn't know that until I thought about it later. Actually, I'm not sure what my expectations were," he admitted. "But I was left . . . empty, unfulfilled."

His grievance set off a whole string of them. "That shitty-assed slip of paper! I didn't understand his stupid little game," another player said. "I didn't even understand his questions. I had all I could do to keep from shouting, 'Imposter, go home!' "

They blamed the guru for setting fire to feelings perhaps better left dormant and untended. "His lousy condescension, that was the worst of it. I felt that we were being used in that paternalistic protective, male-fucking way he has."

"Well, we *let* him use us, didn't we? We *helped* him use us."

"But what really pissed me was the trip he laid on the group about getting out from under *our* high-achievement needs. What about his needs? I looked at that little fucker's schedule for two days and my balls started rattling. I don't work as goddamn hard as he does now. His hypocrisy nearly made me puke."

Already they were feeling somewhat better. "Waving his cock about how wonderful he is, how liberated he is! Then an hour later, he skips over to lecture to a women's group about how men are laying such bad trips on *them!* I never learned a goddamn thing about why men shouldn't."

Righteous indignation worked like Benzedrine. The tone of the meeting grew heartier. "The little son of a bitch never talked about us personally. It was all some esoteric, abstract bullshit about how we're going to get bleeding ulcers and coronaries and knock ten years off our lives if we don't kick the male role," said the sociologist with the mild fixation on abstract bullshit.

"The opportunistic shmuck! I wanted to drop-kick his testicles up to the twentieth floor. Maybe it's easier for men to talk about homosexuality than about housework, as he said. But it's not so easy for most of us to get in touch with our own emotions. We needed more help than holding hands."

"We were fucking well ripped off!"

That seemed to take care of the worst of the hangover. Cigarettes came out, noses were blown, ties loosened. Then by some silent agreement, they returned to the contemplation of that circle on the floor. Their voices grew soft again. The men fell into whispers.

"As soon as we got down on the floor, I felt part of something I really wanted to do. It's very scary to me," said the man who had confessed his "yen for masculine closeness."

"You were speaking for all of us," said another. "When I heard you lay it on the line, I felt relieved. I felt real good about that."

"Genital or non-genital, what the fuck's the difference?" the oldest member of the group asked. "Maybe that's something I'm avoiding. But intimacy is intimacy, isn't it? Shouldn't we prize it, whichever way it's expressed?" His voice was raspy with feeling. "Or else, dear God, how the hell are we going to survive?"

In another part of the country, farther west, a craggy-looking artist who referred to himself as "basically a loner" said that it was some deep-rooted survivor's instinct that was bringing men together now for comfort, sustenance, and the assurance that "somebody cares. But it's no new thing. It's been going on forever. When it really matters, when we're dependent on each other for support, we've always gotten very close—closer than we ever get to women," said this painter who, in his revolutionary past, had spent some time in jail as a political prisoner. "Male camaraderie is a special thing. Take the fighter and his trainer. Take cop partners. Those guys really love each other. In war, or in jail, the 'my buddy' feeling can keep you alive. Sometimes it's really a matter of life and death. In the building trades, when one man heats up rivets and throws them to another, he's pretty damn particular who catches them. 'Not Charlie Smith, he's a fuck-up,' one sandhog says to another. You choose your buddies very carefully when you hit the deepest part of the tunnel," the painter said. "You feel, 'It's the two of us. Do or die. The culture stinks. But maybe we can make a survival unit here.'" It was usually in the absence of women that the survival unit became sexual, he finished. "In prison, even the guards stand in line."

The new thing was that male camaraderie was becoming sexual now even in the presence of wives.

"Alas, the penis is such a ridiculous petitioner," wrote William Gass, unaware that women—the petitioned—might not think so. "It is so unreliable although everything depends on it—the world is balanced on it like a ball on a seal's nose. It is so easily teased, insulted, betrayed, abandoned; yet it must pretend to be invulnerable, a weapon which confers magical powers upon its possessor; consequently this muscleless inchworm must try to swagger through temples and pull apart thighs like the hairiest Samson, the mightiest ram. To enter the cave and escape alive—that is the trick." But the trick, for so many, now seemed hardly worth the effort. The pretense of invulnerability had become exhausting. Even when the thighs were open now, the cave did not warmly beckon.

On a starry night in winter, another men's group, in Virginia, was discussing "Is Brotherhood Possible?" They had come a long way from the halting, tentative candor of the earlier "mixed" meetings. A white-haired vocational guidance counselor spoke frankly. He said he had been married for thirty years. "But I want to be *more* than that to them," he sighed, of the young men who "show up on my doorstep saying, 'I'd like to talk.' I want to know them deeply, not just their surface thoughts, in the way that we have been allowed to know only women until now."

A thin, bland man opposite him wore a cowboy shirt, long hair, and steel-rimmed glasses. He said that he had been divorced. "When I was younger, the big thing was getting close to women. It seemed very hard. I felt submerged up to my eyeballs in warm water, like I was drowning. The goal in life was to get into bed with some chick. When she said, 'You're wonderful,' you were supposed to know what living was all about. But so often, it sounded tinny, without spontaneity. And I was frightened of that falsity. If I had an erection, it all went away."

A mustachioed macho type with slender wrists and soft full lips spoke to the issue of the evening: brotherhood's possibility. "It's a question of coming out from behind the big know-it-all male role and relating to each other nakedly, without the trappings."

Potent new man-to-man feelings, sanctioned now but not yet completely incorporated, drew a lengthening Maginot Line of the emotions. "Brotherhood *is* possible," a small, light-haired man testified, catching the attention of everyone with his quiet conviction. He put out his hands, on one of which a thick gold wedding band gleamed. "But the desire for brotherhood is greater than my ability to get myself together—to do with myself what I have to do to achieve it. I don't want to hurt my wife," he whispered, as if the pain of that was his alone. "So I sabotage the dream of brotherhood with my own fears. But I have that dream."

Some men, like Otto Thompson, had not yet reached such a peak of self-acknowledgment. Thompson was a tall, imposing, exceptionally attractive man. His close-cropped blond hair was just turning silver and his eyes, almost all iris, were like gray clouds. They crinkled into friendly patterns when he smiled. Dressed for dinner in a charcoal-gray silk turtleneck shirt and black trousers of some shiny stuff, he looked like the sort of fellow the girls in grandmother's day would have called a heartthrob. His oldest friend, male, had described him as "a charmer."

"I am not gay," Otto Thompson announced early in the evening with his disarming smile. It would have been a curious demurrer—if his reputation, or rumors of it, had not preceded him. That old friend, once his college roommate, explained that Thompson was "a lifelong heterosexual," only recently "into exploring homosexual relationships. He's a very sweet, sensitive, maybe even a fragile man. And he's been irreparably hurt by women. So where has he got to go?" The rejection of one sex by the other, in response to "irreparable" wounds, was an unpopular analysis among experts in such matters, the former roommate conceded, but how else explain the belated conversions of the middle-aged? "Otto's forty-six. Three kids by his first wife, three stepchildren, married twice, divorced. And he gave those women everything. Not just furs, jewels, duplex penthouses with the whole skyline wrapped around. Otto gave himself. He's always been that kind of guy."

It was a gift, Otto Thompson agreed, wholly accepted by

neither wife. He admitted that much, without—at first—admitting that, yes, he had been hurt. "But I'm still in love with both my wives," he declared more simply than seemed reasonable from a man who was by no means simple. An architect and sculptor of sophisticated gifts, his works adorned the banks and plazas of the Northeastern city where he lived.

Closets were flapping open like swinging doors everywhere in the country, but Thompson was one of those men still too uneasy about his own sexual ambivalence to confront it—except, as it were, through mirrors. His old roommate had probably caught the spirit, if not the fact, of his erotic life. In any event, the architect plunged straight into his marital history. "Marlene, my first wife, was disciplined, coordinated, and completely responsible. There were Germanic overtones in her personality. She came from Wisconsin, suburban middle class. To her, everything was right or wrong, black or white. There was no middle ground. A couple of minor infidelities that meant nothing to me turned out to mean everything to her." He did not specify the sex of his paramours.

"My second wife was a wild, extravagant person, unfettered by convention." Thompson paused. "She was a lesbian. On a lesbian rating scale of one to a hundred, Dominique's rating would be 98.5. Her many attempts to prove her womanliness were all in vain." His cloudy eyes grew brighter. Now he could relax. Dominique was the subject closest to his heart. She might have been, in a sense, his subliminal self, the mirror in which he saw reflected his innermost being. Yet from another point of view, her unsteady sexuality made him seem the picture of stability.

"The feminist movement gave both my wives the courage to start being themselves," the architect went on. "Dominique learned that her lesbianism—or as she prefers, her bisexuality—was not such a terrible thing. She gained support and comfort. Without that encouragement, she could have lived a lie for the rest of her life." Bisexuality, he said sternly, was inauthentic. "Gay people play the straight game as a smoke screen. Men do it. Women do it, too. Dominique's erotic energies were totally focused on women." The rest was performance, Otto Thompson believed.

He spoke of his former wife with emotion and chagrin. "By the time we met, she had already acquired a tremendous hostility toward the whole male sex." An undercurrent of her experience for twenty years, it finally had to erupt, he explained. "Dominique carried with her from her earliest childhood in Brazil a great resentment of her father's freedom and her mother's sequestered life. That animosity lasted a lifetime. She was jealous of men and always full of distrust."

Yet her female conflicts seemed to confirm, for him, some principle of male order. He told a turbulent story with almost unnatural calm. "During her first marriage, to a Hollywood physician, Dominique was already trying to deny her lesbianism. She had numerous flirtations, numerous affairs—not only with me. She slept with all the celebrities from here to Beverly Hills, including several of her husband's patients. In fact, she was considered the raciest thing in town." The architect's tone was as chaste as if he were discussing the taking of clerical vows. "But all that time—and all during her subsequent marriage to me—she was closeted with her female lover. On our seventh anniversary, she came to my office and confessed, 'This is where I am.' Dominique didn't want a divorce. But sexually, she was pretty much through with men. I admired her . . . courage," said Thompson. It might have been the kind of courage denied him.

"At first I became distraught. The truth burst in on me like a white sulphur bomb over a mine field, as you see it the moment before it strikes, exposing enemy installations. Dominique's lover was her best friend. Two artists, they started a studio downtown on the pretext that 'we have our work together.' Weekends, they played the game with their respective husbands. Oh, there had been some catty cocktail gossip about the life they shared, but it was always my nature to be naïve."

Otto Thompson tapped his temple with two fingers—sign

language for "lunatic." But leaving Dominique, although he loved her, testified to his respect for the heterosexual life. He valued *dominus* as the male ideal as fiercely as some men, whom wealth eludes, value money. Divorcing her seemed to satisfy his sense of sexual decorum.

"Nevertheless, I can understand lesbianism," he admitted. "The delicacy and sensitivity and depth of feeling between women—it's very beautiful, even though it may exile men." Then Thompson's tone changed. "But I don't understand male homosexuality," he said harshly. He recoiled, not from the inversion itself, but from the brand of maleness inherent in it. "The responses men ask for from each other are coarse. They're brutal and callous in sex. They're brought up to be tough and aggressive and demanding. But women . . . it's easy to see how they fall in love with each other. They can be yielding, warm, enticing. In analogous circumstances, men can only be . . . hard."

So, wounded or not, he cleaved to women—with some faint hope of making what he called "a sound emotional connection." Yet the two to whom he now turned held, for him, the seeds of disappointment. "One's a hooker and one's a Ph.D. in philosophy." The architect smiled his disarming smile. Neither of them was in the business of making sound connections.

"Marie, the hooker, is a remarkable person. She comes to town from somewhere in Tennessee to do her stint. She's a freaky kind of girl for a prostitute. I've never seen such a hard worker. Checks into a motel in town and stays there twenty-four hours a day, waiting for calls. But I like her very much. Although she's my intellectual inferior, she's a direct and honest person. We've got a decent, strange relationship going—no conniving, nothing to conceal. And it's not based on sex." Little by little, he was purging himself of fragments of the truth. "I take Marie out to dinner when she's around. I want to divert her from that rigorous motel existence," he said in a fatherly tone.

"But I may be in love with Leona." His intellectual equal, the Ph.D., enlisted his deeper emotions. "When I begin writing poetry, that's a sign." The poem he wrote, "To a Middle-aged Feminist," was rejected by several magazines—but not by Leona, who copied it out in calligraphy and hung it on her wall. "She's a woman of great charm, with an incredible kind of beauty and an overwhelming need for independence, who's also been divorced.

"The unshared life is not worth living," the architect mused. "But I've been badly burned. I'm timid, nervous, wary of getting into one more heavy situation destined to collapse. And I can't crack Leona's privacy. That worries me." Then he added, as an afterthought: "Besides, neither of us wants very much to be intimate. So I'm caught between the Scylla and Charybdis of invading her privacy and finding ways to be warm to her . . . other than in sex."

Otto Thompson was the victim of an intolerable dilemma: the sexual encounter with men seemed too brutalizing to endure, but although he admired women, he could not physically love them. "I would like the touch of Leona's head on my shoulder to mean as much as sixteen orgasms. The touching and holding is so important. So is the honesty. Sex does not have to be the cement that keeps two people together," he declared. "Women used to be wives, mothers, sex objects. Now they're fantastic companions. That's better."

He leaned into the subject of the transformed woman. "We can expect no more servile behavior from her now, either as a wife or a colleague, so we've got to tune in on her other qualities. Maybe we can become the recipients of a kind of grace that she'll give to men when it's *not* demanded, when sex is *not* the issue."

Like other visionaries who could see beyond the gender chasm, he imagined a stronger, finer human race. "We can forget the body thing. We can refuse to play the male and female roles assigned to us. That's why I welcomed the feminist movement. Right from the start, I knew that someday women would make it possible for me to say, 'This is what I'm about!' " It was astounding, the numbers of men who were depending on liberated women to liberate them.

The architect thought for a moment. "But of course they've always been less vulnerable. They could always fake the sexual thing. There's no way you can fake an erection. You're nailed to the cross—a position of extreme vulnerability. Nailed to the cross!" he breathed. Then he presented what seemed to him the ultimate paradox. "When women were still just women to me—wives, mothers, sex objects—I thought impotence was a disease of sick old men. But I have learned: It's no disease. It's a kind of involuntary . . . resistance. Something's expected that you can't put out. There's no vibes left. It's just not there."

The architect sighed. "It shouldn't matter, really. Still, you feel you're not a man's man. You lie to your male friends compulsively about your sexual conquests. Everybody bullshits everybody else. But you can't lie to women, can you? So lately I've been saying to Leona, 'I'm too tired to play these little failsafe games. All I want to do is go to bed with you. I don't want to make love. I just want to lie down with you and hold on tight. I hope you'll understand.' " Thompson's eyes had grown stormy now, like gray plains on which showers would soon break.

"Men with men may be freer in all sorts of ways, but they cannot be frail with each other. Men with frailties," the architect said, "need women in their lives."

Harrison Blum, a burly, tough-talking union organizer in Colorado, admitted no frailties. He flaunted the imposing physique and the crude tattoos of a bouncer in a Denver bar. Everything about him asserted invulnerability. In his checkered past, he had sprung open jails with the aplomb of a Houdini. His tattoos were souvenirs of escapades on several continents, any one of which could have annihilated an ordinary man. His favorite game was "doing the dozens" with his favorite friend, "a great, tough black lady. I say to her, 'I balled your mother last night. She was a lousy lay.' Or 'Those coons don't swim because they can't float.' She says to me, 'Jew boy, I won't take such shit from you!'" His rowdy laughter, which was frequent and infectious, almost made the walls shake. He seemed a man designed by nature to dispel whatever remnants of the "pansy-fag-fairy" stereotype of homosexuality still lingered in the cultural air.

When Harrison Blum described his wife of twenty-five years, a civil-rights attorney, he seemed about to burst with uxorious enthusiasm—although he never spoke of love. "We're really good friends. She's an interesting person, she's funny, she's wicked; I dig her." Their marriage, he said, "began without subterfuge and continued in the same way. Shirley started out by telling me, 'I don't intend to cook, I don't want any children, and I don't belong to you.'"

He had taken his bride at her word. For nearly three decades they lived together rather like college roommates—each one following his own inclinations. Now and then, they relaxed long enough to play flamboyant pranks on one another. "I was teasing her unmercifully one night, prancing around stark naked," Blum remembered. "Finally Shirley said, 'Go down and buy bagels.'" They lived on the top floor of a renovated townhouse. "'Like this?' I teased her. 'Just like that,' she said. To call her bluff, I opened the door. She pushed me outside and down the stairs. I found myself out in the street, stark naked!" Stark naked seemed a gloriously defiant state to him. He laughed with such glee at the recollection it was impossible not to laugh with him.

He was delighted by Shirley Blum's audacity, even when it culminated in expelling him nude on the sidewalk. Both of them were bright, outrageous people who nurtured their outrageousness as if it were a hothouse plant. It confirmed their countercultural sense of superiority to expose, by their own spontaneity, the hollow propriety of others.

They did not miss having a family, perhaps because they

themselves had never quite grown up. Blum saw his wife as an adored child as well as his female alter ego. These two roles were not mutually exclusive. After all, at more than fifty, was he not father to the mischievous little boy who still lived within him?

Like Thompson with his Dominique, Blum could hardly stop talking about his Shirley. "She worked as a secretary until she was thirty-five. Then one night she came home, threw her stenographer's pad on the floor, and announced, 'I will never take shorthand again.' Long before it was the fashion, that pad had become a symbol of degradation to my wife. Eventually, she wangled her way into law school. When she graduated, she was the only woman in her class. It was a tough role, but Shirley's a tough woman. She worked it out brilliantly. Today, anyone who gets busted around here calls her."

Anecdotes about the two most fascinating characters he had ever known poured out of him. Like perennial rebellious adolescents, they were still horsing around—and loving it. Surely they must have been soulmates, one thought. "We were at a dinner dance in Aspen with a lot of very posh people." Blum dropped some political and theatrical names. "We got stoned before we went. We knew it was going to be a long evening." One of the most posh of the party people asked his wife, "as if Shirley had committed a felony, 'Is it true that you've been married twenty-five years to just one person? How can you defend that? What's your explanation?' Shirley was dancing. She didn't miss a beat. 'I've always fucked a lot of other guys,' she said. 'That's how we stay married.'" It was the first hint he gave that, if they were soulmates, that was virtually all they were.

Harrison Blum stopped laughing. "What goes on in men's heads today is pretty sad," he said. "Would you believe that all evening, that whole Aspen crowd was asking, 'Is it really true what your wife said, about you and her?'" Worse than anything, he vowed, he hated hypocrisy. "Sure it was really true about us . . . and them . . . and everybody else at the party. But nobody said so out loud."

The story of the Aspen dinner party traveled as far as Princeton, New Jersey. There, months later, Blum met a friend "who was in Princeton just to sleep with his mistress, a staff psychologist at one of those preppy boarding schools. But he grabbed me by the sleeve. 'Harrison, what's this that I heard about Shirley freaking out in Aspen? Did she really say that the reason you stayed married so long was that she had fucked around all her life?' " Blum allowed that Shirley had. The fellow looked stricken. "Well, even if she said it, she didn't *mean* it, did she, Harrison?" he begged. It was a weakness of American men, Blum believed, to refuse to acknowledge what was true, if the truth contradicted the cultural lie.

Now he diverted the conversation from weak men to strong women. He seemed to attract a special breed of fearless female, the way pratfall artists attract banana peels. Harrison Blum spoke of his "tough, hard-nosed secretary, openly hostile to guys. If I holler at her, she hollers right back." These hollering matches, verifying mutual emancipation, were one way to act out the new social equality. Then he told of another woman who had helped him and a male collaborator write a book. "Her research became invaluable. She had worked very hard with us, all the way through, up to the tedium of reading the galleys. One night, when the three of us were checking proofs, I said, 'Cecile, how about getting me the file?' I wanted to validate some fact or other. She blew. 'Fuck you. I'm not your nigger slave!' she screamed." He recalled that with warm approval. Women who screamed at men, by seeming to affirm their own existence, soothed his social conscience.

"Cecile let us have it. 'You fucks!' she screamed. 'I just made up my mind. I don't want that fucking mention in your fucking preface! I want to share the byline with you. I damn well deserve it.' At last we realized she was right. We *had* patronized her. We *had* exploited her. So instead of settling for that measly credit, she wound up sharing the byline."

His admiration of such strong-arm female tactics was effusive. "There's no way for women to get what they want *but* by yelling and fighting and clawing," he declared, with a host of other men. "When you're married to a person like Shirley, you learn to take the whole package. She's mean, nasty, demanding, powerful. But she's also very supportive of me. Shirley upholds my right to act on my own beliefs. You can't draw a sharp line between what you want of a dynamite woman like that and what you don't want . . . between what's admirable and what's abrasive. You live with the defects of her virtues."

But how had he learned to live with his wife's lifelong stream of lovers? Blum was more comfortable offering diverting anecdotes than answering direct questions. "In the beginning, there was some jealousy on both our parts," he admitted after a while. "But we suppressed it, because our rules didn't allow for jealousy. We were always on the level with each other. I was aware of her affairs . . . and she was aware of mine." Wed to a tough woman who took lovers, did not cook, did not bear children, and did not belong to him, this seemed a more than equitable arrangement. But one could wonder: what made it a marriage?

"Shirley frightened off a lot of men because she let them know I knew about them. I wasn't cuckolded; I never felt that way. But they sometimes got scared. After all, I look like a bruiser. And on political grounds, I have been known to take guys apart." As for the sex they sometimes shared together: "Three or four in bed is best," he said with an even smile. "And naturally, I like to ball the same guys Shirley balls. That goes with the scene. If it turns me on so much to watch *her* do it with him, why wouldn't I be intrigued with the notion of balling him myself?"

Harrison Blum remembered their first such partners as other men might remember their first romance. "It was a couple with two sons. The boys are grown up now—one's straight, one isn't. Our relationship used to worry their father, long ago." He might have been speaking of the quaint inhibitions of a bygone time. " 'What if the kids wake up and find you in bed with their mama—or with me?' Well, they did wake up. But it was no disaster. They just got used to a certain way of life. We could all be in bed together, balling, with both kids around, and they thought nothing of it. They accepted it as perfectly natural." Or so Blum preferred to believe.

But recently, he said, Shirley herself had begun to reevaluate the sexual patterns of a lifetime. She wanted to revise the marital agreement that had served them so well for so many years. " 'Let's change the rules,' she suggested. 'From now on, whatever you're doing, if I'm not there, I don't want to know.'

"When Shirley was younger, she used to take my gay life with a grain of salt," he said. "If a man called me, she would say, 'It's your number-two wife, or your number-three wife, on the telephone.' " He professed not to understand why his gay life should aggravate Shirley now, precisely at the moment when history was catching up with them; when "bisexuality" was becoming not only acceptable but practically a mark of status. He blamed it on the fact that she was growing older.

Then he added one more detail. "Not long ago, I had an intense emotional affair," he said. "Shirley and I came close to breaking up, but we couldn't throw away all those years. For the first time in my life, I went to see a shrink." He blew out his breath in a long whoosh, like smoke from a cigarette. "But changing the rules? It's too late. All our lives, we have never been furtive. We have never lied to each other and said, 'I'm going to be in on a late business meeting' when we were really getting into someone's bed. So how could I start lying now?"

However, he could have been lying to himself. With all his contempt for repression, he might have been repressing some visceral animosity toward this tough woman, his wife, whom—intellectually—he so admired. Harrison Blum's persona was devised to reflect a masterful man. *Dominus* was important to him; he had learned to mimic it like a virtuoso actor. So perhaps, less consciously, was sexual revenge.

As for Blum himself, he dealt with his demons (which he did

not regard as such) in his own confident way. "Initially, it takes
a long leap for a man to get past the traditional fears of homosexuality. But once you handle that stuff, you've got it made,"
he said. For him, the subject was no longer fraught with anxiety, if it had ever been.

"Why I can remember the first time I ever had a cock in my
mouth. I marveled about how soft it was even when it was
hard." He smiled and sighed, "Let's say men are my hobby," he
suggested. Were women, then, his chore? Harrison Blum's wide
smile persisted.

15 | Tunnel's End

"So many prominent people now seem to be using bisexuality as a cover for homosexuality," Gore Vidal was informed during a conversation reported in *The Advocate*, a leading gay journal. " 'Oh,' they say, 'I'm bi, isn't that trendy, isn't that clever, love me a little bit more, fans!' Like this writer friend of mine who always bills himself as bi. So you ask him when he last went to bed with a woman and the answer is 1958."

"That's quite recent," Gore Vidal replied.

But for those suffering its pangs, the is-he-or-isn't-he? crisis was often more desperate than droll. Men who dropped the mask of bisexuality were almost always less anguished than those who tried to live double lives. Attempting to straddle both worlds, they were regarded suspiciously not only by much of straight society but by gay society as well. "The one thing I hate is bisexual homosexuals," declared the writer Truman Capote. "I say I'm a homosexual who has had heterosexual experiences. If I were coming down on one side or the other, I would not be one of those marvelous bisexual homosexuals."

"The Anglo-Saxon mind likes to make everything either/or," Vidal had observed. "Everybody must wear his badge and not go moonlighting." This was, of course, quite true. It was also true that up-front homosexuals who did not "swing both ways" on that tricky pendulum were also easier for heterosexual society to accept—or to choose not to accept. So although "coming out" might be at first more agonizing, in the end it could be more comfortable than coming halfway out.

"I had a lot of problems dealing with what society expected, what my family expected . . . and I found myself pushed into a role that just wasn't me," said Leonard Andres, not yet thirty, who had recently given up the masquerade. "I got married when I was twenty years old to a woman who knew I was gay. She was going to change me. It took just one good lay and I'd be all right." He smiled a sadder-but-wiser smile. "My marriage was a mistake. Not because I couldn't and didn't and do still feel . . . something . . . for this woman." But whatever the exact nature of his feelings, they were not husbandly, he said. "It wasn't an emotional situation I could tolerate. It ended in divorce."

Discarding heterosexual drag, however, did not instantly produce inner serenity. Gays required more than self-acceptance to feel at ease in society. Their world, insufficient unto itself, had to be accepted and assimilated by the larger world—not merely tolerated on one hand or idealized on the other. Despite the permissive moral climate of the seventies, this had not yet happened. Leonard Andres, like other homosexuals, was worried by the underlying male standards (in his vocabulary, stereotypes) that prevailed. "You have to have a big penis, be over six feet tall, put the make on every broad you meet, really be aggressive toward other men . . ." He caressed his full dark beard. "Well, I reject the idea that if I gently stroke a brother's hair, I become somehow less a man; that if I touch a man between waist and knee, I'm sick. Oh, a handshake in the pool parlor's all right, or a pat on the ass on the football field. Or occasionally we're allowed to hug a friend at a funeral. But that's it, brother." He gave a wry twist to the word. "So I have pushed my love underground into dimly lit bars and the corners of public parks and subway-station toilets. Sex is important to me. But it has become too important. My whole life is structured around my homosexuality . . ."

According to him, Americans were still punishing those outside the mainstream as pariahs—and it was unfair, not only to them. "We cannot leave homosexuals in the old heroic-martyr position. That moment has passed," one man said, and more agreed. But in this society, so given to extremes, it had brought another moment in its wake. Many of those who had stopped vilifying homosexuality were glorifying it now, not as martyrdom, or as "trendy" and "clever," but as the pinnacle of the erotic life. It was perhaps no coincidence that they were glorifying masturbation too.

This became difficult to overlook at various conferences on "male sexuality," one of which took place in a huge university hospital auditorium in Missouri. The audience was predominantly medical students, mostly male. Long before the talks began, the SRO sign went up. In the second balcony, the overflow crowd was sprawled on the steps. Without preliminaries, one of the panelists—among the country's most outspoken authorities on human sexuality—plunged into the evening's main preoccupation. "Boys discover right away that, despite the admonitions of their gym teachers, they don't get TB or warts from masturbation," he remarked. Indeed, he extolled that act once known as the solitary vice as others extol fitness regimes. In his view (which he shared with other social scientists in the new sex corps), it was totally benign; on the level of sensation, more pleasurable as well as more hassle-free than any other sexual activity.

"Among the married, college-educated male population, masturbation is a significant source of sexual outlet for more than one third of men all their lives. But the other two thirds are engaging in the same behavior, merely substituting a partner's available vagina for their own hands," he maintained. "The real source of sexual arousal is not the interpersonal dynamic between husband and wife but simple physical stimulation."

As he saw it, heterosexual intercourse was something like an awkward substitute for masturbation . . . and masturbation the rehearsal for homosexual encounter. Indeed, the sexologist implied, really satisfying sexual union was all but impossible between two people of opposite sexes, so alienated were they from each other's body, each other's psyche, each other's needs.

From the onset of puberty, males learned to respond to sexual fantasy, but not to sexual women, he went on. To the hassle-free masturbatory release, add the glamour of self-fulfilling erotic daydreams. "All through adolescence, boys are jacking off at a very high rate. And always, in his masturbatory fantasies, the male plays God. In his sexual scripts, which he writes for all the actors, the woman never does anything he doesn't want her to do." In this failure-proof paradise of his own creation, real, live women, with their quirks, kinks, crochets, were only an intrusion. Coming of age needing only to please himself, the onerous obligation of pleasing the other—especially if the other was a female—unnerved him.

And when at last he cranked up the courage (if he did) to wrestle the monster, heterosexuality, it was not because of true erotic impulse, but rather to impress his male peers. The approval of *men* was what he sought, the sexologist said. "Ask anyone whether he would prefer to spend a night in secret with the world's reigning sex goddess or to have his friends believe that's what he's doing without really doing it . . ." A thrill of recognition vibrated through the audience. The rest of his thought was drowned in a sea of applause.

"Women like to screw, they like body trips. Men like head trips," he asserted, stressing the mutual incompatibility of male and female. "When she gets high on screwing, he drops out, demoralized by her constant criticism and her unwillingness to fantasize along with him." Yet his most potent fantasies embarrassed him. If I told her what I'd really like to pretend I'm doing, she'd call the booby hatch, he thinks, alarmed by his own homosexual imaginings.

When he dropped out on women, it was usually only a matter of time until he dropped in on the gay community. "Here, the sexual component is uncorrupted by reconditioning," the sexologist told his audience. "It is uncorrupted by the necessity to adapt to somebody else—a female—whose patterns of socialization are fundamentally different from yours." He construed the primal act itself as unnatural and deficient, except in its procreative function. Heterosexuality, not homosexuality, was "queer." It could make one wonder—briefly—whether coitus itself might not be nature's dirty joke.

Not only the theory was startling. The apparently uncritical acceptance of it by this small army of physicians-in-waiting was even more so. But in a world where *dominus* was in disarray, and more and more men were declining (or euphemistically redefining) the acts and responsibilities of manhood, did it all make perfect sense?

In the new gospel now taking shape, the homosexual—because "'unreconditioned,'" so to speak—was more authentically erotic and more erotically active than other men. He was also more generous. "There is a profoundly higher rate of sexual activity than occurs among heterosexuals," the social scientist said. "The homosexual is not as committed to, or as gratified by, the receiving of pleasure as to the giving of it. He can go to the baths and blow fourteen guys in two hours, while our friendly horny heterosexual is up in his hotel room, safely masturbating with a copy of a sex magazine." It was clear in this cosmology who was the better man. The homosexual was less "goal-oriented," less selfish, less committed to orgasm, and less demanding than the heterosexual. "God knows how many boys get picked up hitchhiking, and blown," the guest speaker mused.

He returned to step 1 in the sexual drama. "Do you cheat your body when you ejaculate into a Kleenex? Do you cheat anybody? Will you be less available for others?" These rhetorical questions needed no response from him. "We've got to get over the attitude that the sex you spend on Kleenex, you don't have left to spend elsewhere. The Kinsey report said, 'The more you spend, the more you have.' Those who masturbate become much more sexual and much more sensually sensitive. Their total rates don't go down, they go up. The more men conceive of themselves as erotic actors in *any* contact or context, the more erotic they're really going to be."

Now he took up the special problems of those fixated on the

heterosexual life. "Men get married and go into boredom," the expert counseled the medical students. "They need other outlets, new encounters, not just the wife. They too ought to translate some of their fantasies into reality and get beyond that into deeper emotional ability. More is more," he pointed out.

These long thoughts provoked little debate among the doctors-to-be, only many earnest questions. "Will I jeopardize my marriage if I extend my repertoire of gratification?" one medical student asked. "It's harder to extend your repertoire if you're straight than if you're gay" was the reply. "Away on a business trip, instead of having extramarital encounters, your average husband just goes back to his hotel room with a copy of that picture magazine and jacks off without worrying about his wife and kids walking in."

"In the gay world, does friendship survive the sexual affair?" another medical student asked. "Yes! Gays fuck first and become friends later" was the reply. "In the straight world, that is painfully reversed. You have to become friends first. Then the sexual activity threatens the structure of the rest of the relationship." Nobody laughed.

It was not only radical men but also radical women who now viewed heterosexual behavior as simplistic and narrow, a mere cultural "adaptation" of the natural homosexual impulse. The sexually radical female agreed. "The very naturalness of lesbianism (and homosexuality) is exactly the cause of strong social and legal rules against it," said *The Hite Report*, a self-styled "new cultural interpretation of female sexuality." "The basing of our social system on gender difference, biological reproductive function, is barbaric . . . It must be clear by now that female sexuality is physically 'pansexual,'" Shere Hite wrote, ". . . certainly not something that is directed at any one type of physical organ to be found in nature. From the point of view of physical pleasure, we are free to relate to all creatures of the planet, according to their individual meaning for us, rather than their specific classifications or gender. Of course it goes without saying that as we move toward a more equitable view of life, the right to love other women will be taken for granted." On that view, phallus-inclined women (whom one feminist called "man junkies") were arrested, if not retarded, in their sexual behavior.

Masturbation was no less popular among the female "pansexualists" than among the male. At one for-women-only workshop (they were scattered around the country now, a veritable growth industry, functioning in hospitals and sex-therapy clinics, as well as under private auspices), an *aficionado* of this newest group activity called it "a beautiful trip . . . in a sex-positive environment! I'm headed for Macy's window with my vibrator!" she whooped. Her manic air was not unusual in such gatherings. Many of these masturbating women were almost as heady as if they had just discovered the wheel—rather than simply their own genitalia. It was, in their favorite word, freeing. At least, it could free them from men. But they also viewed masturbation politically, as yet another aspect of equal opportunity. After centuries of deprivation, why should the all-time preferred male sexual activity still be prohibited to them?

Men spoke, only half jokingly, of "the small-penis liberation." Women spoke of liberation from "cunt inferiority." "At twelve years old, most girls think they're deformed. I had those inner lips that are extended," the *aficionado* confessed. "One was longer than the other. 'It's from playing with myself,' I thought. Well, I was gonna do it just one more time to even things up!" Her group of disciples was regaled by this confession. Later on in life, she told them, she met another woman, similarly afflicted. "Oh, you've got the same kind of cunt!" she cried. Old anxieties relieved, they embraced like long-lost sisters.

But now there were less chancy methods of putting such anatomical anxieties to rest. Nude demonstrations of masturbatory techniques took place routinely in many of the workshops. Close-up color slides of women in the act of showing "three or four different styles" of do-it-yourself sex were sometimes displayed for study. "For years, you could photograph couples making love, but no one would come in and jerk off. That was private, sneaky, naughty," the *aficionado* explained. One breakthrough paved the way for the next. "The cunt slides were invaluable to women. The next trip is orgasm. Already, four of us have masturbated to orgasm in front of the camera." There were many hours already on videotape, she revealed. "You can watch yourself on the monitor," she exulted. "I used to fantasize doing it for pictures. Now I need a new fantasy. I fantasize money, power, Washington, politics!" One could imagine her sitting on the Supreme Court eventually—hands busy underneath her voluminous black robe.

Meanwhile, in the for-women-only workshop, students graduated from techniques of masturbation to techniques of mutual massage. For some, it was the transition to their first lesbian experience.

The Hite Report also ennobled autoeroticism, opening with a long section in praise of masturbation: "It seems to have so much to recommend it—easy and intense orgasms, an unending source of pleasure."

The report on heterosexual intercourse was, predictably, disenchanted. "I am rather hung up when it comes to orgasms. Because I never have them during intercourse I feel deeply ashamed and inferior . . ." "I went along for thirty-four years carrying the burden of not having vaginal orgasms . . ." "Is it uncommon not to have orgasm while you are having sexual intercourse?" "At thirty, and having screwed for over fifteen years, and still not able to come, I'm fed up . . ."

Even women married to men whom they classed as "good lovers" discounted the penis as an all but irrelevant organ. "My husband is the best lover I ever had, and I hope we have sex till we're a hundred and ten years old! I have orgasms from masturbation and clitoral stimulation *only*. I feel very little, and rarely, from penis stimulation, and I've *never* had an orgasm from penis stimulation." Women who did come to orgasm "with" male partners almost always reported that they did so through clitoral contact.

The Hite Report's diagrammatic drawing of the clitoris was virtually indistinguishable from an erect penis, with the bulbous glands on each side resembling the testes. The accompanying text read, "In short, the only real difference between men's and women's erections is that men's are on the outside of their bodies, while women's are on the inside. Think of your clitoris as just the *tip* of your 'penis . . .'" female readers were advised. "Or think of a penis as just the externalization of a woman's interior bulbs and clitoral network." The implicit statement was unmistakable. No woman in her right mind could have penis envy when she had one of her own, tiny but perfectly functioning, and only as inaccessible as her inhibitions made it.

So the "hidden sexuality" of the female was independent, solitary, and/or lesbian. Lesbians, like male homosexuals, simply extended the techniques of masturbation to same-sex coupling. "She's soft and gentle, knowing exactly how to rub my clit and what pressure to use—taking as long as we want and coming—coming—coming!" "Lovemaking with a woman is always more variable than with a man, and the physical actions are more mutual. While the same places are kissed and touched as with a man, the whole feeling is heightened for me when the lover is a woman." "Finally now, with my present female lover of two months, I have orgasms!"

Society has dishonored masturbation and homosexuality, while "legitimizing" intercourse with partners of the other sex, for essentially political (i.e., reproductive and patriarchal) purposes, *The Hite Report* assumed. From the point of view of female sexual pleasure, the penis was little better than a vestigial organ; and the vagina not much more efficient. Once more, erotic love between a man and a woman was implicitly devalued as the true opiate of the masses.

But more deleterious than the propaganda itself was the resistance it provoked within conventional society, further victimizing those whom it intended to set free. Not gay liberation but gay imperialism rankled, as a philosopher said. At one major social-science conference, presumably devoted to marriage and the family, big red GAY LOVE IS THE ONLY KIND buttons sprouted like carnations in countless lapels. Obviously, heterosexuals (who wore no buttons because they had no "cause") could not concur with this sentiment. Yet many might comprehend the human right of homosexuals to create "marriages" and "families" on their own terms.

A young man with long flaxen bangs and a close-cropped beard revealed his frustration in trying to become a foster parent. "Homosexuals aren't supposed to love or want children," he said. "Why not? We are very nurturing people. Why should we be deprived of the experience of parenthood? Why should gay adolescents who need sympathetic-like environments be tormented by trying to survive in a heterosexual household where they are not understood and which they cannot emotionally understand?" The right to adopt children, he said, was the homosexual's last frontier.

Gay liberation was not an exclusively American phenomenon. Just as no major country in Western Europe was without its feminist movement, none was without its beginning crusade for homosexual equality. And the Europeans were sometimes more openly militant than their American counterparts; more outspoken in their commitment to revolutionary change. "The oppression of gay people starts in the most basic unit of society, the family," said the manifesto of London's gay-liberation front. ". . . consisting of the man in charge, a slave as his wife, and their children, on whom they force themselves as the ideal models. The very form of the family works against homosexuality . . . How many of us have been pressured into marriage, sent to psychiatrists, frightened into sexual inertia, ostracized, banned, emotionally destroyed—all by our parents?"

Beside the American slogan "Gay love is the only kind," the Englishman put "Gay shows the way." "We are already more advanced than straight people. We are already outside the family and we have already, in part at least, rejected the 'masculine' and 'feminine' role society has designed for us," a spokesperson said.

"The ultimate success of all forms of oppression is our self-oppression," London's manifesto proclaimed. "Self-oppression is when the gay person has adopted and internalized straight people's definition of what is good and bad . . . Self-oppression is the dolly lesbian who says, 'I can't stand those butch types who look like truck drivers'; the virile gay man who shakes his head at the thought of 'those pathetic queens.' This is self-oppression because it's just another way of saying, 'I'm a nice normal gay, just like an attractive heterosexual.' "

In *Fuori* (translated *Come Out*), Italy's gay-liberation newspaper, homosexuals situated themselves to the left of the left. They vowed "to live our homosexuality fully, not giving a damn for the niceties of bourgeois society . . . to tear down the myth of the sacrilegiousness of the asshole," a myth, it was said, developed among the proletariat. "We are a minority and therefore have revolutionary potential. To make revolution, you have to have one or more antagonists; if they don't exist, you have to create them." High up on *Fuori*'s list of antagonists were certain other homosexuals: "those who camouflage themselves and don't come out."

In France, a participant reported on the burgeoning movement of "revolutionary effeminism: We are what is feared most: effeminists. Men who are struggling to become unmanly, men who oppose the hierarchy and ideology of a masculine fascism that requires domination of one person by another, of one sex, race, or class by another. We will become gentle but strong faggots who will fight their oppression in militant ways, faggots who are vulnerable to each other, able to cry but not passive or paralyzed in our struggle to change."

A self-confident society in which roles were generally steady, identities firmly established, and sexual values clear would not need to fear effeminism or oppress it, outlaw any peaceful way of life or private mode of coupling. Men who felt trapped by masculinity surely deserved a place within their own culture for which they did not have to fight. Those "gentle but strong faggots, struggling to become unmanly," should not feel obliged to remake the world in order to live in it. When being gay was divested of the glamour of the illicit and the drama of the heroic, when it was no longer an excuse for exhibitionism or a spark for revolution, they might even find the nature of their struggle transformed. But while the sexual structure was in shambles and *dominus* with it, too many felt too imperiled. The open society, sustaining diversity (and even perversity), had to remain only a dream.

16 | "Dominus" in Exile: The World without Eros

Maybe, as the old mythologers believed, the gods still dominate man and can forewarn him of his destiny. Two thousand years ago, Ovid, in his *Metamorphoses*, told how they doomed Hermaphroditus to live as half a man, because he surrendered his male strength without a struggle. Apuleius, in *The Golden Ass*, told another cautionary tale—this one, of woman's faithlessness.

Psyche, the incarnation of the human soul, loved Eros as she loved herself. But she was forbidden by the god even to learn who he was, much less to try to become like him. She agreed to know him "only by touch and hearing." But her jealous sisters betrayed her. "They are enemies of your own sex and blood," Eros cautioned his beloved Psyche—in vain. She could hear only her sisters' warnings: "The husband who comes secretly gliding into your bed at night is an enormous snake," they whispered, foreshadowing by millennia Freud's intuition about unconscious association. "Plunge the knife down with all your strength at the nape of the creature's neck and cut off his head."

But how could any woman save herself by murdering the god of love? In the moment before slaughtering (or gelding) him, Psyche "uncovered the lamp and let its light shine on the bed." Not a snake, but Eros himself lay there. She saw her error too late. Burned by oil from his own lamp but wounded deeper yet by Psyche's distrust, Eros flew away to Mount Olympus.

In ancient mythology, their romance had a happy ending. After wandering day and night, searching everywhere for her lost husband, remorseful Psyche begged mercy of the gods for her lack of faith in love. Then Eros intervened in her behalf and she was welcomed on Olympus.

But in present-day America, from which it sometimes seemed too that Eros had vanished, such a reunion was uncertain. Today's Psyche also often disowned and distrusted he whom she might better have cherished. And in Eros' absence, the lament of Apuleius echoed down the centuries: "The whole system of human love is in such complete disorder that it is now considered disgusting for anyone to show even natural affection."

So the breach between men and women widened. For some, sexual union itself degenerated into a struggle almost as ludicrous as it was crude. "The tyranny of the female orgasm is really going to drive male heterosexuality to the wall," Gore Vidal predicted, in language that would have robbed the act of love of its last vestiges of grandeur—if it had not been already stolen blind. "Now it's, 'Herman, are you giving me the big O., are you a considerate person, Herman?' 'Well, Miriam, it has been two hours now, I am still sawing away trying to give you the big O.' 'But if you were a warm and mature person, Herman, I would have had the Big O. by now.' This dialogue is heard every night in the suburbs of America," Gore Vidal reported, as authoritatively as if he had hidden tape recorders under twenty million beds. "And one day Herman is just going to say, 'Oh, shit. Here—take this vibrator and I'll see you later.' "

Unsanctified by Eros, sex became an endurance contest that mortally endangered every man, but that almost none could win. "Lots of male heart attacks are coming out of this too," Vidal said. "Men live under great tensions in the kind of greedy society that most of them have to work in, and now they also have to be good at sex and go on and on and on. I can see how a lot of them just quit the game and go with each other or stay alone."

"Quitting the game" was officially sanctioned in high places.

"Some of us are feeling the need to pull back from relating to women," a social psychologist, esteemed among his colleagues, said. "And the culture is beginning to accept such moratoriums as legitimate." (Moratorium: temporary cessation of an activity considered hostile or dangerous.)

One man, engaged in such a learning process, noted, "In recent years, I have learned to listen to my penis much more and it works out much better. More and more often, my penis says no." Even heterosexual men whose penises were still saying yes sometimes required special circumstances. Many discharged their confused and alienated sexual impulses by making American prostitution a bigger business than ever. In the borough of Manhattan alone, it was conservatively estimated as a multi-million-dollar industry. But the male experience was fundamentally selfish and solitary, the antithesis of union. The "pleasure and massage spas" were masturbation parlors, specializing in hand-jobs, blow-jobs, all the last resorts of men unable, or unwilling, to make love to women—although not yet ready to give up the fleeting illusion of it. The hard-core porn films, the sex magazines, and even some of the sex manuals were all tried-and-true-blue masturbatory accessories for the impotent, the incompetent, and the disaffected. It was not for nothing that *Penthouse, Playboy, Oui,* and *Hustler* were called "stroke books" within the publishing trade. For many female readers, *Viva* and *Playgirl,* those Janey-come-latelies to the newsstand, were probably stroke books too.

However, while humanly estranging, they still honored heterosexuality in some fragmented or symbolic or nostalgic way. But where Eros had fled and Narcissus reigned, often even the pretense of male-and-female connection was abandoned. Many masturbating women debunked the dildo as a piece of camp equipment, ludicrously out of date and inappropriate. At symposiums on human sexuality, all of which now seemed to begin and end with paeans to female masturbation, the new and better vibrators were never shaped like that anachronism of the erotic life, a penis. The phallus itself, once venerated as the first force of nature, was now—at most—a minor toy in the sexual playground of the avant-garde. The disparagement of the male became a political tactic. A man who got around in those circles described the favored "radical woman's" position for copulation: man on his back, legs flung up over his head.

In America's coffeehouses and on college campuses, a new genre of joke was born, aimed with malice toward men. "I don't want to say I got attached to my vibrator, but on Valentine's Day, I sent it two dozen roses," said one college-circuit female comedienne.

Men retaliated in predictable ways. When it was not entirely eliminated from their so-called sexual repertoire, "sport fucking" was the only kind some would dare. It was a game, a giggle, a tickle, a twitch, "no big deal." "Mind fucking" was the only kind some women talked about. "Eating dinner together is really more intimate," one young medical research assistant said. "It's not even sex these guys really want. The turn-on is the challenge itself, the strategy it takes to climb into my head, get into my bed, and get out again, emotionally untouched. They'll do that kind of mind fuck on you and then they'll disappear."

A divorced stockbroker in his middle forties made a counter-accusation. "Liberated women just experiment. They're looking for different kinds of thrills." Sex had become a form of gourmandizing "for most of the girls who still want it," he declared. "A Japanese on Monday, a black on Tuesday, a teenager on Wednesday, another girl on Thursday. If you fall in the wrong category at the wrong time, forget it. And Wasps like me are a dime a dozen. Not exotic enough for the current tastes. What's happening to women?" he asked, echoing scores of other men. "*They* used to be the ones with feeling."

A college professor of economics, married three times, described his own double vision. "In one way, I'm attracted to women who are intelligent, educated, and independent. In another way, I miss the warm, maternal thing, the feeling for romance and tenderness that none of my wives ever had." A buxom black woman passed, glossy-skinned and glossy-eyed, with her small daughter in tow. "I'd like to put my head between her breasts and just lie there for a while. White women aren't built that way any more, I don't mean just physically. If they were, they wouldn't have the time . . . or the inclination." His eyes followed the strong black figure holding the child's hand. "The tenderness of women was one of the few decent things left in the world. Now we've lost even that."

The young were no less victims of the moment than their fathers and mothers. On a TV "family" show, the erstwhile act of love was characterized as "what kids do to keep from getting acne." The studio audience rewarded that line with the biggest laugh of the evening. Many moviegoing adolescents witnessed the primal scene, or a reasonable facsimile, many times before even once engaging in it. They regarded intercourse, if not as a skin treatment, then as a minor escapade almost as cool as swinging from the back of a moving bus; or else as some kind of chore—a rigorous *rite de passage* that carried them beyond the gates of that adult world that they simultaneously envied, feared, and despised. Familiar only with "making out," how could they comprehend making love, except as a played-out idiom of their grandparents' time? All the fornicating pop portrayals of their formative years verified that love had little to do with it, with this sad and sorry tumbling-and-fumbling act that usually looked plain foolish on the wide screen when it did not look repulsive. Their own parents often added confirmation. "What's so sacred about a fuck?" one father responded to his adolescent son in response to a leading question.

Far from being sacred, it had come to seem demeaning to many men, when not dangerous or tedious or petty. Some felt that they could no longer burden their loved ones with the promptings of their lowest, least attractive natures. Instead, they opted for those hit-and-run episodes known as "quickies" or "one-night stands" (usually a euphemism for fifty minutes). Screwing strangers, always a popular daydream, was now a real-life pursuit of some social legitimacy. It located with icy precision where sex, abandoned by Eros, now stood in the hierarchy of human values.

Young husbands often claimed that they reserved what was most pure and noble in themselves (everything going on above the belly button) for the "caring" relationships in their lives. "Caring" was evolving into the direct antithesis of the sexual encounter. "What counts? Where you happen to put your cock on any given Saturday night? Or another kind of commitment?" an Eastern museum's administrative director asked friends of both sexes at a dinner party. Here as elsewhere, the consensus—both male and female—was all on the side of "the other kind" of commitment. The meeting of minds got all the gold stars. The meeting of bodies was viewed as an unmomentous, actually rather tacky occasion.

It was getting on to the moment when to screw your own wife just for the subjugating, domineering thrill of it would seem, well, tasteless—and uncaring. A Texas rancher, father of two children both under four years old, said, wrinkling his un-lined brow, "I wish prostitution were legalized in every state. Men need *somewhere* to go to get those kinds of needs met." Somewhere, but certainly not home. Many sensitive young husbands were apparently convinced that they could not bring "those needs" into their own bedrooms, inflicting their low-minded, exasperating horniness on those equals, those buddies, those *nouveaux* madonnas, their wives.

In the world without Eros, there sometimes seemed only an unsatisfactory choice between varieties of half-women: the madonna, whose high mind was everywhere else but on sex; the whore, whose mind was nowhere else (or so men often believed); and the Donna Juana, who would use them and abuse them, toy with them and trivialize them, as men once were said to have done with women. But the madonna's detachment was chilling, the whore's professionalism was ego-deflating, Donna Juana's voraciousness was unseemly—and the erotic sum was zero zero.

We have been overtaken by "the asexual revolution," philosopher William Barrett said. When love was over, or where it had never lived, carnal acts were the ultimate degradation. "The woman who buries / her head in his lap / swallowing the cock / down / letting his nest blind her / . . . / she feels her belly turn / wishes he'd hurry / but won't sit up till he's come / a woman like this/doesn't want to see where she's going," wrote Lyn Lifshun, whose book of "poems," sometimes unpoetic but ever unambiguous, was published by Shameless Hussy Press.

Yet it was always possible (although some feminists would be aghast) that woman's real peril might lay in wanting to see too clearly where she was going. A deathly objectivity could destroy her deeper vision. Even if her stomach did not turn, "swallowing the cock" without loving the man would stir up no more than small sensations and intimations of her own power.

Although it might not always boggle male understanding, such female detachment could often damage the male sexual drive. "*It scares the shit out of us*," journalist Ross Wetzsteon wrote, "that women are fully as capable as men of feeling a biological, impersonal sexuality, utterly autonomous, completely unconnected to their feelings about a specific man."

Some, apparently, were. "As we learn to love ourselves and stimulate ourselves," one Illinois woman said, "*we're* becomimg the people we once wanted to marry. Like we have fantastic jobs we really dig, we travel, we think interesting thoughts. We really get off on ourselves . . ."

She bristled with self-confidence—and received ideas. "We used to adjust to the male fantasy trip, to male demands in bed . . . and to male masturbation, which just gets transferred into the coital act with women. Now we're asking: What do men really want when they sleep with us? The answer is never just sex," she said, turning the tables somewhat contemptuously. "It's prestige, excitement, the first rush of getting it on with a new person. They want to forget their jobs. They're asking us to give them hope and nurturance, softness, even femininity." Her small, carved nostrils dilated with scorn. "Well, I don't want a man who demands from *me*, takes from *me*. I don't want somebody to drain me of my sexual energy, my time, and my emotions . . ."

Her pretty face was flushed with conviction. "We're on the demanding end now. And there's lots of stuff men have laid on us that we're in the process of examining again . . . like penis size doesn't make any difference." She sniffed. "It sure does! It makes a big difference. There's not just one way to have sex, just the old in-and-out. Penis size makes a difference in *how* it goes in and out, and where, and how successfully." She spoke, in the fashionable new way, of her labia and her clitoris, her vulva and her vagina. "Girth makes a difference, length makes a difference, but not always the kind of difference men believe. If he's smaller, it makes it easier for me to have oral sex with him, to perform freeing types of coital acts, and positions that are fun to try. If he's too big, it hurts. It's uncomfortable, genitally not satisfying. So it isn't necessarily incremental growth that equals success," she said, like a mathematics teacher talking about decimals and square roots.

"Men have a lot to learn from us. I'm not trying to put a performance-anxiety trip on anyone. But men just better get it together. They just better get to know our likes and dislikes. Or there will be a lot more performance-anxiety trips going on."

With Eros in exile, women of experience (and experience often started at age eleven or earlier) were compiling a crass new sexual inventory of their own. In the new folklore, "men with thick dicks fucked better and lasted longer." Scholarly surveys might not confirm it, but empirical evidence did. "It's probably psychological—like a person has more confidence in bigger muscles—but it's real. A small penis performs small feats," one woman said.

Item: the most painstaking and careful lovers cultivated that talent because, it often turned out, "they can hardly fuck at all. Cunt teasers—lots of foreplay, but no main event" was the consensus. Item: Men who felt the urge most keenly sometimes satisfied it just as quickly. These were the "ten-second, hair-trigger men" whose hot but brief passion left their partners frustrated and unfulfilled. Item: The "all-day fuckers" or "maintenance men," as they were called, were sometimes so supercool that, for all their staying power, they seemed almost bored by the act. And long-term erections notwithstanding, they sometimes bored women. "I'm not even sure he feels his own orgasms," one woman said about a man of such low (or no) affectivity. "I think he resents it because I feel mine more intensely. Now there's competition between us about even *that*." Item: Other men, whose emotion might be deeper and more complex, were frequently unable to express it with an adequately serviceable "hard-on." Not uncommonly, they undertook their amorous missions equipped with a veritable plumber's supply of tools and toys, of which the ubiquitous battery-operated vibrator was only one artifact. Some, likewise afflicted, became so adept at the substitute use of another appendage that certain women began to wonder whether they were not attending night classes in cunnilingus. After all, there were classes in everything else, including masturbation, weren't there?

These "cockswomen," self-educated connoisseurs of the male organ, were now painfully aware that nature could play pranks of all sorts on men of all ages. Some were also—more slowly—becoming aware that it was they who were really the butt of the joke in this gigantic comedy of errors. For so much knowledge might have made them wise, but it seldom made them happy. Instead of savoring the hoped-for pleasures of sexual liberation in this world without Eros, they were experiencing more than their own fair share of sexual dysfunction and disappointment. Female anorgasmia (a.k.a. frigidity) was at least as commonplace now as first-, second-, and third-degree male impotency.

"We have become the casualties of our own movement," more than one liberated woman said.

Because so many men were "quitting the game," either voluntarily or not, the new sexual mores produced a new and exasperating breed of Casanova. He seduced vulnerable women with dazzling tales of other women who had achieved not just multiple but *multi*-multiple orgasms in his bed. "Of course, you realize that you don't have to be satisfied any more with coming just two or three times," he promised. Lured into sampling his skills (which did not always include plain, old-fashioned intercourse), and almost always frustrated (because those who promised most usually delivered least), the unlucky lady was sternly chastised. It was she who was frigid, not he who was inept. Twenty or thirty satisfied clients, coming ten or twenty times apiece, had already proved his prowess.

But more than likely, he was just whistling in the dark. The truth of the matter was that "the unlimited orgasmic capacity of women . . . makes men all the more fearful for, in the face of such insatiable lust, such unappeasable appetite, they feel everything dissolve into insubstantiality . . ." Wetzsteon wrote. "If a stiff prick has no conscience, a moist cunt can devour the world."

It would have been foolhardy to expect the god of love to turn up at the "human sex" seminars convened in the national emergency on college campuses and elsewhere by those new American messiahs, the members of the mental-health professions. Maybe only the mythologers, the poets, and the philosophers who had not disowned the spirit in the body, could help us to become whole. "One couldn't make it without love . . . I was unable to budge this belief," said Charlie Citrine in Saul Bellow's *Humboldt's Gift*. Then, musing that perhaps Eros was leading him to wisdom, Citrine added, "That was nice, it had class, but I don't think it was a bit true (for one thing there was not perhaps all that much Eros left)."

At these conferences on human sexuality, there was hardly the faintest breath of Eros left. The professional rescue teams that plunged so eagerly into the jungle of "stiff pricks and moist cunts" where we had foundered only settled into the morass with us. Treating the ailment with the same toxins that had caused it, in this instance, proved no cure.

During a two-day, university-sponsored "workshop in human sex" in the Middle West, a paradigm for many other such programs in other parts of the country, most of the words—and all the pictures—were of steamy penises and vulvas, roaming randomly in a lubricious wonderland. Who put what where did not signify; only that all of us were making joyful—and frequent—use of all available entrances and exits. "Who's promiscuous? Anyone who's getting more than you!" one workshop leader told the audience of young men and women, almost all under thirty. But it seemed to be not the message most of them had come to hear. Promiscuity was perhaps too easy, too empty, and too animalistic for a significant segment of this generation.

"How many really 'fun' relationships, with no serious commitments, can you count among your own friends?" another leader persisted with the guilelessness, or one might say, simple-mindedness, that often prevailed at such proceedings. "Joyful, guilt-free sex, how much of it is really going on?" Already some members of the audience were squirming. Could it be that they had begun to reevaluate the importance of "serious commitments" and even the routes of joy?

But the series of films that would be shown in the course of the long weekend were scrupulously value-free. "They are designed not to keep you comfortable, but to bring out feelings you refuse to acknowledge," Dr. Raoul Patai, the psychiatrist in charge, explained. Small and intense, with slightly accented speech of indeterminate origin, he himself seemed less than comfortable, as if wrestling with feelings he refused to acknowledge. "Everything looks much the same—her and him, her and her, or him and him." The message of the mental-health corps was direct and unembellished by sentiment: Do it! Practice makes perfect. (In one of the movies, two eleven-year-olds were portrayed doing it on a children's sliding pond.)

The warm-up screening of erotic slides depicted lesbian and male homosexual couplings, lots of anal and oral intercourse—and very little copulation. "The art of love, it requires you to have to be free," the narrator declared. "Turn the lights up, turn 'em on, make 'em bright . . . If you're ashamed of yourself, ashamed of your body, don't try to be sexually competent . . . What is required is that you clothe yourself in beauty and pride."

The morning's event, "the Fuckerama," responding to this call for beauty and pride, was a cinematic barrage of such unrelenting carnality as to make even the most dedicated devotee of the bedroom arts sick of sex for a month. Here, a penis loomed in mid-screen, erect as a skyscraper. "Ladies will love it, fellows will love it, you can do tricks with it," the voiceover crooned. Exclamations spewed forth, each one sounding like a Hitlerian command. "Shit! Piss! Fuck! Cunt! Prick! Cocksucker! Motherfucker! The heavy seven! They kept the country from winning the war!" Other sharp satirical sallies landed in swift succession. "On television, it's okay to do certain things. You can prick your finger, but you can't finger your prick."

There, a studious-looking young man, reading a book on his bed, masturbated dreamily. A girl appeared from nowhere to fondle his penis. The lyrical accompaniment blared, "She'll turn on the heat, she'll put you on your feet, she's someone to meet." The girl from nowhere performed fellatio on him. The young man was still reading. Simultaneously, on the same screen, another film strip unfolded; this one, of a Victorian chambermaid and her foppish master. He peeled off her dress and caressed her breasts as she masturbated dreamily.

At last, a quartet of films crowded the split screen. It was a four-ring circus of sex, a phantasmagoria of fingers, tongues, genitalia of assorted shapes, sizes, and species. Several large dogs enlivened the action as it became progressively rougher and more frenzied. Men masturbated each other. Ditto women. Women masturbated men. The Victorian fop removed his trousers and, still wearing ruffled shirt and vest, ejaculated all over the chambermaid. She rubbed the semen on her body. On the sound track, a song, "Fuck You," attended the acts of two lesbians. "You're breaking my heart, you're tearing me apart, so fuck you!"

Now sadomasochism cast its shadow. A man in a black mask whipped a woman, concentrating on her naked groin. He beat her bloody while, in the adjacent film, one lesbian poured wine into the other's vagina and sucked it out. *The Big Schwantz Meets the Wild Wang*, a film of male homosexuality, followed. Two cops arrested two men, in the act of drying each other with Turkish towels. In the police lineup, accompanied by some more naked men, the convicts assaulted the cops, throwing them to the floor and undressing them. Two giant pairs of testicles took over the screen. Scenes of anal penetration. Scenes of gang rape, performed on one of the up-ended policemen who seemed to be enjoying it. At a heterosexual party, a dog licked a woman as she applied a vibrator to herself.

Titles flew across the screen, lacking appropriate films. *Twat's My Line* . . . *The Hump and Suck Club* . . . *The Story of An Eager Beaver Twat* . . . *Where There's a Will There's a Lay* . . . *Dial C for Cunt* . . . *The Cozy Sniffer* . . . *Fifty Million Frenchmen Suck Cunt* . . . *The Cock Tickler* . . . *When My Wife's Away, My Prick Will Stray* . . . *The Art of Asshole Fucking* . . . *Famous Historical Fuckers*. Finally, with a slapstick screwing and a jubilant cry, the Fuckerama ended: "What a wonderful fucking world! They fucked happily ever after!"

There was no applause. No one in the silent auditorium looked wonderfully fucking happy. Most of the young viewers appeared stunned and exhausted. Instead of rousing them out of their supposed prejudices and inhibitions, the films seemed to have plunged them into torpor.

Slowly, in a sort of daze, the men and women shuffled upstairs to the administrative offices of the university, where they dispersed into small discussion groups. In group D, no one spoke for several minutes.

"What are you feeling *now* about the Fuckerama?" the group's so-called facilitator, a psychiatric social worker, asked brightly. She hoped, apparently, to elicit "gut-level reaction" while it was still hot. But it was not even lukewarm. Rather than releasing feelings, as anticipated, the pornographic movies had anesthetized them. Nevertheless, the young people stumbled on, apologizing for apathy, manufacturing responses.

"Well, I've taken gross anatomy already, so I was bored," one man said, without heat. He sat on the floor, wall-eyed and dejected, staring at his shoes.

"That woman giving head to a poor guy who obviously can't get an erection . . . how would *that* be stimulating?"

"Many women have large dogs and use them that way. You don't have to work hard to teach animals."

"The audience for porn movies has changed these days. You walk in expecting to see the trench-coat set, and instead, everybody from suburbia has landed in the theater."

"I've seen a few bestiality films, but hardly any bondage ones. Suppose someone gets kicked by accident in the scenes of sadism?" It was the first ray of feeling anyone displayed.

The psychologist in the group looked disapproving. "Watching intellectually produces boredom," he warned. "It also distances the threat." However, he might have misconstrued the nature of the threat. It was probably not the sexuality in these films, but the debasement of sexuality, that alarmed the young men and women.

The facilitator, disappointed by the damp, unfocused response, eased the discussion into its main arena. Had the men seen any homosexual films before those in the Fuckerama? They eyed her warily now. Were they going to have to defend their heterosexual preference . . . or disown it?

"The guys in my house didn't want to go. We weren't

worried about the films disturbing us. We just didn't want to put up with that crowd."

"As for swishers, the frats wouldn't let them in. Besides, those movies were for men who didn't have dates. So what would be the point of watching guys make it with each other?"

The facilitator looked displeased, but carefully refrained from making judgments. She waited for further comments. Slowly, they came.

"I wouldn't like anyone to put the munch on me. So I stay away."

"Around those theaters, the transvestites are hard to take. Guys pulling up in cars, making offers through the windows. Who needs it?"

The facilitator pressed on, determined to encourage more positive thinking. "I like to see women with women. They're more creative. They're gentle with each other. It can be very tender and beautiful," she said.

The men continued to eye her with suspicion. "More creative than whom?" one asked.

Then, after a brief pause which nobody filled: "What did you men think of the two girls going down on each other?"

Dark glances darted back and forth. "If that's their bag, that's their bag. I hope it makes them happy," one said.

Dissatisfaction with the Fuckerama's lesbian films flared among some of the few women present. "They were so phallic! A dildo or a male figure was always involved," one objected.

"I don't know if outrage is quite the right word to describe what I feel!" another said.

For some of these young men, it was a new thought that sex could be displaced from its natural realm and experienced by non-lesbian women independently of maleness. They were not pleased. Before lunch on the first day, sexual antagonism, rising, smelled almost like smoke in the air.

That afternoon's films, no longer pornographic, were practically pastoral. The tempo, no longer frenetic, was somnabulistic.

In the last brief nod to heterosexuality in the weekend's cinema, two couples—one black, one white—celebrated the simple joys of touching. Then the seminar's "hidden agenda" burst into full view. Same-sex pairing preempted the screen. Two beautiful boys kissed each other hungrily. Then two girls ran naked in the woods. Soon they were licking each other's breasts and fingering each other's genitals. Men with men and women with women absorbed the rest of the long hour—and the rest of the long weekend.

When group D reconvened, most of the young people curled up in fetal positions on the floor. The facilitator, sitting upright on a chair, seemed less disposed than the rest to return to the womb. There was no way now to avoid the central issue—homosexuality. Did the men resent it when the lesbians came to orgasm with each other? Some of them were growing surly.

"Do you mean did I want to come in there with my big prick?" one asked.

"I really don't give a good goddamn what lesbians do together," another added. Their wariness had curdled into outright antipathy. Neither of these two appeared again in small group D.

Trust exercises occupied the rest of that afternoon. The general implication was obvious: to choose between the touch of one person and another, or even one sex and the other, was somehow undemocratic and oppressive. In a long game of blind man's bluff, revised, "sighted" participants in the human sex workshop took turns leading "blind" partners through difficult terrain. Up the stairs and down the stairs, over chairs and couches, into closets, tripping, laughing, growling. "I'd like to know who grabbed my left breast!" one woman growled. "I did, dear," another laughed. "No, ma'am. That wasn't her breast, that was my breast you grabbed!"

No man spoke aloud.

Early Sunday morning, the second day opened with a marathon of sensual massage. Once more the injunction was to "Touch! Feel! Respond!" to anyone—and everyone—who came down the pike. The massagers, in teams of five, pummeled and patted the massagees, who lay on sheets on the floor. The rhythmic sequence of slaps started softly and grew harder and harder until it filled the room, sounding like heavy rain on the windows. There was a pungent aroma of coconut oil and sweat. Then each team of massagers lifted its massagee slowly aloft, far up over their heads. This was surely learning to trust the hard way! Halfway up, one fat man got into trouble. His team, amid much moaning and groaning, could raise him only to shoulder height. The others cheered them on. Finally, the fat young man was hoisted aloft, rocking and swaying precariously. Now, however, his team could not lower him without dropping him. A human net was formed to catch the fellow as he came hurtling down. Dr. Patai, looking even more worried than he had the day before, embraced the fat man, who had miraculously escaped without a broken back. "Your touch communicates your caring," he whispered, clinging to him for a moment before returning him to the group. In such synthetic crises, a transient and synthetic intimacy was forged.

Sunday's films were exclusively homosexual. A lesbian narrated her own story. She spoke feelingly of "loving my best friend, my fiancée. It's terrible to come out then; it's terrible to be that different." In *Lavender*, another such documentary, two formerly "straight" girls at last succumbed to their sexual feelings for one another. "You can just roll over in bed and say, 'Good morning, lover!'" one of them cried. The other, revisiting the conventional world at a heterosexual party, found all the couples "playing roles" and much less content than she. "It didn't broaden my outlook any," she mused. Naked and free, to the strains of "I want your love, I need your love," the young women combed each other's hair in the bathroom.

Then two male homosexuals, wearing football jerseys, kissed in the kitchen. Helping each other out of his shirt, they opened each other's fly and licked each other's penis. As the camera panned up and down on their strong male bodies, orgasm occurred. Tenderly, affectionately, they wiped each other off.

The conference was now reaching its peak of revelation. "Sex takes place other than belly to belly, under the sheets, in marriage," Dr. Patai said, wearing his customary troubled frown. He then introduced several people who were having other kinds of sex in other contexts.

One gentleman, who described himself as a "celibate preacher," pointed out that it could take place, of all places, in the head. He started his sermon by confessing. He had once loved a woman—a long time ago, he said, "but there was nothing physical about it. My love was all psychological. I knew even then I wanted to be a priest. If you acknowledge your sexual feelings," he told the audience, "you don't have to act on them."

Did he never, in any way, act on his own sexual feelings? someone inquired indelicately. "Masturbation! The great unasked question!" Dr. Patai moaned. The celibate preacher answered it. His voice was low. "It didn't happen until I was twenty-four or twenty-five. 'Okay, Charlie Brown,' I said to myself. 'You wanted to be the perfect guy. You really thought you had everything together.' Okay, now you know." Now everybody knew. But who knew better than the clergy that confession cleansed?

A man and woman, the unmarried partners in a new-style *menage à trois*, spoke of their unconventional living arrangement. "The three of us have really hung together," said Anita, the alternate wife. "After three years, it's just as exciting to be with Elaine [the legal wife in the triad] as if I had gone off with a man on a sexual thing. The key to our relationship is basic trust. We don't see each other as competitors."

"Leaving my kids with both Elaine and Anita lessens the emotional load on all of us," Lee, the husband, explained. "They were not getting on very well with their natural mother, but they have an excellent relationship with Anita." In the interests of candor, he added, "On the other hand, I'm doubly married and it's a very oppressive thing. I've multiplied my responsibilities and I'm struggling with that all the time."

"But the third person helps maintain sanity," Anita, the third person, reminded Lee. "She's invaluable to the domestic atmosphere. When there's only two of you, there's a special kind of lunacy. The married people in this audience know what disasters a tense twosome can produce." She took her man's hand. "And Lee's just a good, gentle person who would never pull a mind-fuck game on either of us. I respect him for that."

The Middle Western community where they lived respected them too, she revealed. On parents' night at the children's school, "the teachers have been open-minded enough to put out three name tags, one for Daddy and two others—for Mommy 1 and Mommy 2." It was enriching for the children, Anita felt, to have three parents. "Of course, all of us have sexual friendships. We have all slept with other people outside this primary relationship," she said.

Then, inevitably, the feminist consciousness reared its head. A workshop leader broached the peculiar ordeals of growing up female. She began, inevitably, with the genitalia. "Although it's part of you, it's not like any other part. It's a place that's always handled differently, from the very first moment your parents come in contact with you. Either their hands are too soft and gentle, or they're too hard and vigorous. The girl child learns about this place, between belly button and knee—that she must not look at it, or touch it or, God forbid, put anything in it. 'Keep your panties up, keep your knees together, and don't take bubble gum from strangers.'" In her Catholic girlhood, the leader remembered, she had been enjoined to keep her underpants on, even while getting into the bathtub, so no arousing, almond-shaped reflection of herself appeared in the bath water. "And a little girl can't even pee outdoors when she's playing," she complained. "It splashes. If she gets her shoes wet, her mother will kill her."

So who could blame this deprived female child for growing jealous of that other creature who could pee where he pleased and—power of powers!—even put out fires with his own water? Who could blame her if, forever after, she never quite wholeheartedly accommodated him? "Ultimately, she takes into her body a strange organ where her own familiar fingers have never been. She takes in the enemy. It's damned hard to be sexy with the oppressor!"

Finally, the workshop leader let the oppressor have it right between the legs. "Don't chalk me up as a size queen," she pleaded, reiterating a favorite new theme of emancipated women, "but penis size *is* relevant to sexual pleasure. To Dr. Masters, who insists it just ain't so, I would like to ask, 'When was the last time *you* had a penis in *your* vagina?' If a man's a tender, creative, considerate lover, he may learn to make do with a penis as big as my finger. But if he's a clod, it's got to be *big!*"

Then a male workshop leader asserted that growing up male was no easier than growing up female. He offered his own view of the much-abused organ that, willy-nilly, still took the limelight at most human-sex symposiums. "Guys also face the effort not to look at it or touch it, although when they pee, they must hold it and aim it. Thus men get mixed messages," he said. " 'You may touch it at a certain time in a certain way, but you may only touch your own, not anybody else's.' " He injected another light note. "The average length of the penis, when erect, is 6.3 inches long. The average vagina can accommodate a penis 7.7 inches long. Therefore, there's a hundred miles of unused vagina in this country alone!"

Not all the women thought that was funny. "If something's too big, then something else has got to be too small," the female workshop leader murmured.

The meeting swung into the final movies of the weekend. In the normal order of sexual development, one progressed from masturbation outward to heterosexuality. At the human-sex seminar, the progression was reversed. Intentionally or not, the films retraced the course of society to its current nonpareil, masturbation. First male, then female, performed slow, explicit acts of self-gratification. On the screen, one man rose to orgasm on his back, another on his belly. In her shower stall, a woman was instructed, "Be your own lover. Enjoy the sensuousness of your own body. Touch the parts of you that are particularly exciting. Stroke your genitals, your breasts." This student of self-love had mottled skin, hairy arms and legs, and long auburn hair. She fondled herself with sore red hands. "Now stroke your body with a vibrator. Then stroke your genitals. Enjoy your orgasm fully. Experience the fullness and joy of orgasm." The woman in the shower obeyed. Her vibrator was not, heaven forfend, shaped like a phallus. Autonomous, fulfilled, she had triumphed over that organ, small or large, real or fake. Coming to orgasm with the aid of a box-shaped, battery-driven instrument, she looked stricken, as if she had electrocuted herself by accident. The high, sweet lute music played on.

In the end, the human-sexuality conference evolved into metaphor. Men and women divided into separate camps, playing out the polarization of the times. At last they were shouting across the widening abyss, almost indifferent to being heard on the other side. But they were not really talking about themselves and each other; only, like dismembered people, about their orifices and appendages. The earnest effort of the weekend to advance sexual enlightenment seemed, finally, to retard it.

"We've got to stop worrying about small penises and, for the first time in history, take the responsibility for our own satisfaction," one woman said. "We've got to abandon the idea that, if he presses the right buttons, I'm going to get off."

"But what about the small penis? How does it really affect us? What can we do about it?" one man asked.

"During the sex act, my partner once said to me, 'Is it *there?*' That was a tremendous slap to my masculinity," another declared.

"If I complain, he just says, 'Ha-ha. Why don't you just take a few tucks in your vagina?' "

Across the abyss, the men and women glared.

Then one man spoke softly of his past. "Where I went to school, some of the guys had three-and-a-half-foot dicks. They had to roll them up. And some other guys had half-inch dicks. They could hardly find them to pee. But what the hell, we all worked it out . . . somehow." The events of this weekend, he said with some emotion, made him feel that he was nothing more—and maybe less—than the sum of his parts.

That night, near the end of my journey, I did not sleep. Although I had been alternately amused and appalled by the human-sex workshop, it was only afterward that I realized how much it had troubled me. For all its good intentions, it seemed to compound confusion and elevate anxieties, rather than relieve them. On the whole, the resonances it produced came through as negative static from a society no longer altogether able to deal with its own emotions, no longer even certain what they were.

As they poured out into the winter night, the young participants appeared pensive and disturbed, thrown off balance by the weird, disordered world of human sexuality that the workshop mirrored. After all, I thought, that was the weekend's deepest intention—to combat complacency. Indeed, its sponsors might have been quite satisfied with the response.

"Those homosexual films grossed me out," one young man said. "I was upset with myself for being upset."

"If I don't like to masturbate, is that a form of self-hatred? What's wrong with me?" a young woman asked.

"Maybe we do have to get rid of our heterosexual hang-ups. Maybe it really is a moral sickness, like fascism, to want to dominate women," another young man reflected.

They seemed so vulnerable, so imperiled . . . and so cheated of the simple, ordinary expectations that had once sustained us of the way things were between men and women. Walking down the moonlit road, closed to traffic by the university, some of the students drew together again; some even clasped hands.

But perhaps, alas, it was only for physical warmth. Any other kind might have been already inaccessible to them. In the world without Eros, the temperature and thickness of flesh, the relative moisture and girth of corporeal parts, might be all that they could know of one another. What then, if they tried to make love? Only pressing part to part, it could be a kind of doom. These young women might forever feel the absent inch of erectile tissue instead of the presence of man.

Yet these young men would need to make their presence felt. Defeated by drugstore technology, deterred from *dominus* by a society that refused to honor it, and feeling fatally diminished, how would they reassert their blocked male power?

Sleepless, angry, and frightened, I dressed for my breakfast appointment with Raoul Patai, the psychiatrist in charge of the human-sex program. It was not too farfetched, I thought, to blame him and his associates—with their vested interest in perpetuating dysfunction and distress—for my fretful night and my troubled mind.

When I arrived in the hotel restaurant, Dr. Patai had already finished a pot of coffee. He was rubbing his eyes with both hands. The sad expression I remembered had worsened into gloom. "Forgive me. I haven't slept all night," he explained. "This weekend disconcerted me. Of course it doesn't do to say so before the media and journalists—with your vested interest in the exotic and experimental, your taste for the new and untried. But you see . . ." He spoke delicately, as if afraid of bruising some portion of my brain with ideas too harsh for it. "When men and women move away from fixed roles, from accustomed patterns of relating, they move into . . . unknown territory. Sometimes it can even be dangerous, especially to the young. So much confusion so early . . . Where will it end? But even at my age," he said, "while at first we welcome 'progress,' at last we may come to question it. To advance is not always to improve."

Ever intrigued by the unexpected, I urged him on. "All these

new sexual arrangements, these signposts to the new morality
. . . More and more, they have begun to seem to me markers
on the road to nowhere." He repeated very distinctly, in the
event that I had not caught the words: "*Markers on the road to
nowhere.*"

When I did not protest, Dr. Patai offered me a cigarette. He
lit it with a courtly gesture. "But, of course, *you* saw something
more positive. You saw a new world opening up, eh? Well, who
am I to doubt it? Who am I to judge? You Americans want
always to broaden your horizons. You want always to make life
better for yourselves. And so you should.

"As for me personally . . ." He spread out his hands and
looked somewhat chagrined. "Well, I don't often mention it in
these sex-education groups because they would think me unsympathetic and passé." The idea made him cringe. To become
passé was, for so many, among the worst human fates. "But
actually, right now, I'm in a sedate, closed, one-to-one relationship with a conservative professional woman. Having gone the
other route—entirely open, entirely free, having tried *everything*, you know . . ." He let that word stand for all the sexual
exploits and role innovations the imagination could encompass.
"I found it empty, sterile, leading . . . nowhere."

He stroked his head with some agitation and combed his
beard with his hand. "Of course, one aspect of freedom is the
freedom to doubt, the freedom to become passé." Once more,
the slight apologetic cringe. "There may be some wisdom in the
recognition that we have reached the end of a long road."

He described the road. "Full of all this variety, this multiplicity of options . . . Yet—I speak only for myself—there is a
certain lack of depth. We experience a weariness of the soul.
We yearn for new beginnings." A moment of reflection; then
his eyes lit up. "Recently, I have discovered that within one
person you really care for, within you and within that person,
an entire world can exist. All needs can be met within a single
relationship. Then Raoul Patai broke into unexpected smiles.

"Lately, I have begun to think of getting married," he revealed. "And if I do, believe me, it will be a very closed arrangement—a very traditional husband with a very traditional wife."

He hurried on, seeming to grow happier and more relaxed. "The current trend against exclusivity, against conventional marriage and conventional roles, we can clearly define it. But trend is not destiny," Dr. Patai pointed out. "One finds courage to act against the trend and, when one least expects it, the winds may shift." Leaning intently across the table, he changed his position, and with it, his figure of speech. "These sexual mores we fashion, each generation a little bit differently, they're like nuclear missiles, I think. Once we build them, they're already obsolete. So we've got to build new ones all over again."

Once more the psychiatrist apologized. "Naturally, you cannot agree. For you, the present has not yet become obsolete. You were charmed by the weekend, of course. It's your American appetite for experiment and change," he chided gently. "As for me, I come from an older society. Long ago, we gave up the search for Utopias. We learned to settle . . . just for life. For life on its own terms."

Yet, I reflected, the search for Utopia was indeed at the heart of the American experiment, animating our most honorable achievements, ennobling our most honorable failures—even including that of the human-sex workshop itself. To discard our dream of perfectability would be to discard the best of ourselves.

Nevertheless, for the moment, I was content with a calming thought. "In the renewal of ancient values," as the psychoanalyst Erik H. Erikson suggested, the future might emerge stronger and sounder than we perhaps had any right to hope. In "the century of the adult," as Erikson put it, true liberation could well lie in our heroic refusal to disown the past—while we reconstruct with loving care the terms of that more nearly perfect social order that men and women shall someday share.